SHADOW WORK

SHADOW WORK

LONELINESS AND THE LITERARY LIFE

EMILY HODGSON ANDERSON

Columbia University Press *New York*

Columbia University Press
Publishers Since 1893
New York   Chichester, West Sussex

Copyright © 2025 Columbia University Press
All rights reserved

Library of Congress Cataloging-in-Publication Data
Names: Anderson, Emily Hodgson, 1977– author.
Title: Shadow work : loneliness and the literary life / Emily Hodgson Anderson.
Description: New York : Columbia University Press, 2025. | Includes bibliographical references and index.
Identifiers: LCCN 2024036424 (print) | LCCN 2024036425 (ebook) | ISBN 9780231218498 (hardback) | ISBN 9780231218504 (trade paperback) | ISBN 9780231562317 (ebook)
Subjects: LCSH: Books and reading—Psychological aspects. | Fiction—Psychological aspects. | Motherhood in literature. | Loneliness in literature. | LCGFT: Essays. | Literary criticism.
Classification: LCC Z1003 .A626 2025 (print) | LCC Z1003 (ebook) | DDC 155.6/463—dc23/eng/20240903

Cover design and photograph: Julia Kushnirsky

SHADOW WORK

LONELINESS AND THE LITERARY LIFE

EMILY HODGSON ANDERSON

Columbia University Press *New York*

Columbia University Press
Publishers Since 1893
New York   Chichester, West Sussex

Copyright © 2025 Columbia University Press
All rights reserved

Library of Congress Cataloging-in-Publication Data
Names: Anderson, Emily Hodgson, 1977– author.
Title: Shadow work : loneliness and the literary life / Emily Hodgson Anderson.
Description: New York : Columbia University Press, 2025. | Includes bibliographical references and index.
Identifiers: LCCN 2024036424 (print) | LCCN 2024036425 (ebook) | ISBN 9780231218498 (hardback) | ISBN 9780231218504 (trade paperback) | ISBN 9780231562317 (ebook)
Subjects: LCSH: Books and reading—Psychological aspects. | Fiction—Psychological aspects. | Motherhood in literature. | Loneliness in literature. |
LCGFT: Essays. | Literary criticism.
Classification: LCC Z1003 .A626 2025 (print) | LCC Z1003 (ebook) | DDC 155.6/463—dc23/eng/20240903

Cover design and photograph: Julia Kushnirsky

To Owen and Dylan

I am gradually approaching the period in my life when work comes first. When both the boys were away for Easter, I hardly did anything but work . . . and yet I wonder whether the "blessing" is not missing from such work. No longer diverted by other emotions, I work the way a cow grazes. . . . The hands work and work and the head imagines it is producing God knows what, and yet formerly, in my so wretchedly limited working time, I was more productive, because I was more sensual; I lived as a human being must live, passionately interested in everything.

—Käthe Kollwitz, qtd. in Tillie Olsen, *Silences*

CONTENTS

Acknowledgments xi

Introduction: Loneliness and the Literary Life   1

PART I. LOSING

1 The Shadow Life of Books: William Shakespeare, William Hazlitt, Alexander Chee   19
2 Reading to a Child: Roald Dahl, Shakespeare, T. H. White   29
3 The Detective's Mind: Arthur Conan Doyle   43
4 Shaking Hands: Ludwig Wittgenstein, Percival Everett   55
5 Pool of Tears: Lewis Carroll   67
6 Obedience Training: John Milton, William Koehler   81

PART II. LONGING

7 Perfection and Platonic Love: Plato, Aristotle   95
8 (An Aside): Shakespeare   105

9 The One and Only Jane: Jane Austen   117

10 Of Pain, Paralysis, and Pursuit:
Samuel Beckett, Mary Shelley   125

PART III. LOVING

11 Shadow Work: J. M. Barrie,
Toni Morrison, Mark Twain   135

12 Animal Love: Miguel de Cervantes,
Jilly Cooper, Laurence Sterne   147

13 Pioneer Girl: Laura Ingalls Wilder   169

14 The Efficiency Expert: William Wordsworth,
Frank and Ernestine Gilbreth   185

15 Invisible Labor, Invisible Hands:
Adam Smith, Zadie Smith   197

16 No Room of One's Own: Homer, Virginia Woolf   213

Notes   223

Bibliography   251

Index   263

ACKNOWLEDGMENTS

Many thanks to Philip Leventhal at Columbia University Press for getting—and staying—interested in this work.

Much appreciation to my various anonymous readers for Columbia University Press; I learned something from each response.

Thanks to the office of the Dean of USC Dornsife for a generous publication subvention grant.

Thanks to David Ulin for reading early drafts of this collection. Thanks to David St. John for reading drafts before they were drafts. Thanks to Maggie Nelson and Alexis Landau for reading messy versions. Thanks to Bill Handley for reading essays in real time, and thanks to Joseph Boone for reading the entire thing. Thanks to Percival Everett for many phone conversations and much horse, dog, parenting, and writing advice. Thanks to Grace Franklin for helping me with the final steps.

Diana Starr Cooper is the friend who set me on the right path in "Obedience Training." The unstintingly generous Deborah Friedell was the editor friend on the phone with me in "The Efficiency Expert"—and for much of this book. Melissa Farman is the Parisian friend I quote in "Pioneer Girl"; many thanks to

Meli for reading, inspiration, writing retreats, and other forms of support. Thanks to Sarah Kareem for multiple conversations and references, also acknowledged in my notes ("Shadow Work," "The One and Only Jane," "Animal Love," "Shaking Hands"). Thanks to Emily Setina for impeccable edits on several essays and longstanding friendship over the years. Thanks to Jessica Leiman for the same. Thanks to Joseph Roach for launching me on the path of scholarship and for writing the essay that features in "No Room of One's Own."

For the more general idea of "shadow work" that started this whole thought process, I'm indebted to Bonnie Nadzam and to the journal editor who rejected the essay Bonnie asked me to write.

The following chapters previously appeared in other venues, often in a shorter form and under different titles, as acknowledged in my notes: "The Shadow Life of Books," "Reading to a Child," "Obedience Training," "The One and Only Jane," "Of Pain, Paralysis, and Pursuit," "Invisible Labor, Invisible Hands," and "No Room of One's Own." Thanks to those editors for the permission to reprint.

For companionship and support, thanks to my parents, John and Susan Hodgson; my brother, Michael Hodgson; my dog, Tater; and the horses that have accompanied me through the years (Rio, Miami, Santi, Malone, Vorme, Sukha, Simon).

Most thanks to my sons.

This collection in its entirety pays tribute to the sentiment of my epigraph, and I think what Kollwitz is getting at there is that when a writing life is necessarily, inescapably, and sometimes infuriatingly knotted into other lives, these knots and braids can produce writing that is emotional, hard won, real. I know that the times I set aside to be "productive" are not always as full as the writing moments I find hidden, like little gems, inside my days. I know that the diversions of my children anchor me. I know that going on means progress but also giving up a life that has been as dear to me as it has been hard.

They will grow older; they will need less care; my writing will be but a shadow of their tending.

SHADOW WORK

INTRODUCTION
Loneliness and the Literary Life

As writer and a single mom, when I really want to work, I go out to the garage. This isn't because I'm an aspirational mechanic or home gym fanatic but because I've set my garage up with some bookshelves and a desk. It is a place I use for a certain kind of thinking, and I'll even announce to my boys as I head out the back door that I'm "going to work."

Understandably perhaps, given their young ages and my proximity, they find this boundary hard to respect. The garage is only a few steps from our kitchen, and it contains plenty of objects they don't associate with work: spare paint cans, old Christmas decorations, an ancient bike. When I'm out there writing, the detritus tends to become magnetic, my presence signaling that previously peripheral objects are now fascinating toys. "Twenty minutes of quiet," I once heard myself bargaining with them, only to be rewarded with a series of Post-it notes that narrated to me, silently, a litany of requests. ("Come qwik mom," read one. "He is touching my tings.")

Reflecting on their interruptions again recently, I've come to think that maybe their confusion isn't related to age alone. Were one to install a hidden camera in my garage, a horrifying thought, it would show scenes of nail biting, doodling, internet browsing, and long stretches of me staring off into space. What must my writing look like to an outside observer? What am I *doing* out there? Why do I need, in those moments, to be so completely on my own? My assumptions are telling in this regard. "Room? Clean? Now?" I asked my younger child, recently, as he sat, like me, staring into space. "Ah I can't, mom," he answered. "I'm not done thinking yet."[1]

The same child who answered me so cogently a few months ago had just turned two when I first found myself parenting on my own. Back then, he didn't answer me in complete sentences but with toddler language and a lisp. Back then, he was still in Pampers and, a true boy, would remain so for some time. My oldest was five years old, eloquent and "mature," on the cusp of kindergarten and having logic battles with me that included defending his door slamming as a strategy he'd adopted to "keep all the love inside the room." I was a thirty-nine-year-old English professor, a long-married, rule-following, successful academic who considered myself articulate and who believed I'd be shielded from life's vicissitudes as a result.

Our tipping point happened on the day before my oldest and I started school, which meant kindergarten for him and fall semester teaching and a new batch of college undergraduates for me. In the morning, their dad was there. In the afternoon, he was not. He wouldn't be there for several years. *What happened?* friends ask. *And then what happened? And what did you do?* I either don't have the answers, or the memories, or those questions invite a story I don't know how to tell. I know family was three thousand miles away. I know I was lonely. I know this hasn't been a story about coparenting until more recently, a new chapter with their dad that I've been happy to add.

But these chapters were written in the years before that, when our life as an unexpected trio caused me to reexamine my work habits and life choices, as well as my own childhood, my current lifestyle, and my approaches to moving on. What I realized in retrospect was how this personal trajectory—that sense of excavation, for the sake of understanding; the feeling of sadness and stuckness when working on something doesn't seem to work; the subsequent experience of momentum, even hope—is one I live through, in microcosm, every time I write.

So this book tells that story, one about how a life lived in books—a life spent reading, writing, and teaching the written word—had prepared me for certain kinds of solitary work. I wrote these pages to weave together my own often contradictory thoughts on labor, literature, and companionship and to explore how books had taught me about solitude and also brought me closer to the people I most love. I wrote this book to figure out how writing relates to longing, and I wrote it to figure out how I could be both a writer and a mom. I wrote it to understand how writing and parenting could feel simultaneously like so much work and passion, and I wrote it to figure out what forms of work I felt I needed to do or resented doing in my life, on my own. Most personally, I wrote this book to understand how the invisible and often isolating work of reading and writing might coexist with my ability to have a communal, not-solitary life.

In telling that story, I realized that this book was also about how studying literature creates the opportunity to talk about our lives though books. Maybe this experience is why Deidre Lynch finds the teaching of literature to be an "oddly intimate profession," with an intimacy that works against the confessional impulse that now dominates so much of contemporary memoir writing and online public life.[2] These days, it seems we find it ever easier to confide in strangers, just as we find it very easy, even addictive, to consume these proliferating confessions. Yet intimacy and vulnerability feel to me diluted when I can know, instantly, the deepest secrets of someone I've never actually met. Why should the popular understanding of self-expression remain confessional? Why shouldn't we work a bit to figure out those (books or people) we want to know? My artistic preferences, the books I choose to read and teach and the elements of them I work to understand, are as revelatory about my heart and mind as a statement about my frustrations with a colleague or my struggles with boundaries or all the hard things I can or can't do. A long-lasting relationship to literature can help us better understand what, despite our shadows, we show and hide about ourselves.

In my case, the books that put words to my life as a single mom were the ones I was teaching, intermixed with those I had read as a kid and was usually now reading to my own. I didn't go searching specifically for other writers who had written about single motherhood or other writers who were discussing loneliness or invisibility or feeling overworked. Instead, I leaned upon the books that had previously provided me comfort or had inspired me with their craftsmanship or were figuring in the conversations I was having with my friends. There were contours to my choices, choices that mapped out long-held artistic preferences, a certain childhood upbringing, an educational background to embrace and confront. There was also a serendipity I could see only in hindsight, and new discoveries, and new life experiences that have reshaped how I write and read. But when I began this project, I was writing about what I believed to be familiar. I was writing about what I thought I knew. More than anything, I was trying to figure out how I *could* keep writing, now that I was alone with two young boys.

Several years into my own struggles with these questions, discussions of loneliness started circulating on a larger stage.

Governments mandated quarantines, and when we were able to leave our houses and see other people, we were scared to get too close. Under those requirements, I pretty much surrendered up my house to my kids during their school days, and my kids pretty much came into my office-garage constantly during mine. Friends and colleagues coped or didn't cope in similar ways. Discussions of burnout, loneliness, and "Zoom fatigue" spread, as we all—regardless of our parenting, romantic, or employment status—came to feel a bit more invisible and a lot more overworked.

There were, for me, certain ironies to this experience, longstanding tensions in my life just now more on view. I was and had been sharing my home exclusively with two younger humans, and much of my loneliness came from feeling that I didn't have enough of what is popularly referred to as "personal space." But I also felt, now with a sense of heightened visibility, the lack of another adult with whom to share my experience or daily life. Books and movies make much of the harried, hard-working parent, yet the tiny steps that had been required to get my two boys to school every morning—dressed, fed, and somewhat clean—had always seemed intended to remain behind the scenes. Societal expectations surrounding parenting encourage us to obscure the effort of our preparatory negotiations, a fact I realized anew when parental expectations expanded to include a homeschooling hidden within the adult workday. These phenomena made me wonder if the cultural structure of the "nuclear family" developed not just so that extra hands could be available for child-rearing but so someone else could bear witness to these backstage attempts. In my family, no one else shares this space regularly with the three of us, and the dailiness of watching my boys grow up mostly on my own can feel unrelenting because unseen by anyone else.

And yet—close friends of mine, suddenly confined with a romantic partner, reminded me that such sharing was not always a consummation devoutly to be wished. Other friends, living on their own without the company of partners or kids, spoke of feeling desperately alone. A few friends described isolation as an "introvert's dream." Clearly, being alone was not so much an objective status as a subjective state of mind. When John Milton kicks Adam and Eve out of Paradise at the conclusion to his epic retelling of the fall of man, he describes them as being "solitary" and also "hand in hand."[3] How can they be solitary yet feel in union? What is it that makes us feel lonely versus just alone? My own feelings of isolation made these questions even more pressing. They also made me more curious about how writers struggle with these questions in books.

I read a lot during this time period, and I became more aware of how the nature of my reading has changed as technology has developed and as I have aged.[4] I experienced a heightened sense, too, of how feelings of isolation increasingly coexist with the sense of "connection" offered to us all by social media and the web. My days often still start by scrolling through headlines; they are then filled with dozens of text messages and check-ins or meetings via Zoom. I reach out to people, or I think I reach out to people, more frequently than before. And yet this kind of reading—scrolling, headline hopping, rereading the same story fed through different mouths—often adds to my anxiety, and constant texting leaves me feeling unsustained.

I mention these feelings because they are so distinct from those I usually get from reading or writing a book. Good books have the power to absorb me; a writing project can suck me in. But I notice that I am now more apt to read many books simultaneously, without the sense of laser focus that I previously thought I owed a page. Similarly, I am more likely to write without the same throughline or devotion that I'd been told governs a sense of intellectual "research." Some of this shift has had to do with external factors (homeschooling or different work and life obligations); some of it has had to do with the distractions of social media and the internet; some of it has been my general mood. It can be hard to turn my eyes to a book from a reality that I wish, by watching it, I could change. It can be hard to lift my eyes back up to that reality from the page. Writing can feel silly, in the face of global chaos; intellectual labor can feel like an oxymoron and effete.

Yet writing, as Zadie Smith has recently articulated, has always ever been for writers "something to do."[5] Reading, and particularly reading works of fiction, similarly continues to toggle ever-more unsteadily between entertainment and a waste of time. A recent statistic in one of my children's magazines told me that the average American reads twelve books a year, a statistic I announced in a fall seminar class with horror and that my students and colleagues then assured me was way too high.[6] "My mom works fourteen hours a day and comes home tired," a freshman student told me last year. "She loves reading, and she also doesn't have the time or energy any more to read books."

For people like my student's mom (or maybe not, depending on her job), isolation can come with certain potential perks. When, for a time, the categories of "essential" and "nonessential" labeled who got to circulate physically in the world while the rest of us were kept at home, many nonessential individuals chose to reapportion time and lifestyles to make available solitary activities previously shoved aside. Burdened with a seemingly never-ending online workday, certain demographics announced that now was the time to learn Greek, take up piano, bake sourdough bread, or read all those "classic" books. Yet I've found that many friends have jettisoned such hobbies now that the pace of life has picked back up. I don't think feeling isolated necessarily inspires a new cohort of readers and writers. I think it causes existing readers and writers to experience on steroids the pros and cons of what it is we, as readers and writers, do.

And as my children's intrusions into my garage attest, what readers and writers do and their motivations for doing it can be hard to discern. Writing occurs in secret spaces, often physical spaces of privacy and also a mental world of inspiration that is difficult to reach. Writing requires an intellectual effort that cannot in and of itself be seen. Reading, too, takes place internally, and the absorption promoted by the practice can take an individual and remove her from a group. There's a sense of pride I feel in this hiding, as if this intellectual activity is a secret treasure that only I can access or a secret superpower that will lose its potency if more generally revealed. To strangers, I'm mild-mannered and even self-effacing, that nondescript person who carries out her own grocery bags and avoids eye contact and reads a book through most of her kid's game. But I know I'm a single mom who is also a professor and an academic dean; I know that if challenged I can duck into a telephone booth and come out brandishing a child's first-aid kit and spouting statistics on tuition revenue and a lecture on *King Lear*. Still, there's a shame to this hiding, too, since writing, like parenting, can often feel harder for having to grapple with it alone. My most secret fear is that I've ended up as a writer and a single parent because no one wants to work with me and that this aloneness is not just an alternate, secret identity but one that threatens to engulf all the others and define me for all time. Intellectual labor is predicated on a link between invisibility and isolation, between work done in the "shadows" and the loneliness that can ensue.

At the same time, work, for me, has also always been one antidote to loneliness, whether that work means staying busy on the surface or digging into a piece of writing or a book. I've just found living a life in books means regularly confronting the question of why this "digging in" matters, perhaps more regularly than in professions for which the preparatory labor is more visible and the end result is life saving or life advancing, in some physiological and essential sense. I've found that the question of why books matter can feel disingenuous, since those asking the question often don't believe they do. I've found answering the question difficult, since the individuals who answer it must do so from a secret and private place.[7]

I also think that this bind, of how to defend or describe publicly a private need, can, for those of us in the humanities, be our bond. I believe that reading and writing inspire unique and crucial forms of human connection. They are activities that require from their participants a level of hiding or isolation that paradoxically acts in a larger service of this experience of visibility, connection, or being seen. As a lifelong reader, I find in books a promise that heads and hearts can actually be shared. As a writer, I find in the pull of the page a promise that through words I can make hearts and heads visible to all. To be alone yet together is the sense of companionship or community that I find within the written word. Reading the work of really good writers can offer what Toni Morrison calls an experience of "intimacy[,] in which the reader is under the impression that he isn't really reading . . . [but] that he is participating . . . as he goes along."[8] It is through "the *act* of reading," states Ralph Ellison, "that marvelous collaboration between the writer's artful vision and the reader's sense of life," that we may "become acquainted with other possible selves."[9] Reading, as Morrison and Ellison describe it, doesn't just train us to be empathetic, as the old, pro-humanities chestnut goes. It counters loneliness, as it lets a reader test her consciousness against other communities, other lives. That practice reassures me that I can listen to, even identify deeply, with others without surrendering myself.

Still, if reading and writing matter to me because they offer the promise of engagement, I live in a world in which I have often struggled to connect. Feeling isolated can make me ask with heightened urgency if what I do as a writer is in any way essential. Isolation can accentuate for me the experience of loneliness because it puts pressure on the nature of my "work."

Growing up, I was always aware that my family worked hard. There was my mom, up at five in the New England darkness to run before she went to work, and there was my dad, down in the basement at 2 a.m. working to finish something unresolvable during the daylight hours. There was my mom, the experienced physician with the call schedule of an intern, admitting patients to the hospital while the rest of us were asleep, and there was my dad, the English professor, commuting long hours to adjunct teaching jobs, grading papers after my bedtime, and working, always working, at finishing books.

The labor required by life seemed thrust in our faces, my brother and me. Yet that labor also felt overwhelming because so much of it transpired just out of sight. I had a sense of tasks lurking on the other side of dinner or of a frenetic motion vibrating through the predawn hours. I saw my parents as dual Atlases, that mythological figure who carries the world, and if they hid from us the full range of their efforts, they showed us, through this hiding, the effort that was in store. While we might be free from adult responsibilities, our childhood chores were clearly rehearsals for some vaster task.

I experienced this parental effort as that which protected me from ambiguous hardships, but it also communicated to me a sense that what my parents were doing was barely keeping the world at bay. One must work very hard, in our family model, not necessarily to succeed at life but merely to keep up. Success must mean moving even faster, the kind of doubled-down effort that the Red Queen explains to Alice in *Through the Looking Glass*, that childhood novel by Lewis Carroll. "Now, here, you see," the Red Queen asserts, "it takes all the running you can do, to keep in the same place. If you want to get somewhere else, you must run at least twice as fast as that!"[10] My family lived in looking-glass land, always running, it seemed, but never quite getting to where we wanted to go. I just figured we must not have been running fast enough.

Rereading the tales of Alice recently, I find that the tasks of life are confusing to Carroll's heroine, too. "Are we nearly there?" asks a tired Alice, only to reveal that she has no idea what she had been running toward.[11] Running *very* fast means you are likely to get lost, especially since looking-glass land is a place in which it can be hard to see. Alice is first drawn into her parallel universe because parts of it are beyond her sight. "I can see all of it when I get upon a chair," Alice exclaims, looking in the mirror room reflected over her mantel, "all but the bit behind the fireplace. Oh! I do so wish I could see *that* bit!"[12] In her efforts to visualize what is down the passage, behind the fireplace, on the back of the reflected clock, she finds herself pressed up against the glass, pressing upon it, and stepping through.

As a child, I was also drawn toward what I could not see. The adult world was lurking, though unlike the desirous Alice, I was lured forward by trepidation as much as desire. Curiosity, the buzz word of the Alice books, can take on many additional valences, and the adult world seemed important to explore preemptively, so that I'd be strong enough to handle it once it was mine.

But in looking-glass land there are also books, and I like to think the books are part of what draws Alice in. They are odd books—"something like our books," Alice states, "only the words go the wrong way"—but books nonetheless, and they provide an element of familiarity in a world that is yet unknown.[13] If the child can recognize but not (yet?) read those other words, she still has the security of knowing that these objects exist. For me, too, books were not only a part of my childhood but also promised to be a part of the otherwise mysterious experience of growing up.

Books troubled, in the best of ways, my vision of the adult world as a place of constant work. Books gave one permission to sit in stillness, even as they made space for a different kind of exertion, intellectual labor, which, I intuited, was invisible labor at its most refined. Books also represented the respite from that labor, an atypical and exceptional source of joy. In my family, we as children grew up being read to, and the ritual continued until we were just on the brink of adulthood, long past when it would end for other kids. We grew up around the physical objects, in bookshelves, on end tables, splayed open on countertops, or stacked pristinely in matching sets. And we grew up witnessing many book-inspired activities of consumption and production in which books were offered to us as a form of comfort, companionship, and rest. My parents were and are both avid readers, their nightstands a teetering testament to this commitment and demarcated only by small differences in literary tastes: my mom's, holding mystery stories and more paperbacks; my dad's, filled with academic books, hardcovers, classics. My dad was and is also a writer, and from him we learned to revere the act of composition and the fact that he could produce the thing that represented to us work and pleasure both. One summer, in an act of emulation, I filled multiple notebooks longhand with a childhood novel and spent just as much time typing out my words. I then asked my father to send the typed manuscript off to his publisher, stat.

This final step reveals me to be seduced by a still-held conviction that words take on additional value when acknowledged by another, printed out, and bound. Think of how satisfying it is—or was—to print a term paper or thesis, tap the pages together on a table, and riffle through the stack. As a child writer, I also intended to make money. Growing up with bibliophiles meant I knew the concept of a "bestseller," as well as the concept of "vanity publishing" or a "vanity press." Earning money for my writing, I (and Adam Smith) believed, would both bring me attention and define what I did as "work." And yet, as an economic commodity, books are unique, existing as lasting, physical receptacles for an experience that comes and goes. I'm a carnal versus courtly book lover, my books bearing the brunt of my deep love—stains, rips, broken spines, their bodies deformed after being lost among my bedcovers and rolled upon at night.[14] But even after such use, they never get used up. Books can time travel, existing when I first read them and with me here as I read them again, and books are at once always in process and always complete. No writer, I now know, goes into the profession for the money, but supply and demand among a readership notwithstanding, writing contradicts all the lessons I learned in college chemistry, the ones that taught me I couldn't introduce new matter into the world. Working as a writer instead reinforces that one supposedly botched lab report I completed, in which I assessed my final compound and announced to my professor that it was "115% pure." That one's mental activity, the intangible wisp of an idea, can unfurl into sentences and paragraphs and chapters, can be typed up and printed, can be bound and dust-jacketed and given depth and volume and heft: these realities seem like magic to me, and the one who can accomplish them the greatest magician of all.

But as a child, I had always already known that books were magic. After all, sitting silently in front of a book and moving one's eyes was doing something, and those still and silent postures somehow caused stories or information to be transferred. The secret, I figured, must be in the physical motions, so I, too, would sit in front of books, sometimes big ones, and scan my eyes while turning pages at what I perceived to be the correct pace. "I'm reading to myself," I'd announce, though I would have been lost had anyone asked me what I'd read. I watched grown-ups carefully to see when and how the act of silent "reading" occurred. I watched my dad sometimes in his study, from a quiet distance, by himself typing, pausing, typing again.

Still, that mysterious spark, and the nature of such labor, always eluded me. There was nothing beside the physical motions I could emulate, nothing that gave me a sense of the internal machinery that told a reader when to turn a page or told my father to hit the keyboard *now* but not then. What was he *doing* in there? Why did he need, in those moments, to be so completely on his own? No wonder *Frankenstein* was early on one of my keystone texts, that novel about a protagonist who similarly yearns to understand the spark of life, an invisible secret that he thinks he can locate by viewing, repeatedly, anatomy and gravesites and decay. There must be something he can learn by looking. There must be a way for such learning to lead to creation, companionship, some vital bond. And in the fiction of the novel, there is.

Yet in pursuing that secret, Victor Frankenstein also finds, for a time, all the companionship he needs. The character Walton announces on the first pages of the novel that he has no friends and then immediately sets out on an expedition to the uninhabited North Pole. "I'd just really rather stay home and finish reading my book," I'd announce regularly to my parents throughout my preadolescence, once I did know how to read and write, myself an allegedly lonely school-aged kid.

And so back to my garage or my armchair, my school office, a car dealership, a doctor's waiting room, my dining room table filled with stuff. I don't always need to hide myself to write, I've learned, since if it needs to the work of writing can take place in many locales. And I don't need to worry about loneliness, either, connected as I am to my potential readers and those invisible friends, my thoughts. Or maybe what I mean is that the work of writing always hides itself and its writer, regardless of where it is done. Maybe the work of writing keeps us at our most solitary, our most alone.

It is like those parts of looking-glass land that Alice can't quite see, and so it draws me toward it, toward the words of others and the spaces between their words.

A Note to the Reader:

My life and mind work associatively these days, though I feel in this shift more peace and less chaos that I did when this book began. Can any of us ever, outside of literature or art, see the throughline of a life? The words that follow are an attempt to organize my thoughts on loneliness, companionship, labor, and books, but at times I weave these threads together tightly, and at times I unbraid them to look at one more closely or just to watch them fray. And while I have my own sense of this collection's arc—with subheadings to indicate different components of loneliness and with subtitles to name salient authors who have been, while I negotiated these components, my literary friends—you may read these chapters in whatever order and at whatever pace and level of attention that your life allows. Mainly, as Alice found in looking-glass land and as I found with Alice, I hope you find my words in some way inviting. And I hope you find in the spaces between them some place to put your own.

I

LOSING

1

THE SHADOW LIFE OF BOOKS

William Shakespeare, William Hazlitt, Alexander Chee

Each book is something of a mask of the troubles that went into it and so is the writer's visible career.

—Alexander Chee, *How to Write an Autobiographical Novel*

I wrote my second book under a shadow, though that shadow is, by definition, nowhere obviously apparent.[1]

I'm an English professor who specializes in eighteenth-century British literature, and the book I wrote was about eighteenth-century actors who reenact Shakespeare as a way to counteract their fears of death. It was a book, I came to realize, that charts various responses to loss: how actors responded to the near-erasure of Shakespeare from cultural memory, how spectators and actors responded to fact that the "liveness" of live performance can never be preserved, how audiences responded to the experience of saying goodbye to a beloved actor who had died or left the stage.[2]

Yet at no point within my writing did I reflect on the ways that my lived experience ran parallel to my research. Nowhere did I discuss the fantasy that all writers have at some point: that abandoning the project would be easier than forging on. Nowhere did I invoke the fact that I'd written the book while pregnant with my second child, while in the fallout of a postpartum depression, while living through the breakup of my marriage and the various symptoms of a broken heart. Nowhere did I meditate on how those experiences forced me to acknowledge the inevitability of the experience—loss—that the actors I described tried their hardest to resist. Instead, the completed book stands as a testament to epiphanies I had during a time of semidarkness, and its pages communicate the vitality and sustenance that came from creating them when other things in my life were being stripped away.

I'm not alone in the choices I made about how to hide myself within my work. Many writers keep their writing process in the shadows, as if by acknowledging the false starts and messiness that preceded our final drafts, we will somehow undermine our final success or compromise what success may come. For many writers, too, writing emerges from the shadows of personal experiences that aren't, in many genres at least, explicitly described. Alexander Pope, the eighteenth-century satirical poet, produced comic jibes that jar with his extratextual depression; afflicted at age twelve with a painful tuberculosis of the spine, he would declare (though not in his poetry) that he suffered forever after from "this long disease, my life."[3] Laurence Sterne—another author I thought about in my second book—wrote his comic, often-profane novel *Tristram Shandy* "under the greatest heaviness of heart" and "to fence against" the evils of his life.[4] Much like Pope, he penned jokes under the shadows of some of life's greatest trials: a terminal illness, his mother's death, his wife's mental break. These experiences lend an urgency and desperation to his novel even as they remain mostly hidden behind his playful style.

My book was about another writer famed for both his seamless writing process and his hidden personal life. "His mind and hand went together," declared Shakespeare's fellow actors and first editors, John Heminges and Henry Condell. "And what he thought he uttered with that easiness that we have scarce received from him a blot in his papers."[5] "I REMEMBER," reflects his contemporary Ben Jonson, "the players have often mentioned . . . that in his writing . . . he never blotted out a line."[6] In this myth, Shakespeare's genius derives not just from the profundity of his observations on the human condition or his eloquence in rendering those observations into prose but the ease with which these observations flowed from him and the idea that there was no struggle involved in transforming experience into expression. Nor, some scholars believe, did Shakespeare likely experience the life struggles he so eloquently describes. Shakespearean authorship controversies emerge from and are rebutted by debates about how convincingly he can describe the state of being a king, or a magician, or a shipwrecked maid. If Shakespeare did in fact write all the plays attributed to him (which I believe he did), then autobiography must not have been his goal.[7]

And yet, confronted with the absence of Shakespeare's biography, fans of Shakespeare nonetheless try to pull the personal back into his work. Might not the tragedy of Hamlet tug at us, as Freud once suggested, because Shakespeare was channeling into his creative work his grief at the death of his own, similarly named son? Might it even pull at us *more* because this personal grief is hidden and uninvoked?[8]

I had these thoughts frequently as I wrote, especially when this myth of seamless process and the intersection between personal struggle and artistic creation were taken up by other writers I discussed. "I writ it in a few hours," the seventeenth-century novelist and dramatist Aphra Behn pronounced, describing her tragic and supposedly true account of the murdered slave prince Oroonoko she claimed to have loved without being able to protect. "I never rested my pen a moment for thought."[9]

A part of me always sympathizes with Behn, since maybe, I think, when the events you want to describe are painful, you don't or can't stop to edit. Another part of me objects—and not merely because the "facts" of her story are debatable or because she waited more than twenty years to describe the events that she then ostensibly churned out. The sense that writing flows painlessly from any of us—regardless of the genre we pursue or the genius we possess—seems a little too pat. Those of us who write for a living have experienced the high of having words and ideas come together just so. We've also experienced the antithesis: the lack of inspiration, the creeping paralysis of self-doubt. I wrote parts of my book in joyful moments, and at times, like Behn, I felt as if I "never rested my pen a moment in thought." Other times, however, I would edit my work down to almost nothing at all, or I would look despairingly on my own system of renumbering drafts as I restarted them (my record, I think, was 25). Something is hiding behind the depiction of Shakespeare's or Behn's easy process. So too, I know, is something hiding behind the vitality communicated by my completed book.

Within academia, reflections on how we write and how our identities resonate with our scholarship wax and wane. The goal of academic writing seems to be to transcend process and not indulge it, so that in graduate school, dissertation "boot camps" and working groups are individually organized and few. Advice and strategies for how to write an academic book are hard to implement, and our PhD programs aren't typically set up to workshop literary critical work. The one piece of writing advice I remember receiving as a graduate student was that if I wrote one page a day, I'd have a 365-page dissertation by year's end.

Eventually, those of us who finished our degrees just figured out a process that worked. How one writes, I realized midway through my dissertation, is an absolute expression of who one is.[10]

This question of who one is also often remains in the shadows of academic writing. In some subsets of scholarship, identity remains, quite rightfully, in the forefront. Performance studies, for example—a field of scholarship devoted to studying the nature of the social and theatrical behaviors that, through their repetition, constitute performance—often attracts practitioners and scholars who draw upon their experiences as evidence for what they discuss. One also encounters these scholars within the fields of queer theory, cultural studies, and the various areas of criticism devoted to minority cultures, literature, and art—fields that tend to attract scholars who acknowledge a personal investment in the subjects they peruse. In other areas of academia, however—especially those devoted to the cultural productions of prior historical periods or to writers who don't share a demographic with their critic or both—autobiography can feel misplaced.

And yet we are like each other in so many different ways. As a writer, "you are like the child who believes they are invisible because they stood in a shadow," writes the biracial, gay author Alexander Chee. No wonder he was so frustrated when editors kept asking him how to characterize his first book: as a gay novel or as an Asian American novel. "It's a novel," he keeps repeating to his agent, "I wrote a *novel*."[11] To label it more specifically threatens to exclude readers who don't see him in terms of those particular labels—the readers who don't, because he remains in shadow, enter into their interaction with the assumption that they would be left out.

In my case, I am a white, straight, forty-something-year-old woman living in Los Angeles, a single soccer mom to two boys and one dog. I've got one boy who looks like me, one who looks more like his mixed-race dad. They've got another family and background across the ocean in Hawaii—physically as far, I remember thinking when I met their father, and culturally as different as one could get from my New England upbringing while still staying in the United States. I can only ever tell them stories about what it was like to get to know this other family, this other home. I'm emphatically not an actor, though I'm a teacher who imagines, sometimes, that her best lectures might rival the performances of the actors she admires. My experiences are mostly peripheral to my fascination with the long-dead, childless, male actor David Garrick, who emerged as the main character in my latest academic research.

And even when I identified with Garrick, I wondered: would readers benefit from hearing that my reflections on Garrick and his anxieties about mortality helped me put words to my own anxieties about death and loss? Should they know that I almost abandoned chapter 5, a chapter ironically about another actor's persistent refusal to retire, at least five different times? Or that I, trapped in my un-air-conditioned garage one summer, stared hopelessly at one ineffectual draft in the unique haze that descends during the final weeks of pregnancy, sweat pooling in crevasses and folds known only to those about to give birth? (My struggles, in this sense, so different from those of the men in my research and my life.)

I chose to keep such memories out of my scholarship, in part because they weren't events that succeeded in overpowering it. Indeed, much of what still draws me to scholarly research is the desire to discover and communicate something beyond myself. Much of what sustains me during times of sadness is the overt disparity between my research and my life. My work lets me define myself broadly, a safety net so that if or when a facet of my identity is torpedoed (free spirit, good writer, runner, friend), I have other identities at the ready to adopt. More privately I think, while watching a student struggle during my office hours or a friend despair over ever finishing a piece, that I would, if I could, protect those I love from such pain. As I do with my children, I want to treat my readers to the fruits of my labors and save them the labor in turn. In this regard, a finished academic book, like a highly polished lecture—or, in its own way, like a carefully made school lunch, a mysteriously folded pile of laundry, or a freshly made bed—is a gift.

There can be benefits, both artistic and personal, to keeping the writing process and autobiography in the shadows. Writing directly about personal experience can, when rendered in a certain way, feel self-indulgent and flat. "Nor will it seem to thee, my friend," writes William Wordsworth to Samuel Taylor Coleridge at the end of the first book of his magnum opus—an autobiographical poem that Wordsworth meant to be but a "Prelude" to his much larger, never-finished, philosophic work—"that I have lengthened out . . . / With fond and feeble tongue a tedious tale."[12] Despite (and because of) his prolixity on the subject of himself, Wordsworth remained hyperconscious that critics might describe his project as self-absorbed, and he was vigilant to avoid becoming the target of such critique. Exposing the work of writing, which Wordsworth also does by continuing to revise *The Prelude* throughout his life, is autobiography at its most intense. As I told one of my most-trusted writing friends, sharing writing-in-progress is terrifyingly intimate, like letting someone see you naked, unwashed, unshaven, and under fluorescent lights. No matter how much you love that person, and how impressive her final product is, that image can be hard to forget.

There can also be benefits, however, to illuminating the cracks and flaws that make up who we are and what it is we make. If the idea that writing always came easily for Shakespeare is a fallacy, so too is the idea that every word he wrote should be revered. "Would he had blotted a thousand!" Jonson famously quipped, and Jonson had his own favorite examples of Shakespearean duds.[13] Perhaps the most frequently referenced Shakespearean faux pas (though not by Jonson) occurs midway through *The Winter's Tale,* when the hapless Antigonus, in accordance with one of Shakespeare's very few stage directions, is told to "*Exit. Pursued by a bear.*" (In Shakespeare's day, a real bear may or may not have appeared onstage.)[14] Another such moment comes at the end of *King Lear.* "'Tis hot, it smokes!" exclaims a nameless gentleman, trying to describe a bloody knife, "It came even from the heart of —O, she's dead!"[15]

These lines risk eliciting laughter at moments of insupportable grief, yet despite Jonson's push for more editing, there are advantages to keeping them intact. "His flawed heart," mourns Edgar of his father's demise, in *Lear,* "'twixt two extremes of passion, joy and grief, burst smilingly."[16] Any emotion, when experienced unstintingly, can feel fatal to its possessor—and not just joy or grief but so too with adulation. Finding moments of inconsistency within a poet or a critic or a parent humanizes the role models we are apt to adore and renders them and ourselves more open to being loved. Just so, the pull and poignancy of art can reside in its cracks and imperfections, as offset by its achievements, and the cracks in our own creations can be reminders of our dedication to our craft. Like our children, the books we write matter to us not because they have been easy or because they are perfect but because the experience of shepherding them through to adulthood is often so painful and takes so long.

This analogy between books and children comes to mind as another book is finally, almost, between its covers—a turn of phrase that conjures up the security I feel when tucking my children into bed. I can reflect now, as I do in those brief moments between my children's descent into unconsciousness and my own, on all that has come before: on the fact that I finished that other book during a time of personal struggle and also during a research sabbatical that kept me out of the classroom and coincided with the 2016 election and the global feelings of fear and isolation that kept emerging in response. Back in the classroom, I watched these feelings play out, as my students reflected for me the daily uncertainties that our news, and the experience of college, can produce. And yet, as I told my crying six-year-old one night, I don't always know how to help.

I think about their struggles in my teaching too, as I guide students again through *The Odyssey* and the trials and tribulations that Odysseus craves. Pain stands in for experience in this epic, as the oblivion offered by the Lotus Eaters, or Calypso, or even Helen, as she attempts to drug her husband's wine, are risks to be avoided at all costs. Odysseus's very name, according to some translators, means "Son of Pain," and Telemachus arrives at Menelaus's palace just in time to celebrate the wedding of his son Megapenthes, a name that similarly means "the great sorrow."[17] No shadows, here; pain and personality in this work are intertwined. Most scholarship, by contrast, seems designed to disguise the struggle that precedes epiphany or conclusion. In our worst moments in academia, we can seem to bury our humanity beneath the appearance of being certain, or of being right.

Yet, as I also reflect while teaching, such an assessment threatens to overlook that exposing our humanity can take on many different forms. "Milton loved me in childhood," the poet William Blake wrote, describing his experience reading John Milton's epic account of the fall of man, "and shewed me his face."[18] Describing a text that is autobiographical only in the sense that it narrates the prehistory of the human condition, Blake reminds us that we can share our struggles with writing or with life in sometimes shadowed ways. The writers I thought about in my second book knew this, too. "Who shall give us Mrs. Siddons again," the nineteenth-century critic William Hazlitt lamented on losing one of the greatest Shakespearean actresses of the late-eighteenth-century stage: "Who shall in our time (or can ever to the eye of fancy) fill the stage, like her, with the dignity of their persons, and the emanations of their minds? . . . Who shall walk in sleepless ecstasy of soul, and haunt the mind's eye ever after with the dread pageantry of suffering and guilt? Who shall make tragedy once more stand with its feet upon the earth, and with its head raised above the skies, weeping tears and blood? That loss is not to be repaired."[19]

Hazlitt's lament for a beloved actress—so impassioned and so out of keeping with his other criticisms of the theater—is also a recognition of all the kinds of losses that life will bring. "The life of a favourite performer," Hazlitt admits elsewhere, "glances a mortifying reflection on the shortness of human life."[20] I don't begrudge Hazlitt the chance to mourn his own mortality through the theater and criticism. If he needs to look askance at tragedy, or to channel his deeper sadness through some smaller loss, that is no more than we all need from time to time. Such moments can teach us how better to read the personal revelations that we all, constantly and indirectly, share. The folded laundry, the freshly made lunch, the retroactive clarity of thought: they are gifts, and they contain, within them, the secrets of their making, too.

2

READING TO A CHILD
Roald Dahl, Shakespeare, T. H. White

*O dear father,
It is thy business that I go about*
—*King Lear*, 4.4.25–26

I decided I would read the first graders Roald Dahl.

I began with *The Witches*, the same book my first-grade teacher had read to my class years ago and a book that I'd also read aloud to my two boys several times already at home. One class into the reading, it failed. "Explain to the children about 'genre,'" my son's teacher had said: "fiction and nonfiction—what isn't true versus what is." Putting aside my literature-professor thoughts on this topic, I had defined the story as fictional only to encounter at the very outset these lines: "In fairy-tales, witches always wear silly black hats and black cloaks, and they ride on broomsticks. But this is not a fairy-tale. This is about REAL WITCHES."[1]

Despite reading the story at home, I had forgotten it began that way: "Real witches dress in ordinary clothes . . . they live in ordinary houses and they work in ordinary jobs . . . for all you know, a witch might be living next door to you right now. Or she might have been the woman with the bright eyes who sat opposite to you on the bus this morning. . . . She might even—and this will make you jump—she might even be your lovely school-teacher who is reading these words to you at this very moment."[2]

I jumped a bit myself; it feels very different to read those words aloud to a class of listening students than it does to read them to yourself, or even to your children, at home. "Let's take a vote," I said at the end of chapter 1, "show of hands. Too scary and stop, or not too scary and keep going?" A solid majority wanted to pause.

To be clear, I wasn't their teacher, so Dahl's accusation somewhat missed the mark. I was a school parent who had volunteered for this weekly activity in lieu of registering for the PTA, organizing a holiday party, leading classroom sessions on character building, or chaperoning twenty-four children on a field trip through LA. I had suggested this activity to make myself feel like a good parent, to deploy one of my few translatable professional skills, and, on some semiconscious level, to offset the possibility that I had, through my recent divorce, irreparably traumatized my first-grade son.

That I'd envisioned my reception differently was no doubt colored by my own memories of being read to as a child. According to the essayist Adam Gopnik, children's books have to please two audiences at the same time: the child, who uses stories to escape childhood, and the adult, who uses children's books to recapture it.[3] In the childhood I remembered, there were the hours spent with the books I paged through but, even more, the hours spent with the books I heard. More specifically, there was my English professor father, who had taught me to revere the act of reading aloud not as a domestic duty or as a ritual for only the very young but as a deeply felt display. For years, he'd read me bedtime stories from the novels that lined his shelves, my mother listening, often sleeping, at my feet. Love, and be silent: I'd worshipped him as a result.

Such memories pushed me to try my hand with the first graders again, this time with *Matilda*, Dahl's last published children's book.[4] Now we all got on swimmingly, reading a couple of chapters every week. I read to them, then, about corporal punishment—a cabinet in the school studded with glass shards called the "Chokey," into which bad children were forced to stand. I read to them about the dreaded Miss Trunchbull, the professional hammer thrower now turned headmistress, who keeps in training by launching disobedient children over her head. I read to them about verbal abuse and emotional neglect: parents who didn't love their children, who ignored them in favor of the "telly" or bingo or at best called them nitwits, idiots, and scabs. I read to them about Bruce Bogtrotter, the greedy upperformer who steals a sweet from Miss Trunchbull's tea and who is force-fed as a result, before the assembled student body, an entire, enormous chocolate cake.

The thing is: most of Dahl's stories are pretty dark, particularly by today's standards, and the darkness is usually exactly what appeals. "The prevalent parental belief," writes the child psychologist Bruno Bettelheim, "is that a child must be diverted from what troubles him most . . . we want our children to believe that, inherently, all men are good. But children know that *they* are not always good; and often, even when they are, they would prefer not to be."[5] For Bettelheim, this fact underscores why fairy tales are so valuable to children, as they, in their darkness, put words to the existential dilemmas that grip us all. Despite his disavowal of fairy tales, Dahl's stories have something of this quality, too. Traumatized by his own time in the British boarding school system, Dahl empowers the young, the small, the overlooked. His tiny protagonists find magic beans, golden tickets, giant peaches. They are also abused, starved, orphaned, and permitted to act out their revenge.

Matilda shared this violence with our abortive first attempt. Indeed, many of the students started taking "notes" in their journals as they read: pictures from the reading, which often replicated the violent scenes we'd just shared. "That's the Chokey," I remember an otherwise quiet girl named Illaria saying to me, calmly identifying the cabinet of student torture. "And that's Miss Trunchbull throwing Amanda Thripp"—a stick figure in pigtails sailed across the page.

Rereading Dahl in these classroom sessions reminded me of how writers such as Claire Dederer and Toni Morrison have engaged the question of loving the writing of writers whose life choices you may hate.[6] As I learned, later, from reading his biographies, Dahl had a tangled personal life and a vicious antisemitic streak. His edges show more in his writing for adults, the stories he published in the *New Yorker* and *Playboy* that ended up in the collections *Kiss Kiss, Someone Like You, Switch Bitch*. I was definitely Dahl-satiated by the time I finished reading those. As a friend once told me, it can be dangerous to learn too much about the writers one loves. In my son's classroom, I kept cringing at how Dahl's not nice to grown women, in life or on the page.

But as a kid, I hadn't known or cared. Like the child audience to whom I now read, I had taken pleasure in Dahl's violence, and I don't remember wondering why the witches were all female or why he would single out Miss Trunchbull, also Miss Honey, as a "Miss." I don't remember being bothered by the way he depicts Matilda's mother, aside from the fact that I was happy she wasn't my own.

Morrison, reflecting on writers such as Hemmingway and Cather, explains that she "loved those books . . . so when they said these things that were profoundly racist, I forgave them."[7] Dederer similarly struggles to make her peace with troubling artists she admires, men such as Roman Polanski, Miles Davis, Carl Andre. The capacity of these critics to forgive feels admirable to me, and right. Except, the danger for the child reader is that in our earliest readings we encounter such depictions as descriptions. The danger is that we accept as ideological reality that which the godlike writer portrays. When does not knowing enough to forgive tip over into thinking that nothing needs to be forgiven?

And yet, we can always take new purchase on our childhood perspectives; we can revisit the books and people we thought we knew.

The early difference, I reflected, between *Matilda* and *The Witches* was Dahl's opening "truth claim," an assertion made even more unsettling by the moment at which Dahl announces that he knows you are being read to aloud. I've always liked those moments in *Tom Jones* or *Jane Eyre*, in which the narrator calls out to the reader directly from the page. In those cases, however, these relationships feel private, insular: a secret shared between reader and book. Dahl, by contrast, manipulates the communal relationship that he creates. "Look carefully at that teacher," he orders the listening child. "Perhaps she is smiling at the absurdity of such a suggestion [that she is a witch]. Don't let that put you off. It could be part of her cleverness."[8] And I was smiling as I read those lines; he was right. The truth claim in and of itself might not be a deterrent—after all, children want both to push and find the limits of their belief. But my own childhood experiences listening to stories told me that I was lulled by the unspoken presence of the adult. Stories fulfill the same role played at a dinner party by a baby or the family dog: they mediate how we engage with others, so that the pressure to see and acknowledge, or to be seen and acknowledged, can be channeled through a book. Dahl disrupts this. He doesn't just remind listeners that the adult reader might be bad; he reminds them first and foremost that the adult reader is there. He reminds me, too, of my own potential influence over listeners, a relationship that in my nostalgia or enjoyment or absorption I am tempted to forget.

To forget that others are present, or to erase others from your mind. Is this what happens when we read aloud? Stanley Cavell has an essay on *King Lear* in which he argues that the play is about "the avoidance of love." What Lear wants, Cavell suggests, is faux love, and so Cordelia cannot repeat the scripts of Goneril and Regan because—were she to say those words of love—they would be true. Similarly, it is only in his meeting with Gloucester that Lear can bear recognition, and this is only because Gloucester at this moment is blind.[9]

Reading books to others can also blind us to those we love; acts of bonding are, if mediated, also complicated by books. When I first became a mother, I realized that my relationship to my own parents would be forever changed, since I now had a maternal bond that required me to be a mother and not a child. Or, that's one way to describe postpartum depression: the belief that being a mother meant I had lost my own childhood for good. Can a child of thirty-seven crawl back into the womb? A mother for the second time, blessed with a newborn who somehow slept, I found that I could rest only if curled next to my own mother on our pull-out couch. Even here, adrenaline would awaken me, launching me into a silent house in which the only cure for loneliness was shelves of books.

And so, at 3 a.m. one morning, I reread a scene about killing a unicorn. It begins like this: "We have not seen our Mammy for one week . . . she has forgotten us . . . if we could do a unicorn hunt . . . and bring this unicorn which she requires, perhaps . . . she will be pleased."[10] The boys planning this quest are future knights of the Round Table—Gareth, Gawaine, Gaheris, and Agravaine, sons to the queen-witch Morgause—and the scene occurs midway through T. H. White's retelling of the King Arthur story, his novel *The Once and Future King*. I read this book for the first time as a child, trapped between the same worlds of fantasy and reality as the boy-knights of whom I read. The boy-knights, however, will soon leave the world of make-believe far behind. "'That girl,'" says Agravaine, of the kitchen maid they lure to pose as bait, "'is my mother. And I am going to be Sir Grummore.' . . . They had abstracted real boar-spears from the armoury, so they were properly armed."[11] The animal killing that follows has none of the comedy of Dahl or the nonchalance of fairy tale. Here, violence marks the departure from childhood and not the fantasy of it.

Yet even for the boys, the true tragedy is not the brutality they enact but the fact that their loss of innocence will be all for naught. They hope for maternal approval; they fear, or perhaps desire, their mother's ire. Instead, at the end of their butchered quest, Queen Morgause "did not notice her four sons . . . dirty, excited, their breasts beating with hope. . . . Queen Morgause did not see the unicorn. Her mind was busy with other things."[12] The passage isn't overtly about readings or readers; it has none of the self-address of Dahl. On the contrary, it is a scene about adult absorption and about children being ignored. Yet it mirrored a sensation that I felt as a child, when I turned to books to forget the world. Lonely children are also often avid readers, substituting the fantasy world of story for the real-world attachments they cannot attain. I used reading to avoid household chores and homework but also to avoid the other types of avoidance that I'd otherwise have to confront: the kids who didn't want to play with me, the parental distraction that can shatter a child's solipsistic world. I read to shut out others and so that my absorption would preempt the sensation of being alone.

When I reread White's book as an adult, this scene put words to my existential dread about being forgotten, a fate in which I was passed over in favor of a book.[13]

Reading to first graders wasn't the first time I'd read aloud. When I began graduate school, I was paid to read to an emeritus professor from our home department who was recovering from a stroke.[14] The circumstances leading up to the employment were comic, bleak: the nurses had called the family to say that their physically incapacitated yet heretofore still lucid patient was beginning to suffer from confusion, possibly dementia; the symptoms were that he was muttering in tongues. A family visit verified instead that he was quoting from the *Metamorphoses*, in Latin, and that he was deeply, even despairingly, bored.

He wanted to be read to, or maybe the family came up with this idea on their own. Either way, a few of my classmates were interested, but the family chose me, perhaps in no little part because I was energetic, enthusiastic, and blonde. I seem to remember he had requested a woman, though how or why this preference would have been publicized now seems unclear. I do know my own enthusiasm for the opportunity bordered on the hyperbolic and that I'd registered the departmental email request for volunteers as a contest to be won. Which of all the students in our department could say they loved books most? "With a love that makes breath poor, and speech unable; beyond all manner of so much," surely I did.[15]

I read, once I was appointed to the post, two evenings a week, at the same time of night each time I came. I read sitting beside a hospital bed, and I brought my own books. I also brought to the readings—and we read mostly poetry, again and again—all the naïveté that in our graduate coursework we were required to suppress. I read the poems and poets I'd grown up with and that I liked to read: Frost, Keats, Ransom, Shelley, Coleridge, Stevens, Eliot, Bishop, Yeats, Auden, Lewis Carroll, Ogden Nash. I read them to him, and he said them back at me: "Arcady," the professor told me, scans with "ecstasy"; "fillet," when referring to a headband for the hair, is not pronounced as if it were a piece of fish; "progress," in the context of "Prufrock," must be said with a long *o*.

My visits took on a formulaic sameness, with occasional variation. Sometimes the nurses or aides stayed to listen; I remember one in particular who stayed for many visits in a row. He was also the aide whom I found the time I arrived early, changing the professor as one would change a child, the unaccommodated man laid out before me, bare and fork'd. Another visit I arrived, only to find the professor on the phone, raging at a family member, in a fight. "I've been a beast," he explained, when I later reentered the room. Once I never arrived at all, after a snowstorm, an icy road, and a message left at the nurses' station that never got delivered. "One must have a mind of winter," I thought, riffing on Wallace Stevens's "The Snow Man," when I heard the professor's voice that night on my answering machine at home. Odd how storm winds figure in both Stevens and *Lear*.[16]

What can reading offer to combat such storms? At this point in life, I had no prior experience reading aloud. Instead, I brought to my new "job" all my years of being read to, by a father who had once been a professor in this same department and who had experienced the vocation they shared as an unrequited love. For years I'd listened to my father read the books I now studied and about which I aspired to write. For years I'd sensed how artistic passion vies with more personal connection: how writers and readers can lose themselves so completely in a book. And yet, for years I'd loved books and, through them, him, and for years I'd struggled, as we all do with our parents, to heave my heart into my mouth.

Reading to the professor seemed, for me and the man in the hospital bed, to put words to the experiences we couldn't otherwise parse out. But if we both had our portion as Cordelia, the professor was more obviously Lear. All we have left to us when we have come full circle is our infantile temper and strength of will. Lear begins the play by choosing to relinquish everything that he has had throughout his life: he's the aging parent who voluntarily gives up the right to drive, the toddler who willingly gives away his favorite toy. Strange that no one sees the courage in this act. If afterward he should ask for flattery and the trappings of adulthood, which he himself has rendered hollow, he's asking for that which can barely compensate for his own presumptive leap of faith. In our final moments, we need those around us to remind us of who we were. Look, there: if I read to the professor by his bedside, the way one does to a sleepy child, I was also the disciple who sat at his feet. When he died, I sat in the back of the church, the stony dignitaries from my university gathered around. I remember being one of the very few people to cry. He had been, after all, so important, and so old.

I know that with my own children, I am often beyond their reach. Sometimes I'm preoccupied with a work email, a shopping list, my phone. But there are also times I tune them out by stealing time to read a few pages in a novel or to work on a few paragraphs in a piece of writing I can't forget. This phenomenon goes back as far as novels themselves. Antinovel sentiment in the eighteenth century was often motivated by anecdotes of fiction's disruptive social effect: scullery maids who stopped cleaning in order to read, aristocratic mistresses setting a bad example for servants by "losing hours" to a book.[17] Other complaints, however, hit the more primal chord of maternal neglect. "I have actually seen mothers, in miserable garrets, crying for the imaginary distress of an heroine, while their children were crying for bread," states one reviewer, horrified that the experiences of an imaginary person would take precedence over the real-world needs of the woman's own kids.[18]

Can this effect be in play even when my children are ostensibly the audience to whom I read?[19] Quite possibly, if we consider that the most frequent reason for adults to read to children is to get them to fall asleep. The critic Maria Tartar presents the bedtime story as the end result of a cultural progression "from the fireside to the nursery," in which communal nighttime rituals around the hearth—rituals in which adults and children commingled in broad kinship units—were replaced by separate nighttime rooms and rituals for children.[20] As these routines became increasingly individuated, late-night communal storytelling shifted to storytelling with a very specific, soporific goal. An adult reader focused on a hopefully sleepy child-listener, one often too young yet to read alone. A "successful" reading meant the reader would supplant (or supplement) the syrups and strategies—from threats, to whippings, to warm milk, to opium-laced drops—that parents used, and perhaps to some extent still use, to get their children to stay in bed.

In the bedtime tradition that Tartar narrates, the practice of reading aloud seems to sever bonds, not forge them: the goal of reading seems to be to subdue the child, not engage him or her. Yet a child lulled by reading can equally demonstrate confidence in the adult attachment and an assurance, hopefully reinforced through the sharing of a story, that the adult will be there when the child awakes. To witness such comfort brings reassurance to the parent, too. "Dear Babe," writes Coleridge in his "conversation" poem to his infant son Hartley, "that sleepest cradled by my side,"

> Whose gentle breathings, heard in this deep calm,
> Fill up the interspersed vacancies
> And momentary pauses of the thought!
> My babe so beautiful! It thrills my heart
> With tender gladness, thus to look at thee . . .[21]

Coleridge "reads" his poem, as it were, to the sleeping Hartley, an act of communion made possible because Hartley cannot respond.

I know I had been, contra Hartley, a difficult bedtime child. Sometimes, in our longstanding evening family readings, I would drift off like my mother, lulled to sleep only a few pages in. Sometimes, I would stay awake, either captivated by the story or anxious about the departure that I knew would accompany the story's end, or both. And I wonder, too, if on some level I always felt the way that the books could pull my dad away. I remember him reading to me from the tales of Paul Bunyan—the episode about the white snowball Paul brings back during the winter of the blue snow—and getting excited about "synecdoche" and pausing to mark the passage and make notes. Who wins this contest for her father's heart? I stumbled across that moment years later, cited in the introduction to his Coleridge book.[22]

It hasn't been until I myself have become a parent that I can feel, from the other perspective, what my resistance to comfort must have felt like to my father and how I myself have used books to perform or disappear. As someone who regularly sneaks into her children's bedroom late at night, I know how quickly we can oscillate between a desire for detachment and outpourings of love. I know, too, how feelings of attachment intensify when our children are unresponsive, vulnerable, or incapable of making reciprocal demands. I also feel a certain amount of cynicism toward Coleridge's peaceful scene. It's easy to have warm, poetic thoughts about your child at midnight, when that child is sleeping and can't contradict your love. How different the acts of parent-child bonding that occur at 11 p.m. on a weeknight when your child is fretful, 5 p.m. on a school night before soccer practice, or at 8:05 on a Monday morning when the school bell rings at 8:15.

Reflecting on these times of parent-child chaos, however, also helps me understand the unique balance between cathexis and independence that reading together can provide: it gives my children and me a compromise between a love predicated on their unconsciousness and the entropy produced by three independent wills. In our moments of most successful reading, it's as if we were standing side by side, admiring some great work of art—each with our own impressions, each absorbed completely by what we see, yet conscious, at the same time, of sharing this experience and sustained by the reactions we reveal. It makes me think, too, that this was the experience I shared during those nighttime readings with my dad.

The worlds of adulthood and childhood can otherwise seem so far apart. In everyday life, so much of what separates parent from child takes the form of competing interests and therefore competing demands: the child who can't understand the parental ambivalence toward a newly imagined game of "ghost hunters," the parent who would choose a cup of tea and a *New Yorker* article over hunting phantoms for the fifteenth time. Behind this scene, further, the adult emotional complexities that feel impossible to translate. My years of reading to the professor were my first of graduate school, a career I'd embraced in part to compensate for the frustrations I'd sensed my father had experienced on that same path; my year of classroom reading was the year I got divorced. But if mine were semiconscious efforts to make reparations for a primal trauma, then I must have thought I could provide, through reading, something akin to the holding environment of analysis: something that would enable my son and me and my father to start again. What I found instead was a transitional space, a place of meeting and departure all at once.[23] As our children race toward adulthood and we dodder, Lear-like, toward our graves, reading to a child can give us a moment to pause in the middle and greet each other as we pass.

3

THE DETECTIVE'S MIND
Arthur Conan Doyle

"You see, but you do not observe."
—Sir Arthur Conan Doyle, "A Scandal in Bohemia"

As the only grownup in my house, the chaos of my living or working space often hits me as a reproach. How can I be a good writer, mom, or person if I live in such disorder? And if I live in disorder, how can anything about my life ever change? Stepping over a makeshift obstacle course on my way to the kitchen, finding Lego pieces embedded in my feet, sitting down to relax on the couch only to be impaled by a plastic sword: I read these circumstances as signs of my inchoate parenting, threats to any aspirational professional identity, and emblems of my inability to keep up.[1]

But if the sword or Lego piece can easily and quite reasonably set me roaring, the irony of my reaction is that these habits predate my current circumstances and aren't attributable to them alone. I'm not a particularly neat person, nor have I ever been. I am instead the worst combination of a somewhat messy person who can't always make peace with her mess. In college, the dorm room I shared with my friend was whispered about as the place you could find jelly stains on keyboards, spoons glued to cereal bowls with long-ago evaporated milk, and coffee mugs that were refilled without removing the remnants of drinks past. Long before I had children, my car was accruing a range of clutter, from snacks to dog hair to library books to spare pens, and my "work" spaces, to the extent that there is a distinction, have always been similarly full of piles and scraps. I keep my notepads everywhere and my books stacked around me in strategic cairns. These writing habits go back to my earliest student days.

Or, if I'm honest, they go back far earlier than that. I believe these are habits I inherited—an approach to living and writing embedded in my DNA.

How can one with neat habits of mind be so chaotic in his space? The question opens one of Sir Arthur Conan Doyle's short detective stories, in which Sherlock Holmes's biographer and roommate John Watson describes his methodical, mentally precise friend as "one of the most untidy men that ever drove a fellow lodger to distraction."[2] To be fair, Holmes isn't dirty, so much as cluttered. He keeps "his cigars in the coal scuttle, his tobacco in the toe end of a Persian slipper, and his unanswered correspondence transfixed by a jack-knife" to the mantle, just below the morocco case that, as we learn in a different story, contains the hypodermic and liquid cocaine that he turns to when the "dull routine of existence" becomes too much.[3] Bullet holes pockmark an adjacent wall, left over from an at-home target practice taken when Holmes was feeling at once lazy and bored. Apparently housekeeping is a dull commentary on existence, indeed.

Sherlock Holmes and my dad have the same housekeeping style. In our home, my father is required to relegate his Holmesian habits (of organization, not of drugs) to his study, but they, by definition, encroach. Chocolate chips, the substitute for hypodermics, migrate from the kitchen to the study; newspapers proliferate outward; scraps of paper on the breakfast table contain partial solutions to a diagramless puzzle, a cryptoquip. We have bookshelves everywhere, yet his books end up on endtables, nightstands, the floor. He may never yet have deposited criminal relics in the butter dish, but "his papers were my great crux," I can imagine my mother saying, as Holmes's biographer also laments.[4]

As cruxes go, these habits remind me of another crux popularized in eighteenth-century philosophy, that of the absolute inaccessibility of the human mind. Theories of sympathy proliferate in this time period; newly minted novelists offer up, via fiction, the experience of psychological access. And yet, at the end of the day, the century's thinkers are hamstrung by the conclusion that still confronts us all: we can never know precisely what is going on in another's mind. Not only that, we aren't even the best observers of these functions in ourselves. John Locke describes the understanding as "like the eye," which, "whilst it makes us see and perceive all other things, takes no notice of itself."[5] An eyeball can't see itself, I often paraphrase to my kids, to justify the concept of a blind spot usually while demonstrating one of my own. Still, we desire this access, and we gravitate toward those who seem to have it: therapist, fortune teller, detective, priest.

But what if habits of housekeeping *could* provide the key to an otherwise inaccessible mental space? With both Holmes and my father, there's a method to their madness, since one can imagine a fireplace and slippers and tobacco as activities that all align. And what better place for a week's worth of the *New York Times* than the kitchen floor? Clutter, my mom calls it, and there's definitely a tipping point, when piles that have been old friends become suddenly infuriating, and I set off in search of trash bags and that other Lockean metaphor of existence, the blank slate. The puzzles and papers make it hard for me to see those at their center, hard for me to be seen by those whose attention is otherwise engaged. But must they always function in such a manner? Holmes, after all, has also long trained me to suspect that what I'm looking for might be right before me, invisible because it is too near.

Sherlock Holmes is famous for his powers of observation—famous, as my epigraph indicates, for being able to register what most of us merely "see." His first illustration of this distinction occurs in "A Scandal in Bohemia," when he asks Watson to tally from memory the steps leading from the street to their apartment: Holmes can immediately name the number, whereas Watson, despite climbing these steps numerous times, cannot.[6] Another example is the episode of "mind reading" Doyle initially included in "The Adventure of the Cardboard Box" (he moved it in later editions of his tales to "The Adventure of the Resident Patient"). In this second case, Watson, lost in a reverie, is first pleased then baffled when Holmes times an interjection to coincide with his friend's "inmost thought." "What is this, Holmes!" exclaims Watson, as he realizes that Holmes's speech has articulated perfectly with his own silent musings. "This is beyond anything which I could have imagined."[7] Holmes can do, in other words, what eighteenth-century philosophers aspire to do: see inside the mind itself.

He can't, of course. Instead, he explains, he has merely seen—and observed—the way Watson's eyes have been traveling around their cluttered room, then interpreting the sequence of Watson's thoughts based upon the associations he guesses each object will inspire. The trick, too, is a learned behavior, modeled as Holmes admits upon the behavior of Edgar Allan Poe's literary detective August Dupin, who had done the same.⁸ Poe, as Doyle well knew, had been the first to make famous via literature the detective's powers of observation, with Dupin solving the case of "The Purloined Letter" by discovering the titular document "hidden" in a public card rack: hidden, in other words, in plain sight. And Poe, like Doyle and Holmes, himself gravitated toward the puzzles and mysteries of life. He was fascinated by cryptography, with his short story "The Gold Bug" turning on an example of what Poe elsewhere called "secret writing," and he tantalized readers of *Graham's Magazine* by challenging them to send him a cipher he couldn't crack.⁹ All these examples show faith in a precise kind of discernment: a belief in a mind that is able to see what other minds cannot, a mind that, if it can't quite see inside other minds, can nonetheless see meaning in nonsense or treasure in what others perceive as trash.

Such a mind shows an ability to make sense of clutter, which, as the detective knows, can disguise a sense of hierarchy waiting for the detective, or the critic, to discern. Archival research is similarly motivated by the belief that individual documents have the potential to increase in value based on a researcher's ability to synthesize and contextualize the materials that remain. Scholars are like detectives trained to "read a room," not based on emotional intelligence but on how the component physical parts of a room matter and add up. That water stain on the floor, ignored by most observers, may be the crucial clue; that unsigned letter in a collections box may reveal long-lost secrets; that scribble on a Post-it note may be a writer's key prompt. Scholar and detective alike sequence, prioritize, and create narrative out of what appears to be random life. To do so, they need a room to remain crowded, its materials, intact.

The objects that crowd the apartment on Baker Street are reminders of this mental activity; equally, they are invitations to join in, or retrace, the chase. Take, for example, the relics from "The Musgrave Ritual," a title whose words describe an actual act and the tale—told by Holmes to Watson and then recorded by Watson for us—of the same name. The tale begins in a fit of tidying, as Watson, finally at his hygienic limit, urges his friend to spend the next couple of hours cleaning up. But Holmes's dedication to the task lasts only minutes, as he soon emerges dragging a large box. In the box are early case records—the titles of which Holmes rattles out as another form of provocation, a strategy that Doyle developed early in the Holmes series, of planting within existing stories allusions to stories possibly yet to come— and a seemingly random collection of objects: a smaller box containing "a crumpled piece of paper, an old-fashioned brass key, a peg of wood with a ball of string attached to it, and three rusty old discs of metal."[10]

Holmes's rediscovery of these objects reminds me of moments when I've been similarly derailed in my own acts of cleaning, distracted by a clutter that suddenly becomes a sentimental, mnemonic prod. The objects are reminiscent of assortments I've found in my children's closet, a space that I refer to only semi-facetiously as the "toy compost pile." But I've been chastised by my children, too, for disposing of their unassuming strings, discs, and pegs. Far from trash, I learn, these were crucial transitional objects, treasures, props. "It is a curious collection," states Watson, sounding like me as I empty a backpack (but curious why? And to whom?). "Very curious," confirms Holmes, "and the story that hangs round it will strike you as being more curious still."[11] These objects provide the scaffolding for stories; they are like the seamstress's dummy upon which she creates.

The story that Holmes spins around these objects similarly exposes value in chaos and hidden puzzles where no puzzles were thought to exist. The titular Musgrave Ritual, as it unravels, shifts from a series of phrases as recorded on that saved, crumpled piece of paper and repeated by every aristocratic Musgrave man upon his coming of age to a much larger coming-of-age story: a series of phrases saved and first recorded years ago by the Cavaliers to help the exiled Charles recover his crown and riches once the monarchy had been restored. The repetitions of the titular ritual carry through the process by which Holmes reveals the ritual's true purpose, which doesn't begin as an investigation into lost treasure at all but a response to the current Lord Musgrave as to the whereabouts of his butler, Brunton, and his troubled housemaid, with whom Brunton had had an affair. But the former, older mystery becomes visible as the current household affair is addressed, with Holmes identifying the phrases as not merely a descriptive utterance but a list of directions, a verbal map of sorts. Brunton, too, he realizes, had perceived the same, and as Holmes retraces the cryptic directions, he locates first evidence of Brunton's following this same path and then, finally, the (dead) butler himself. The final piece of the puzzle has to do with the human psychology that has left a dead corpse where once the crown jewels had been laid to rest, and Holmes resolves this puzzle too, explaining that the butler must have been betrayed by the spurned housemaid he called upon as an accomplice and that this same housemaid has not drowned herself but cast what she perceived as a worthless assortment of objects into the nearby lake and fled. The rusty discs of metal, dredged up when the household dragged the lake for the housemaid's corpse and now saved in Holmes's crowded Baker Street flat, are remainders of these relics: gold sovereigns from the time of the Stuart reign.[12]

There's a final, spatial dimension to this tale, fitting for an experience that has yielded some of the objects that Watson feels infringe upon his space. It turns out that the instructions on that crumpled paper plot a trigonometry problem, in which the treasure hunter must use the saved peg and string to map out an appropriate distance from the top of a specified tree to the end of the shadow it casts. What the critic Peter Brooks calls the "thread of the plot" becomes the same thread or string that Holmes saves; the key to the mystery is the same old brass key that Holmes finds in the lock of the finally located brassbound chest. The plot of the story is overlaid onto the plot of ground that is the Musgrave estate, with the solution to this tale, which is actually a math problem, a plotted point upon grounds that have become a graph. The instructions that enable any intellectual with the power to identify them as instructions also provide a prompt to repetition, with the reader being invited to redo, recreate, both plot and plot.

In this context, the peg and the thread saved by Holmes feel especially poignant, functioning as they do to literalize points of reference and functioning as they did to link the top of a now missing oak tree to the end point of the shadow it would cast at noon. The tree and the shadow are both no more, but the length of string Holmes saves gives him a way to tether that relationship in place and to render tangible a relationship that cannot be, could never be, quantified, outside of math.

As Watson is to Holmes, so is the top of the tree to the shadow that it casts.

Holmes keeps the relics of the Musgrave ritual as mnemonic anchors, things that, in times of lassitude or agon, can give his restless mind a way to re-create. Still, there can be a slippery slope between random stimulation and the thrill of pursuit. See Holmes's cocaine habit, which he defends on the grounds that his mind "rebels at stagnation" and as that which eases him when his detective cases, his cryptograms, aren't providing the mental stimulation that he needs.[13] He buzzes with the same energy I see in my family members, who need to offset sedentary activities—such as eating breakfast—with puzzles, headlines, requests for crossword clues. Such a mind craves momentum; such a mind hurts when not in use. But the mind so titillated also defines "use" in very particular ways, and what Holmes defines as boredom may actually be closer to "fear of pain." After all, after cocaine, opiates are his drug of choice.

Holmes's ability to make sense of chaos has long been the foundation for a godlike intellectual hierarchy between detective and sidekick, with the detective as the enviable figure whose mental powers the sidekick and reader should both admire. And yet, for all of the fun Holmes regularly makes of his friend, Watson's brain has the capacity to do something that Holmes's cannot. Watson has a knack for reverie, whereas Holmes reminds me of Tennyson's Ulysses, tortured by the "pause" that will, he claims, cause one to "rust unburnished, not to shine in use."[14] Why is it so hard to be unstructured? Why so hard to rest? Faced with a lazy day, Holmes must find in his friend's wandering mind a challenge whereby to focus his own. Maybe I'm bothered because such activity can make the daydreaming companion feel indolent by comparison; maybe because a mind in motion feels hard to share.

Maybe, though, Holmes's love of puzzles is its own act of exposure, and maybe my task is to take up Holmes's gauntlet and play what Sherlockians call "the game." "Come Watson, come!" cries Holmes, at the beginning of "The Adventure of the Abbey Grange," "the game is afoot," thus launching both tale and men into motion, with a once-sleeping Watson "rattling," just ten minutes after being awakened by this expression, down the streets in a hansom cab.[15] Such a mind is exciting; such a mind requests companionship, if only one can keep up.

My dad tells Holmesian stories from time to time. He's an introvert, yet he's happy enough in the limelight if his audience is rapt. He's got a good dinner party story about a winter snow sculpture from college, another story about sledding down a hill on swivel chairs bolted to cafeteria trays. My own memory here is fuzzy, though; I have no tangible evidence of these accounts.

I do, however, have many of his old books, dotted with marginalia, thin, penciled numbers running down the side of the page in a secret code. Those are cross-references, pagination that locates how the idea asserted on this page anticipates or echoes an idea somewhere else.[16] I have some of his papers, too, old lecture notes from when he was just starting out. Some are mimeographed, now faint purple marks on paper that's been long creased. Some are jotted down on index cards in pencil, pen. Aristotle's *Poetics* is also a collection of lecture notes, I explain to one of my classes, and that's one reason you may find it hard to understand.[17] I keep my father's notes in a filing cabinet in my garage, in a folder next to saved thank-you cards, birthday greetings, my old college work. To this day, I give my version of his lecture on *Oedipus Rex*. I read his essay on Conan Doyle to write this piece.[18]

Perhaps I should digitize these papers so they'd be less fragile, take up less space. But I'd miss the paper, the touch of his hand. Since Daedalus and his labyrinth we have needed clues—which are also clews, which are balls of yarn—to keep us on a path. Those notes are my anchor, so when he wanders, I can bring him back.[19]

Is there a difference, at the end of the day, between a mind that wanders and a mind that is lost? For all their dedication to direction, there is, between detective and academic, the shared quality of a mind that evades attention and a mind that is always busy running off to something else. To be "absentminded" isn't to lack a mind or even to lack a focus but merely to have a mind that isn't *here*. Parson Adams, the Quixotic intellectual in Henry

Fielding's novel *Joseph Andrews*, once walks away from an inn without his horse because he's thinking about his friend Joseph and because he's reading his beloved Aeschylus, too.[20] My dad once biked himself the two miles to work and then walked himself home without his bike. I've walked into traffic while thinking; I've given a lecture with my shirt on inside out. "Zoned out" is my eldest son's term for himself in these phases; "wanderous" is his term for me: easily distracted, mesmerized, absorbed by other things.

For all his precise mental focus, Holmes similarly lets personal interactions, aspects of his wardrobe, fall away when he is on a case. When I was in graduate school, I sometimes wondered if the bodies tucked away in various reading rooms were important, researching professors or members of our homeless population who had wandered into the library to get warm. Holmes toes this same line, disguising himself as a mendicant in "The Man with the Twisted Lip" and languishing in opium dens in a manner that may not always be a disguise. Drugs and detection, both, take him away from human attachments, with his one possible romantic interest being Irene Adler—"the woman," from "The Scandal in Bohemia"—and the nature of the attachment resting on her ability to outwit him (interestingly, the two figures share a facility with disguise). Even his bond with Watson, established over years and stories, is one that can feel tenuous to Watson and readers, given Holmes's lack of emotional demonstration on this front—given his ability to focus so precisely on the task at hand.

I sometimes wonder if Holmes even sees Watson when, in his game of mind reading, he interrupts Watson after observing his friend's wandering eye. And yet, Holmes makes informed guesses, bred of long acquaintance and cohabitation, and his demonstration reveals his close knowledge of the mind he tracks.

He's bonded to his subject, and if Watson may feel at times crowded by Holmes's habits, Watson is the one who becomes engaged to Mary Morstan and who, for a time at least, moves out.

Baker Street's fullness becomes touching in this context; the piles and puzzles could almost make me cry. For, between detective and academic, there is, finally, the shared quality of a mind that is at capacity and, because of such, a mind that thinks it has to pick and choose. Holmes famously isn't aware of the Copernican theory of the universe—the simple fact that the earth revolves around the sun—and he defends his ignorance as predicated on choice. "What the deuce is it to me?" he responds to Watson's astonishment. "If we went around the moon it would not make a pennyworth of difference to me or to my work." He has chosen not to pursue certain branches of knowledge because he recognizes his mind as capacious and finite, both. "I consider that a man's brain originally is like a little empty attic," states Holmes, evoking Baker Street as it was before Watson and Holmes, but "it is a mistake to think that that little room has elastic walls and can distend to any extent." When does absent-mindedness become something more pernicious? "Depend upon it," states Holmes, "there comes a time when for every addition of knowledge you forget something that you knew before."[21] The critic, like the detective, works to fill his or her mental spaces, and as memorabilia accrue, we stack and coordinate as best we can. No wonder Holmes secrets relics in every niche and cranny. No wonder I keep those papers by my desk. I'd hide in the toe of a slipper, if it meant I could remain in the orbit of such a mind.

4

SHAKING HANDS

Ludwig Wittgenstein, Percival Everett

"You know the thing with a handshake?" he asks. "When you shake someone's hand for the first time and you get that limp, floppy 'grip.'" His voice on the phone is raspy, full of gravitas or extra phlegm. He's offering up non sequiturs while I make dinner and he, miles away, walks his dogs.

We'd been talking about human connection instead of the more philosophical discussion I'd wanted to have on how categories of likeness or difference are understood. What I'd wanted was something closer to a Wittgensteinian language game, about the functions of language that flag sameness or difference, about how similes call attention to the act of comparison and how metaphors disguise it, about how metonymy and synecdoche show us understanding one thing by reference to something else. As a fan of the philosopher, as someone who knows that Wittgenstein finds language to be game-like in its dependence upon external rules, he of all people should play along. Since all language is itself metaphorical, I had wanted to say, aren't we constantly using language both to accentuate the space of difference and to overcome it? And shouldn't this function of language matter to us, especially when we are using it to talk about likeness and difference in some cultural sense? But somehow the conversation has shifted, and we are talking about how we reach out to each other across cultural and experiential divides. We are also talking about when and why such attempts at human connection—at finding, perhaps, a point of "likeness"—fall short.[1]

We are talking, in other words, about actual people, here.

But then I remember a writing teacher once told me that a good introduction should be like a "firm handshake," and I get distracted by that thought. "Words don't have hands!" I can hear my youngest son protesting, though to me the teacher's simile had made perfect sense. To shake hands is to meet someone by touching them; to shake hands is to confirm an agreement, even when you are just saying hello. To shake hands is a sign that I might like you, even if I'm only being polite. To shake hands means I'm agreeing, for a time at least, to hear what you have to say.

"Well," he says, "you may learn to like more about the person later, but you'll never forget that first grasp."

When I think about why I like reading, I think about what it feels like to meet a book. Reading a new book brings out my closet introvert, as if I'm gearing up for a cocktail party at which I will need to smile and smile and shake hands and nod. Usually, I'm gratified I made the effort; sometimes my energy disappears into the void. I *like* reading, but cracking the cover is almost always for me a heavy lift. No matter what techniques this new author chooses, I'm being asked to bring something or someone new into the middle of my life. I'm agreeing to take the current flow of my life and redirect it a bit. There's a contract here in which the book holds out a hand that I, for a time at least, take up. And my attention at the beginning is apt to wander; it can take me several pages till I'm "sucked in." Sometimes, I flip back and reread the beginning, but usually I just forge ahead. Authors know, I'm convinced, that my attention will be accretive and that we are both going to need some time to get to know each other, to adjust. It wouldn't be fair or possible to ask that my entire understanding of a book rest on some detail in that opening page.

But what he says about the limp handshake means that a firm handshake should have some effect. Certainly, I think my writing teacher meant as much. A firm handshake emphasizes not only the importance of first impressions—introductions, first sentences, an offhand hello—but also the importance of first practices for setting a standard of engagement with the world. A firm handshake says *I'm here, you're here, and I'm interested in that fact.* A firm handshake means taking a position of civility and attunement toward another; it means agreeing to be the one greeting and agreeing to return the grasp. Also, you don't tend to change your handshake from person to person (except, my friend points out, if the person you are greeting is very old). The firm handshakers bring the same hands to all the varied individuals they meet in life.

"I don't want to write something just to fill a void," I say.

"Did I ever tell you the story about . . ." he answers.

Probably, I think. Writers tend to tell the same stories. We just find new people to tell.

When I think about why I like writing, I think about what it feels like to start a piece. No matter how many essays or articles or chapters I've completed, starting a new piece—like cracking the cover of an unread novel—requires gearing up. Everyone has their own approach, but I'm a jumper who doesn't even pretend to know where she is going to land. I dive in, in media res, trusting that eventually the new environment will feel like home. Still, it never seems to get easier, that first jump. It reminds me of how, as a longtime swimmer, I hesitate every morning on deck, stripped down to my swimsuit but not yet ready to leave the edge. To dive in represents not just the speed or decisiveness with which you enter something but the shock, the effort of that change. To dive into something always, momentarily, takes away my breath.

Diving makes more sense here than shaking, since I can't meet my writing until it's done. Hello you, I remember thinking, when my youngest first curled those tiniest of fingers around my thumb. Who else shakes hands like this, after the fact?

Well, but think about the handshake in athletics, he says. Think of the postgame congratulations; think of the high five, the chest bump, the butt slap. He's done different sports than I. I like my swim friends immensely, but on the pool deck, maybe because we are all so nearly naked, we never touch. In running, too, we rarely used our hands. My running coach wasn't much of a hugger, though in a picture of the two of us, by the finish line, she's holding me up by the shoulders while we both grin.

When I was in graduate school, I tell him, I wanted to brag once to one of my professors about reading a book. It was a really long book by a well-known eighteenth-century author, but of the books he had written this one was probably the least frequently read or taught.[2] I'm talking about Samuel Richardson's *Sir Charles Grandison*, which wasn't at the time in print. Anyway, this professor had told us about the book, and I had found an old one-volume edition of it in our library, leather bound, with tiny text printed in double columns on each page. I remember these double columns, since I felt I was reading a dictionary the entire time. I'd spent my whole spring break reading it, and I wanted to tell my professor that I'd finished reading it as soon as I returned. Sure enough, on my first day back I saw her walking through our student lounge. "Professor," I cried, "Professor! I read this book," and she made a noise in her throat and started walking toward me with outstretched arms. Ah, I thought, we are hugging, and this is an appropriate reaction given what I have just shared. But as we made contact, I saw in her face that we were shaking hands. So we ended up clasping forearms, kind of grappling each other in the lounge. I wonder if any of my British transplant friends struggle with this phenomenon—the confusion over the American handshake or the European kiss and hug? That's how I made myself feel better at the time. But another friend told me I had lived through the embodiment of graduate school, since graduate students all expect, or are starved for, more affection and approbation than we actually receive. I have wanted to write about this story for years; I just never knew how to start. My point is that the handshake keeps the other person at arm's length.

What does it really mean to like someone? What does it really mean to be *like* someone else? We all approach one another at some remove.

The story he tells me this time turns out to be one I haven't heard before, about an essay he was asked to contribute to a journal doing a retrospective issue on John Howard Griffin's 1961 book, *Black Like Me*. (The invitation suggests that the journal editors must have seen some kind of likeness between my friend's thinking, Griffin's project, and their journal's intellectual work.) Griffin's book, published at the height of the civil rights movement, was meant to narrate what it was like to be a Black man in a world that went to great legal and schematic lengths to assert the discrepancies between—or, to put this another way, the fundamental unlikeness of—Blacks and whites. "This may not be all of it," Griffin reflects, as a white man, on the experience he is about to claim and recount, "but it is what it is like." He's very sure, and he's a philosopher at heart. How to compare that which has been defined as uncomparable? Blackness, Griffin implies in his title, can only be known by "likeness," and the "like" announces the descriptor and the object being described as similar but not the same. There are implications that accompany the act of comparison; there is an imposition of solidarity, since comparison means that more than one person is in the room. (Imagine this same book retitled *I Am Black*.) Another way to make this point is that instead of shedding light on the 1960s Black experience, Griffin's book sheds light on the experience of being a white man pretending to be a Black man in a white world. Griffin had taken skin-altering prescription medicine, sat under an ultraviolet light, shaved his head, dyed his skin, and set off on a trip to live, as he put it, "as a Negro" in the deep South. Six weeks later, he holed up in a hotel for a few days, stopped taking his medicine, then left his room to rejoin his normal white life.[3]

My friend is a storyteller too, except "I never write nonfiction," he asserts. So to fulfill his assignment he crafts a fictionalized scene. Midway through Griffin's tour, he sets Griffin and a Black man next to each other somewhere, with Griffin about to take a piss. "I'm trying to see how Negroes are treated," the fictionalized real-life Griffin explains. His companion is casting strange looks at his skin. Griffin didn't look Black, after all; he looked diseased. "You could have just asked," the Black man responds.

Well yes, it's a good punch line, I say, when he recites the story. (Why did you stage it while they were peeing? And why is this the question I fail to ask?) But that wasn't the question Griffin had in mind.

Does reading let me ask the questions I might otherwise avoid? I think about the range of characters that, while reading, I think

I've known: men, women, boys, girls, gay, straight, Black, white, Asian, alien, talking horses, talking dogs. The characters I've found unknowable are wide-ranging as well. There are the authors and characters I simply *do not like*, and there are also the characters I like reading about and can't understand at all: Kinbote, Dorian Gray, Humbert Humbert, Becky Sharp.

This estrangement is another pleasurable effect of reading, what Rita Felski calls the allure of "shock" and what I usually experience more mildly as novelty or disgust. We read to explore other lives, other places, other minds.[4] I can understand a character enough to render that character legible, but I can also appreciate the character as profoundly different from myself. I inhabit this other life to an extent, while my consciousness is occupied through the act of reading, but I don't feel "like" this other character. Instead, I'm fascinated to see all the things about human existence I haven't felt or didn't know. The feeling is similar to the one I have when, on rare occasions, I stay out past 9:30 p.m.

"That's why I think you are more interested in Wittgenstein's family resemblances," he says. "You like people as much as language games. Think of Wittgenstein's story about the beetle in the box. I see a lot of myself in you." (He's speaking figuratively; how else do we look alike?) Well, I say, Wittgenstein says that no one can see inside anyone else's box, so what I call a beetle and what you call a beetle may not be the same. And by "beetle," Wittgenstein means pain. There are things about each other we cannot compare.[5] Except, when I was very young, I made a bug collection for school, and because I didn't want any of the bugs to suffer, I put them in plastic bags in the freezer before I mounted them in a box. That way I didn't have to watch them die in alcohol fumes in a jar, and then I pinned them in the box carefully and put identifying labels under each pin. I matched up genus and species so that Wittgensteinian family resemblances were in full effect. Overlapping similarities, you know, with no one feature exactly the same. Then on my way to school, I sat with my beetles and my box, on my lap, and I started to hear faint sounds. And because it was my box I could look inside it, and when I did I saw that all my beetles had been sleeping but not dead. They were reanimating now, like so many carapaced Lazaruses, back from the dead. Or maybe the better simile really is beetle-Jesuses, since I, afraid of inflicting pain, had crucified them all.

"What do *you* think he really wanted?" I write to him later, in reference to Griffin, over text.

"He wanted to be a hero," he responds.

I wrote a lot about likeness, a while back. I liked the enigma of it—the idea that you could be similar to something or someone but not the same. I wrote about similes that bled into metaphors; I wrote about statues that came to life. I was fascinated with the idea of an actor or object being *so* similar to something that maybe you became the thing itself. Sarah Siddons was famous in the early nineteenth century for playing the character of Hermione in Shakespeare's play *The Winter's Tale*, a character who poses as a living statue of herself. Audiences loved not only the Pygmalion wish fulfillment but the promise that art could approach a realism that would spill over into life.[6]

But what happens to solidarity when we all become the same? Likeness or emulation may not always be a gift. In graduate school, I learned that mimicry could become menace, though I think my own acts of mimicry have always fallen short. A difference that is barely noticeable can become overwhelming. The one trained in mimicry can learn to supersede. The child can get frightened of her shadow, the playwright Derek Walcott states.[7] Yet I like to think that I have a talent for finding aspects of likeness in ideas most people dismiss as being different. The effort feels welcoming more than threatening, I hope, more like stretching out a hand in greeting, a taking up and a letting go.

On the eighteenth-century stage, I tell him, you know white men always played Black parts. In London, a Black man didn't play a Black character until 1825. (He was playing Othello, and his name was Ira; he was only seventeen.)[8] It took longer in the States. So eighteenth-century audiences who came to see plays that featured a Black character knew, on a foundational level, that they were watching a white man pretend to be Black. They would accept this rendition of Blackness for the duration of the play. But sometimes their illusions were disturbed. The actor Barton Booth came onstage once in blackface, sweating, and when he wiped his face, half his makeup was gone. The actor James Quin stepped out once as Othello, wearing an all-white costume with a large-powdered wig and white gloves. The audience laughed at him for a "magpye," strutting onstage in his black and white, until he took off his gloves to reveal that his hands were black.[9]

In stagecraft, we call it black*face*, this problematic practice of appropriating race as a performance of makeup, only skin deep. We call it blackface, indicating that we can pick and choose how extensive we want this illusion of verisimilitude—this likeness of likeness—to be. We trade in on synecdoche, the idea that the part, the face, stands in for the whole. Think of all the body parts that Griffin, on his tour of the South, didn't need to show. If he had taken that imaginary piss in public, would he have dyed his dick? But when Quin took off his gloves, the audience gasped.[10]

In jazz, my friend tells me, the handshake develops complicated permutations, among them the low five, a touching of palms, a more casual request to "gimme some skin." You can also say, he says, "gimme some skin on the dark side," when you turn your hand over, in sign of solidarity and experiences shared. Except in minstrelsy, a handshake explodes connection as a myth. I wonder if Quin would have blacked his palms. I wonder what touching him would have brought to light. When Laurence Olivier performed Othello in blackface in 1965, he left his makeup smudges on Maggie Smith. Paul Robeson, the first Black actor to take the role since the nineteenth century, played it in 1930s London opposite Peggy Ashcroft, before bringing the performance to New York. He was popular, in the main; he was a good actor; he was just pretending to be Othello. But: he handles Desdemona roughly. He kisses her onstage. "Why should a black actor be allowed to kiss a white actress?" he reports hearing from spectators, in interviews with the press.[11] In the very crucible of likeness, in the space of similitude that always approaches yet falls short, he is Black, and he touches Ashcroft like Othello.

"I've been reading interviews of Nabokov," I say, in a different conversation. "And they make me think he would have been a hard man to know. I mean—you know, really *know*."[12]

"That's because you don't know him," he says. "People say that a lot about my work."

But would he *want* me to know him? Is he reaching toward me at all? Strange, how the hand of a lover can also tremble. Or, I mean, a hand can shake.

Griffin couldn't just have asked 1960s Black Americans about the Black experience, because there is a difference between being the listener and the live-r, just as there is a difference between reading a novel and being in a play. Griffin didn't want to know what it was like to be Black. He wanted to be Black, and then he wanted to be able to put down the book or walk off the stage.

He also believed that the experience of likeness could be narrated only by him.

There is a difference, he tells me, between saying you know someone and saying you want to know what someone else is like. There is a difference between insisting that you know a person's experience and acknowledging that your desire to know that experience can only come so close.

No matter how firm the handshake, you always have to let them go.

A friend once told me that during a period of loneliness she would pay for manicures so that she could enjoy the sensation of another person grasping her hands. She didn't go for the nail-painting part but the part at the end when they put lotion on your hands and arms and usually interlace, for a moment, their fingers with yours. It isn't a handshake so much as a clasp, when two hands are brought together as close as hands can be. Palm to palm, the manicurist will roll your wrist around and maybe press the back of your hand with her thumb.[13] I never know the person who holds my hand like this. I have no sense how deeply similar or different we may be. Still, the difference is no obstacle to a temporary joining. Saints have hands that pilgrims' hands do touch.

To this day, I'm afraid that I choose words instead of people. I'm afraid that words take the place of physical connection, so that writing or reading becomes a way to avoid any "real" reaching out. But words touch me, all the time. When I taught my first son the elements of baby sign language, I could feel my hands making letters in my mind. Language is metaphorical, and language is produced and shared in the physical world. I touch with the same hands that type these words; I kiss with the same mouth that says "I kiss." The word and gesture are separate and the same. "A handshake is a performative act," he tells me, and a performative utterance performs the action it describes. So what if I say "I greet you." What if I shake your hand without speaking at all? "That's why they call it body language," he says.[14]

We are talking about actual people, here.

5

POOL OF TEARS

Lewis Carroll

My dad was a math major when he started college, and I always found it funny how someone so numbers oriented could go on to make a career out of words. Weren't the two disciplines so very different, even opposed? Maybe not. I remember a visiting mathematician once talking to me about the beauty of a proof and sounding as impassioned as I could be about a turn of phrase. Wordsmiths don't have the final word on aesthetics, and numbers are a language I just don't know how to read. Remembering that professor, I still feel a little sad to think of all the extra beauty out there, hidden in numbers, that I can't see.

My dad switched majors, he told me, because he realized that as much as he liked his math classes, his English assignments were the ones that he kept thinking about after the assignment was done. I remembered that story when I made my own science-to-literature switch, and I decided to follow the activities that didn't feel like work. But I can still see shades of my father's math beginnings in his writing, just as, occasionally, I can see scientific characteristics in my own. He's precise with his language, schematic in his thought. He likes puzzles and patterns, and he reads literature as if it were a secret code. He's the

English professor father who surrounded me with books but who also quizzed me on Pythagorean triplets when he walked me to the bus.

He's not the only writer who had a second, left-brain secret life. In fact, the proliferation of these overlaps makes me wonder if those of us who dabble in subjectivity need sometimes the reassurance of numbers, patterns, and natural laws. Maybe without the latter, life can feel just too chaotic, and the unpredictability of human tragedy, so vast. Wallace Stevens sold insurance, William Carlos Williams was a physician, and Sir Arthur Conan Doyle was primarily an ophthalmologist: he studied eyes. Charles Dodgson, too, was a mathematician at Oxford, though we know him better by a different name. He wrote under the pseudonym Lewis Carroll. He never married. He kept his two lives even more separate than some.[1]

I can't remember if I knew Lewis Carroll was a mathematician when I read *Alice's Adventures in Wonderland* for the first time. I certainly didn't know anything else about him, such as his penchant for photography or the disturbing discussions surrounding his friendships with young kids. Those other discussions share the narrative of trauma, or the logic that our childhood hurts will give shape to our grownup wounds. But I fell into his stories the way so many children have done, for their magic and mayhem and for the mischievousness of Alice, who reminded me of me. (In the famous Sir John Tenniel illustrations, we even look a bit alike.) And yet, maybe because of Carroll's background with numbers, I always felt there was something in the stories I wasn't quite seeing, like the garden Alice can peep at through the keyhole but cannot reach. There's a concept for this sensation in mathematics: the asymptote, that line of a graph in calculus that approaches a curve it strains toward and will never touch. I felt this sensation in *Alice*. Maybe it was all the falling. Maybe it was all the tears.[2]

In *Alice's Adventures in Wonderland*, Alice falls twice. First, and most famously, she falls down the rabbit hole, a plunge that takes some time. "Would the fall NEVER come to an end!" she wonders, and it lasts long enough to let her think and joke, pick up marmalade jars, and even sleep.[3] The duration of this first fall has made "down the rabbit hole" its own idiom for pursuits that seem unending or interests that take us, often without our intention, far out of our way.

But since rabbit holes are not tunnels we typically explore, Carroll also has Alice describe this first falling as into something that feels to her like "a very deep well." We rarely remark on this comparison: the fact that she imagines her conduit to Wonderland as that which will bring her to water, at the end. As idioms go, "down the well" doesn't have the same ring to it as "down the rabbit hole," perhaps because falling into wells posed, especially in Alice's day, a real childhood risk. A descent into water promises an end more tragic, more clear cut.

Or does it? For once Alice is in Wonderland, she falls again, this time into a salty pool that she herself has wept into being. These tears, shed when she finds herself suddenly nine feet tall, are emblematic of the lack of control any of us have over maturation and the inarticulable sadness we feel over the lost opportunities that accompany "growing up." Except, these tears also remain awash in the hallway once Alice shrinks back to Wonderland size, and now they pose something of a threat:

> As she said these words her foot slipped, and in another moment, splash! She was up to her chin in salt water. Her first idea was

that she had somehow fallen into the sea, "and in that case I can go back by railway," she said to herself. (Alice had been to the seaside once in her life, and had come to the general conclusion, that wherever you go to on the English coast you find a number of bathing machines in the sea, some children digging in the sand with wooden spades, then a row of lodging houses, and behind them a railway station.) However, she soon made out that she was in the pool of tears which she had wept when she was nine feet high.

"I wish I hadn't cried so much!" said Alice, as she swam about, trying to find her way out.[4]

This is her second fall, though Carroll dubs the moment but a "slip."

This second fall produces an idiom, too. Alice is a capable swimmer, but her condition, when she finds herself in the pool of tears, literalizes how we feel when we find ourselves "at sea." This sensation is different from being "at the seaside," with its Alice-associations of vacations, sandcastles, opportunities to bathe. This idiom instead describes a sense of aimlessness, the ocean water conveying the experience of being lost. Maybe this idiomatic sense comes from the difference in scale we experience when in the ocean, surrounded as we are by a presence tangible yet so massive that we cannot but feel powerless and very small. Maybe it also comes from the lack of coordinates in a landscape that is now a seascape, with only waves for "landmarks," and with those markers rolling by repetitively, identically, without end. Even Alice, though fearless, seems confused. When we are "at sea," we are also often "adrift"—stripped of agency, control, and at the mercy of some higher power.

It is amazing what ocean currents and biomechanics can do to one's sense of place. I'm a late-in-life swimmer, and I do most of my swimming in a pool where black lines on the bottom and lane lines on the side keep me in check. But my brief forays into ocean swimming have reinforced how easy it is, like Alice, randomly "to swim about." I pull harder with my right arm, and my catch is funny on my left side. In the pool, this means I'll occasionally hit a lane line or smack a lane mate with a wide left arm. But in the ocean, I skew left, and if I'm not sighting every three or so strokes, I'll go far off course. Back when I did more ocean swimming, buddies would joke that I was determinedly "heading off to Catalina" (the island twenty-six miles off the Los Angeles coast), while they all dutifully hugged the shoreline north.

The confusion doesn't come just from trying to swim straight. In Greek mythology, Narcissus drowns when the verisimilitude of his reflection convinces him to exchange water for air; John Milton's Eve is similarly if temporarily deceived. Back when I spent actual time on Catalina (a locale I finally reached by boat), I experienced one nighttime free dive during the season of bioluminescence, when the algae flashing around me mimicked the constellations above. Far from any light pollution, I lost myself in an underwater somersault and had to exhale all my air to track the direction of my bubbles, to figure out which way to swim to breathe.

The ocean can be disorienting in this manner, even when it is calm. In *Moby-Dick*, that tale of whaling in which the ocean is a character of its own, the cabin boy Pip falls twice out of a whaling boat, and the second time he is "left behind on the sea" by the second mate, Stubb. The day is lovely; the scene, pristine: "It was a beautiful, bounteous, blue day! The spangled sea calm and cool, and flatly stretching away, all round, to the horizon, like gold-beater's skin hammered out to the extremest. Bobbing up and down in that sea, Pip's ebon head showed like a head of cloves. No boat-knife was lifted when he fell so rapidly astern. Stubb's inexorable back was turned upon him; and the whale was winged. In three minutes, a whole mile of shoreless ocean was between Pip and Stubb."[5]

"Like gold-beater's skin hammered out to the extremest": the water forms a picturesque contrast to the Black cabin boy Pip, while the mile of "shoreless ocean" offers a vast expanse. Pip is rescued, ultimately, but not until he has spent substantial time in this idyllic scene, and once he is back on the ship, his wits are gone. He has suffered from neither storms nor true overexposure—his rescue doesn't take that long—but from something less visible, more pernicious. "Now, in calm weather, to swim in the open ocean is as easy to the practiced swimmer as to ride in a spring-carriage ashore," explains the narrator (and Pip, like Alice, seems a capable swimmer, able to navigate the element that stretches away on every side), "but . . . the intense concentration of self in the middle of such a heartless immensity, my God! Who can tell it?"[6] I always enjoyed the isolation of the ocean—the sensory deprivation produced from diving under a wave or floating on my back with my peripheral vision obscured—but only by choice, and only when I could, if needed, quickly leave it behind. I can't imagine being, like Pip, by myself in an ocean with no shore or ship in sight. The very idea makes my mind recoil.

The other irony of Pip's condition is that he could have died from dehydration, if he hadn't instead been rescued, if he hadn't instead just lost his mind. "Water, water everywhere, / Nor any a drop to drink," states Samuel Taylor Coleridge's Ancient Mariner, recalling his shipboard ordeals and now, like Pip, similarly crazed.[7] The curse of the shipwrecked mariner is to be surrounded by the substance he desires yet cannot consume, as drinking seawater will incite the excessive urination that speeds up dehydration and leaves the kidneys clogged with salt. "Drink me," reads a bottle in Wonderland, which contains a substance that will make Alice small, but she is careful not to follow orders until she has checked to see "whether it's marked 'poison' or not."[8] "Beaver fever," we were warned of, as kids: parasites one could get from ingesting water in which forest animals lived, defecated, ate. And yet, mountain idylls include those random swimming holes in which water is so obviously a home to others, full of muck and murk. We grew up swimming with salamanders, bullfrogs, leeches; treading water in even the deepest areas of our pond would churn up moss. I'm sure we swallowed much of that water, in our day, and I don't remember any of us being the worse for it.

We were the lucky ones, in this regard, bathed in childhood but not becalmed. More predictably, we drank from the natural spring that still emerges from the hillside near our New Hampshire home. Someone during my lifetime has mounted a little poem on a plaque next to it, a bit of Carroll-esque doggerel summoning others to stop and drink. Unlike our pond, this water comes from so far underground that it is safe to consume, and visitors wedge spare buckets and bottles under the stream to fill up and take back home. It comes from so far underground that it emerges frigid from the hillside, on even a ninety-degree day. Decades ago someone tapped into it in some formal, if haphazard, way, and now PVC piping protrudes from the hillside to widen and direct the stream; the end of the pipe is propped up on supports. The contraption exists to redirect something already there, but the constant flow feels wasteful to me; the water runs and runs, with no faucet to turn it off. As I type these words, it is flowing steadily. In the winters it creates ice sheets and walls around the pipe.

Alice, immersed in this same abundance, immersed in the tangible evidence of a sadness that can now engulf, also connects her experience to happy childhood times. To be in the sea is to have a possibility, for Alice, to "go back," even though her prior experience of the sea is brief. "When . . . people get weary of life," the often-melancholic Carroll once wrote to some fans, "and can't find happiness in town or books, then they rush off to the seaside, to see what bathing-machines will do."[9] "Thou know'st that from the first time that we smell the air / We wawl and cry," states Shakespeare's Lear, confirming that, as babies, we cry at birth to draw air into the lungs that until that moment had drawn in fluid.[10] But maybe we cry, too, for the lifestyle we have lost. My children clung to their life as swimmers; for both pregnancies, my waters refused to break. In the human fetus, the jaw and ear bones begin as gills.

Even those of us who are land dwellers retain some affinity for our liquid home. Consider the moment when, at the outset of Kenneth Grahame's *A Wind in the Willows*, the normally earthbound Mole emerges from his burrow:

> He thought his happiness was complete when, as he meandered aimlessly along, suddenly he stood by the edge of a full-fed river. Never in his life had he seen a river before—this sleek, sinuous, full-bodied animal, chasing and chuckling, gripping things with a gurgle and leaving them with a laugh, to fling itself on fresh playmates that shook themselves free, and were caught and held again. All was a-shake and a-shiver—glints and gleams and sparkles, rustle and swirl, chatter and bubble. The Mole was bewitched, entranced, fascinated. By the side of the river he

trotted as one trots, when very small, by the side of a man who holds one spell-bound by exciting stories; and when tired at last, he sat on the bank, while the river still chattered on to him, a babbling procession of the best stories in the world, sent from the heart of the earth to be told at last to the insatiable sea.[11]

Here, the power and vitality of water entrance as well as overwhelm, as the childlike Mole is comforted by the adult figure of the river who streams alongside. Here, the motion of the water mimics the vitality of the animals that live in it, sleek and sinuous, like otter, or snake, or (as Grahame will soon introduce) Mole's friend the water rat. Here, that disorienting tug experienced by anyone who has ever gone fishing—that sense of as-of-yet invisible liveness communicated from water to pole to arm—dissolves into the water itself, that can laugh and hold and talk. In Wordsworth's poem "The Daffodils," the first poem I ever learned to recite, the titular flowers grow alongside a bay, and winds ruffle both flowers and sea into a euphoric minuet: "The waves beside them danced; but they / Out-did the sparkling waves in glee."[12] The same water that drains Pip's mind has a mind of its own, and feelings, too. As Mole's meandering emulates the meandering of the river, he recognizes, without ever before having seen it, the river as artery that joins earth to sea—as that which renders his solid environment and this fluid one one and the same.

Here is another way water can revitalize as well as kill. I've always been enamored of those humans who recognize water as a natural habitat and who find in water a source of buoyancy and peace. My former husband was like this, and watching him free dive reminded me of watching yoga or ballet. Then there are the postcollegiate swimmers at my morning workouts, whom I gaze at underwater and admire. A woman who swims two lanes down from me lost her son four months ago to an overdose, and I've seen her on the pool deck or in the ocean every day since. She's like the sea lions that line the California coast: easy into the water, labored as she returns to land. I swim for very different reasons, but every plunge reminds me of those childhood somersaults that I watch water bring out in my own children, and that being in water seems to inspire. Maybe water comforts us because the movement of the ocean models for us a way of moving that in our hardest times is hard to feel; maybe this movement can be lent to us, appropriately by osmosis, until we can resume these behaviors on our own. After all, the membranes of our cells are porous. Sixty percent of our bodies are constituted by water. We will die in roughly three to four days from thirst.

The assurance of movement must have been intoxicating to Carroll, who suffered all his life from the speech impediment he referred to as a "hesitation": a moment when he would open his mouth but make no noise. How reassuring, then, to have water exhibit a loquacity and rhythm of its own. Time on water was crucial to Carroll's composition of *Alice*, which he recollects as:

> A tale begun in other days,
> When summer suns were glowing—
> A simple chime, that served to time
> The rhythm of our rowing.[13]

As apocrypha has it, Carroll first began the "Alice" tale on July 4, 1862, during a summer outing, in response to three girls badgering him to tell a story that would keep them amused while their group rowed. These were the daughters of his colleague Henry Liddell, the dean of Christ Church College, one of whom was the real-life Alice upon which Carroll's famous adventure stories were based.

As an Oxonian, Carroll spent the majority of his life by the Thames, and the river provided an occasion for communal gatherings otherwise missing in his quiet, bachelor-scholar life. According to diary accounts of his boat outings (which he enjoyed with the Liddells and with other families, too), his children friends did most of the rowing while Carroll acted as storytelling-coxswain, to help the rowers pace their boat smoothly through the waves. In reality, the Liddell children as oarsmen were probably less practiced. Alice, in Carroll's sequel *Through the Looking Glass*, suddenly finds herself transported from store to rowboat, where she receives an (only vaguely understood) lesson in rowing from a talking sheep. "Feather!" the sheep keeps insisting, as the boat-novice Alice keeps digging her oars too deeply in the water so that they seem to stick. ("You'll be catching a crab directly!" the sheep protests, an idiom used to describe Alice's misjudged stroke but that also seems to signify literally in looking-glass land.)[14] Ideally, a savvy oarsman will "feather," or rotate the oar handle as the oar emerges from the water, so the blade is parallel to the water's surface on the recovery stroke. The episode suggests that Carroll's boats probably moved with a jerkier motion, one more in keeping with his hesitations in speech.

Yet in the fantasy of memory, the water, children, and oars all move rhythmically ahead, much like the story Carroll tells, which is much like the story Mole hears from his babbling river, which tells a "procession of the best stories in the world." Consider how, in Joseph Conrad's *Heart of Darkness*, the progression along the Congo River emblematizes the forward momentum (and imperial project) of the novel's plot. Or how, for Mark Twain, journeys along the Mississippi River provide the content for his most famous works. When handled in an expert manner, a boat, like a story, like a river, will truly glide along.

Such movement doesn't always depend on the skills of those who float upon it, as, in water, we are all interlopers in this regard. Maybe this effect explains the associative, dreamlike quality of so many of Carroll's tales (and this chapter): suddenly you open your eyes, and you are in a different place. Or think of Jim and Huck's raft, in Twain's *Huckleberry Finn*, and how the relative freedom of their water expedition so often seems problematically to eclipse the much more literal freedom, for Jim, that they are moving toward. Think of how they can be on the run yet seemingly content, while on the river, to "lazy along."[15] "It knew now where it was going," asserts A. A. Milne, of the river that figures in his childhood tales of Christopher Robin and friends, "and it said to itself, 'There is no hurry. We shall get there some day.'"[16] Twain's river says the same, for as the Mississippi widens it takes on gravity, gravitas. Huck and Jim can spend their time on the river simply "listening to the stillness."[17] "Sometimes someone would speak in a boat," Ernest Hemingway writes, in his classic *The Old Man and the Sea*, "but most of the boats were silent except for the dip of the oars."[18] Maybe our silence develops as water does the talking. Maybe it is accentuated by the fact that sound travels so easily over water, with casual conversation carrying over it for miles.

But what about those moments before we've been fed by the necessary tributaries, before we have the volume and substance necessary to carry us along? "But all the little streams higher up in the Forest went this way and that," writes Milne, "quickly, eagerly, having so much to find out before it was too late."[19] I talked constantly when my grandfather would take me fishing; the Liddells wanted Carroll to tell them stories as they rowed along. In Milne's world, the young are fascinated by the river's determinism; Carroll's fascination with the young will always be mysterious, suspect. In my own childhood summers, I'd take a rowboat by myself to the shallows of our pond and enjoy a Huck Finn–like existence of looking for tadpoles, while my oars (not very feathered) punched through the underlying leaf mulch to release bubbles of methane gas. And still, I laughed quietly. I don't yet have the river's assurance. Who am I to say that I will have more time?

Carroll apparently spent many afternoons on the river with the Liddells, where he entertained them, and many other children, with many other stories that he never transcribed. These tales were written on water in a different sense: ephemeral, idiomatic, with but fleeting impact. Water holds no imprint; equally, water erases sandcastles, footprints, all signs of human life. "One day I wrote her name upon the strand," writes Edmund Spenser of his love interest in the sonnet sequence the *Amoretti*, "but came the waves and washed it away."[20] We weep for that which we have lost; our tears threaten to wash away that for which we mourn.

Consider, in this vein, the moment in Laurence Sterne's novel *Tristram Shandy* when the protagonist celebrates water as that "impetuous fluid" which "pressest against the flood-gates of the brain." Instead of overwhelming the mind, as it does for Pip, water for Sterne is that force that sets creativity awash. Water, with its fluid motion, models the momentum of effective writing, and writing (in Sterne's "Shandy-istic" style) emblematizes and impels the experience of life itself: "True *Shandeism* . . . opens the heart and lungs, and like all those affections which partake of its nature, it forces the blood and other vital fluids of the body to run freely through its channels, makes the wheel of life run long and chearfully round."[21]

Sterne's writing runs freely like the waters of Mole's river; it bubbles up in unexpected places; its tributaries pursue tangents;

it presses ever onward; it provides us with an energetic source. If we sit (mostly) still while writing, in our best moments we feel carried, caught up, borne away. We are born in water, but we are borne in water, too. Not for nothing do we say that good writing "flows."

And not for nothing did Sterne and Carroll celebrate the vitality communicated by the sensation of reading or writing well. Did Dodgson's other life as a mathematician prove lacking in this regard? Like my friend on the pool deck, we take vitality where we can find it. Sterne and his fictional protagonist were dying from tuberculosis, a disease that systematically liquefies the lungs; Carroll would die of pneumonia, after nursing his godson through Sterne's complaint. Seventy-one percent of Earth is covered with water. Almost the same percentage marks out the molecular content of the water in our cells. But let us not tip too far the other way. In *Hamlet*, when Laertes learns of his sister's "muddy death," he forbids himself to cry: "too much of water hast thou, poor Ophelia. / And therefore I forbid my tears."[22] Virginia Woolf chose to walk into the Ouse River, her pockets loaded with stones. What is the tipping point between too much water and not enough? Tuberculosis patients usually die of respiratory failure; more accurately, as the organs meant to supply oxygen are replaced by fluid, the patients drown.

In Wonderland, we have a chance to navigate these waters and come out safely on the other side. In the real world, we often lack Alice's powers of adjustment; we lack her ability to recognize, finally, the substance around us not as foreign but as of ourselves. How frequently we risk falling into a pool of our own making; how frequently we risk drowning to death in a sadness that we've made. But our tears, like the ocean, contain electrolytes, which make both salty to the taste. At the end of it all, Alice's second fall is but a slip.

6

OBEDIENCE TRAINING

John Milton, William Koehler

*"Would thou approve thy constancy, approve
First thy obedience, the other who can know,
Not seeing thee attempted, who attest?"*
—John Milton, *Paradise Lost*, 9.367–69

I had leaped into puppy ownership the way many of us do: a long and tentative thought process followed by an impulsive move. "Have a dog before you have children," friends had said to me when I first got married, and I planned for our as-of-yet imaginary dog as the trial run for the children that my husband and I would, I was positive, later share. I named her long before she existed, and we jokingly referred to her in her absence as we waited for living situation, landlord, and stars to align. Then one day there was notice of a litter on Petfinder, a trip to the shelter, and a tiny girl puppy who crawled, trembling, into my lap. She had a white blaze, a spike of hair protruding from her head, and a tiny black nose that would turn pink as she grew up. Her ears were velvet; the rest of her coat, rough. I walked out holding her in my arms only to realize once we'd gotten home that we were in possession of almost no supplies.[1]

My approach to pet ownership would prove prophetic. I had imagined my dog as a companion who would stare at me adoringly, who would romp when I wanted to romp and snuggle when I wanted to be still. I'd imagined that we'd enjoy long walks, games of fetch, and that at night she'd leave her armchair for my bedroom, launch herself from floor to mattress, climb over the hump of my body, and curl herself beside my back.

I'd learn quickly, however, that puppies have a mind of their own. Housebreaking aside (and that's a big aside), her energy in those first months was relentless. She chewed; she whimpered; she howled. She tangled herself in my feet when I walked; she contracted a parasite and shit in every corner of the house. She ate one pair of indestructible flip flops, then, twenty-four hours later, another. She never wanted to sleep when we did, or, if she did want to sleep, she certainly didn't want to sleep alone. Something on the internet told me that she had separation anxiety and would need Prozac if she were ever to function by herself.

In a moment of panic, I abandoned the internet and called a long-distance friend who specialized in training Labradors for field trials. Was there an alternative to pet antidepressants? She recommended obedience school. Specifically, she recommended a trainer approved to teach something called the "Koehler Method."

Earlier than my puppy's nervousness, the world's first version of separation anxiety occurs in book 9 of John Milton's epic *Paradise Lost*. Eve incites it, in the context of a conversation she has with Adam about how best to run their garden home. Even in paradise they have work, though it is work of such a nature that it hardly seems as such, and Adam reminds her that their task is far from "strict." God has said they can take breaks, for food, for conversation, for "looks and smiles"; they are made, after all, "not to irksome toil but to delight." Eve, however, wants to get their garden tidy, and she remains insistent that their pruning and tending can be more efficiently accomplished if they split up.

I'm on Eve's side throughout the entire conversation. To this day, nothing distracts me like a messy home; to this day, I live in a constant state of distraction. But the part I find most fascinating is the length of their discussion and her response to Adam at the end. She wants something from Adam, and it isn't help. He finishes by saying, well, if you think this way, then "go, for thy stay, not free, absents thee more." And Eve replies, "with thy permission, then . . . the willinger I go."[2]

Except, I always think, he never gives her permission. Except, I always think, he never could. That's the sticking point of free will, that capacity to reason that sets man apart from beast. We choose how we stay together or come apart.

Well, my friend responded, you asked for my advice.

The Koehler method is a mode of dog training named after William Koehler, a man who began his animal-training career in the military, at the Pomona Ordinance Base. In 1946, he started teaching public classes and private sessions, and, as the current Koehler Dog Training website indicates, his has been a recognized form of dog training ever since.[3]

While the Koehler method has various identifying characteristics, the most singular remains its focus on producing dogs who behave "reliably off leash." In Koehler's theory, control of your dog off lead is *the* most telling indication of obedience, though "control" becomes something of an oxymoron as your dog's training matures. Koehler promises the ability to stop a free-standing dog with a single command but also suggests that you won't need this ability once you have it: your dog will choose, of his or her own accord, not to chase that squirrel, run out that door, cross that street. The Koehler method produces dogs who can be trusted with autonomy, who can make "better choices for [themselves]."[4]

Koehler dogs can, in other words, execute safely the workings of free will.

Koehler was also famous, as the subtitle to his first book declares, for being "movieland's most experienced dog trainer." Koehler had gone on from the military to become the head animal trainer for Walt Disney Studios, where he handled some of cinema's best-known dogs. Celebrity, however—among any species—apparently comes at a cost. As indicated by the defensive tone of the introduction to his 1962 book *The Koehler Method of Dog Training: Certified Techniques by Movieland's Most Experience Dog Trainer*, Koehler's techniques were registering as controversial with readers and owners even decades ago. Koehler advocates using choke chains and throw chains, types of negative reinforcement that many trainers nowadays forgo. "Because it proclaims the kindness of adequate discipline when needed to correct a fault that cannot be condoned, the book might disturb some folks who have nothing to offer but their own emotions," Koehler states.[5] He'd long been the last resort for people with dogs so problematic that it was either his training methods or euthanasia, and he defends his most extreme procedures in the context of that choice.

Luckily, I'd grown up as a WASP-y New England kid, so keeping my emotions in check was no big deal. While my family didn't practice any kind of organized religion, Puritanical ideologies ran in our blood. Discomfort was a mark of character; self-denial a virtue to be praised. We walked to school through blizzards, and I moved to California convinced that "self-care" was merely a West Coast rationalization for sloth. Rhetorically, characterologically, it was clear to me which sort of "some folk" the aspiring dog trainer should be. I called the listing in Ontario, California, and signed us up.

It turns out that that property in Ontario was the site of Bill Koehler's original Southern California kennel. The man I would be working with, Pat Smith, had purchased it from Koehler in the nineties when the Koehlers had retired to Washington State. I didn't know this when I registered us, and the place, when I first sighted it, was not prepossessing—all adjacent strip malls, dirt, and heat. Train tracks ran near the kennel, and the noise at times was loud.

I'd signed up for private training sessions on Saturdays, since I couldn't manage the commute to group classes during the week. My then-husband and I went to most of the sessions together, eight, maybe ten, weeks in total to complete the novice course. It took an effort to drive out there, and I'd had to promise Pat up front that I'd do a minimum of twenty minutes of training each day between our lessons. I knew that, like an omniscient god, he'd be able to tell if we did not.

Pat and his wife, Marilyn, were religious, I believed. I'd seen Bible verses printed in their little sign-in shed on my first visit, Christian iconography here and there. But in all our time together we never talked about anything but dogs. Our training was conducted on a bare field at the upper end of the property, just past the kennel and near the train tracks, whose noise sometimes required us to pause. Each of our sessions had a clear goal that Pat would demonstrate and then ask me to repeat: from drills on a long line, to encourage my puppy to stay close to my side; to leash work involving heeling and abrupt changes of direction; to off-lead work requiring careful attention from both of us and prolonged sit-stays.

Still, it was true: I liked the training method because it involved work, a very Protestant ideal. My dog liked to work, as well. She was always excited when I pulled out her leash and training collar, always bouncing as we set out. Each week we'd go home with discrete homework and come back to show Pat what we had learned. In between, we practiced on our home sidewalks, at a local park, and by the baseball field as maintenance guys manicured the grass. We had a great training session near the football field while the marching band rehearsed, the color guard threw flags, and the tubas sounded like things possessed. We practiced in a church parking lot, too, the stained-glass windows casting color on the asphalt, both of us oblivious to their scenes.

Our locations for training were influenced in part by the charge that we should seek out distractions, not avoid them. Koehler's second obedience manual—*The Koehler Method of Open Obedience for Ring, Home, and Field*, first published in 1970—has a memorable black-and-white photo of a German shepherd sitting at attention while surrounded by a cat, an agility board, a plate of food, a duck, a bag of dog treats, and a horse. "In addition to visible distractions," the caption reads, "this area is covered with tempting scents."[6] The dog sits stoic, staring straight ahead at cameraman or trainer or me. My goal, similarly, was to tempt my dog so that I'd have the opportunity to intervene. "Open wide the favorite gate," reads a favorite passage in manual 1. "Prop it lest a roughish wind spoil your moment . . . you're not heeling, you're hoping—that he'll spot the open gate."[7] A bolt, a break, a correction, and she'd be one step closer to the statuesque shepherd, who demonstrates obedience by willfully ignoring the temptations that encompass him round.

Logically, I understood. In practice, as I set about finding scary trash cans, small children, and brazen squirrels, I came to feel that I wasn't always playing fair. I was teaching my dog self-control, and every time I had to discipline her (in the etymological sense of "teach"), I was theoretically bringing her that much closer to disciplining herself. But as I would wait with her on that sidewalk, envisioning the horse and duck that couldn't lure the German shepherd from his post, I didn't know if I should be happier when she bolted away from the monster tuba or when the previously scary skateboard zipped by and she didn't turn her head. If she didn't bolt: had I failed in my job as a trainer, since I hadn't anticipated some supreme temptation yet awaiting her canine will? If she did bolt: had I failed in my job, since her reaction proved that she wasn't yet fit to govern herself?

It was during these sessions that *Paradise Lost* started weighing heavily on my mind. I teach the epic about once a year, and students (and Milton's original readers, too) regularly get tangled up in the Miltonic presentation of predestination versus foreknowledge and, specifically, Milton's contention that the two are not the same. "If I foreknew, / Foreknowledge had no influence on their fault, / Which had no less proved certain unforeknown," states Milton's God, in describing his knowledge of original sin.[8] God means that free will still exists among mortals, even though he already knows everything they are going to do. God knows Adam and Eve are going to succumb to temptation, but that doesn't mean he makes them do it.

The distinction mattered to Milton for political and personal reasons both. As a Puritan on the losing side of the English Civil War, he needed to feel himself "sufficient to have stood, though free to fall," and if free to fall, then free to rise again.[9] (I've been tempted to quote this statement when students ask me if it is "OK" to miss a class, a deadline, a quiz.) But students also get tangled up in the fact that God plants the very tree that marks man's fall and fault. Adam explains God's reasoning to Eve thus: obedience is meaningless unless tested, so if you are obedient simply by default and not by choice, the virtue doesn't hold. Still, it is hard not to feel that God sets them up, hard not to notice how the enlightenment that follows disobedience can hurt. Milton's epic ends with both parents shedding tears, barred from their garden by a flaming sword. They bear the inheritance now of effort: the promise of difficulty in tilling the ground to grow crops that previously flourished, the agony of childbirth for a process yet required to fulfill God's mandate that we populate the earth.

Back to our sidewalk, featuring an old ice cream sandwich, a pile of poop, a hot dog bun plus flies. Maybe I do have more of those "emotions" that Koehler cautions the trainer against. I seem to feel a doggy pull of desire, a postlapsarian guilt, a sadness that doesn't come from her. She loves the sandwich yet forgives me my correction, moving seamlessly from correction to task. She doesn't know what in the world could be more interesting than what's on that sidewalk, but the fact that I'm telling her to look at me suggests that something could. She doesn't know I've engineered her temptation. She trusts me, every time.

Milton himself wasn't the most trustworthy of men. He wrote *Paradise Lost* in 1667 as a "reformed Puritan" who had newly declared allegiance to the king. Ostensibly a retelling of the war in Heaven and the biblical creation and fall of man, his epic easily reads as a political allegory too, with royalists invited to read Milton as a now-devoted subject of the crown, Oliver Cromwell as the rebellious Satan, and Charles II as the omnipotent

God who punishes disobedience and restores glory and order to us all. And yet, the epic also has the potential to reflect on the "lost" paradise of Cromwell's Republic and the alternative forms of government that Milton and his kind had hoped to maintain. Even Milton's first readers often found Satan the most charismatic of his characters and his God as tyrannical, hard to like.

I love teaching the epic to undergraduates because Milton is so good at playing to both sides. And Milton may not have known, fully, where his own sympathies lay. By the time he writes *Paradise Lost*, his work of "long choosing, beginning late," he is in his fifties and completely blind.[10] He composes the poem orally and dictates it to his daughters to be transcribed; throughout the poem, his blindness provides a constant source of anxiety and fear. "But not to me returns / Day, or the sweet approach of even or morn," he laments, describing himself as one "in darkness, and with dangers compassed round."[11] His agony doesn't simply concern the condition of his blindness, as Milton hopes to claim the disability as a sign of grace, of proof that as his life is harder than that of others, so he must be more important to this world than most. Suffering, however, can also simply be punishment for past crimes. As a royalist, Milton should believe in the monarch as God's deputy on earth. As a Puritan, Milton supported the execution of a king. Might not his blindness be the result?

Every time I read the epic, Milton seems trapped between these readings, desperate to prove his election, tortured by his guilt. And yet, in either reading, suffering resonates as a requirement of attention. To be noticed by God, in any capacity, is to feel pain.

No wonder those of us who grow up in his tradition feel at times the need to hide. My dad, my gentle and most beloved teacher, once told me that his job as a parent was to discipline me: to see and show me my mistakes.

Write two sentences, my son's first-grade teacher says, using the words "I can." "I can see god," my six-year old writes, his *g* sprawling across the page. He's dyslexic sometimes, but he tells me he sees God at night when he, the youngest, takes his bath. "I can dig."

The thing Milton also doesn't acknowledge is how tempting it can be not to see. Oedipus, Homer, Tiresias, Vergil: all the great prophets in this tradition present physical blindness as productive of insight, but blindness, as blindness, has comforts of its own. Take the moment in *Paradise Lost* when God corrects Eve for becoming enamored of her own image, that watery shape she sees reflected in a shady pool. She doesn't know initially that what she sees is a reflection, so God corrects her and asks her to move away. Moving will allow her to meet Adam and also to encounter shapes that won't be insubstantial—shapes that can't be erased by a chance shadow or a passing cloud.

And yet Eve wants to stay put. Even after being told what she sees is a reflection, even after meeting Adam, she wants to go back.

This kind of self-love feels painful to me, especially once she knows shadows have the potential to erase the image for which she pines. But maybe she loves herself because the shadows come intermittently, to give her eyes a break.

The thing about dogs is the way they look at you. Even today, the cataracts cloudy in my old dog's eyes, she meets my gaze.

After a full course of novice obedience lessons, we drove to Pat's property for our final exam. My dog had mastered, to a point, heeling off lead, sit-stays for a long duration, the drop-on-recall, and various other techniques. The point of the exam was to walk her through these skills one final time in front of Pat. It would mark the end of our training treks to Ontario, though not the end of the rituals we had rehearsed. "Once a dog has a solid course of novice training," Pat had told me, "it sets. The dog can get rusty, but the skills are ingrained." He's been right: over a decade later, she'll periodically ignore me, but when I go back to our basic routines, she proves that all her training habits remain intact.

Her ignorance these days, then, is willful. She races out the door after that squirrel by choice.

I don't remember a lot about her exam. I do remember that the morning began atypically gloomy and that, as we drove east, the clouds piled up. By the time we got to Pat's house, it was windy, wet, and cold, and my little dog became bedraggled as she marched about her tasks. Our last test was an off-lead sit-stay from a distance, in which I stood about thirty yards in front of her and was supposed to ask her to come. I placed her on her stay, turned heel, and walked off.

When I turned back, she was sitting there, small and solitary, her coat matted with water, her little face peering ahead. Would it have been so hard to stay together? Would life have been so different if one of us had not strayed? I waited a few moments before I issued the recall, the two of us getting ever damper in the rain. Her anticipation was palpable, the moment of connection, rich. I felt that "invisible string" I conjure up for my children; I felt her eyes fixed on me from across the field.

The sky darkened, and still I stayed.

II
LONGING

7

PERFECTION AND PLATONIC LOVE

Plato, Aristotle

> SOCRATES: *Undoubtedly, such captives would consider the truth to be nothing but the shadows...*
> GLAUKON: *Most certainly.*
> —Plato, *Allegory of the Cave*

Plato can be a good author to read when you are focused on being right. He is famous for his dialogues, which feature his teacher Socrates in conversation with one or more individuals, in a technique known as "dialectical cross examination" that I've never found to be effective with an angry friend or spouse. Socrates, however, manages to ask questions that persuade his interlocutors to reconsider a familiar topic, while the individual being questioned unfailingly comes around to seeing things from the Socratic point of view. By recording these dialogues, Plato implies that those of us who never had the privilege of meeting Socrates can be improved upon by his intelligence. By holding these dialogues, Socrates indicates that the smartest person can always keep at least two people together, in conversation, in the room.

I came to these conclusions as a teenager by extrapolating, very broadly, from what I learned in an introductory philosophy class about these dialogues in the context of the Platonic theory of forms. Plato teaches that there exists somewhere up in the ether an idealized "region of forms," where one can find the universalized, perfect, and all-encompassing version of any object that one may encounter here on earth.[1] For me, the region of forms implied that everything we see and feel around us can be improved. Your dog, whom you believe to be the world's most perfect dog? She is just one, inferior instantiation of the Platonic Dog Form. Your table, for some reason the object that many philosophers use to illustrate this idea? It is also just one pale and partial approximation of the spirit-ideal-table that exists. You, yourself, the "Emily" who is reading these dialogues? An intangible concept such as "loyalty," or "justice," or even "marriage"? My professor didn't get that far in our introductory class.

Since I was a teenager by the time I read these theories, I don't think I believed in the region of forms in any palpable sense. But I did find that thinking about the world in this way brought with it a very real feeling of relief. Plato made sense of my adolescent frustrations, given that the perfect version of the world was hovering just above me, out of reach. The region of forms explained why my experience of life might feel shadowed or my specialness as a child might feel obscured. Plato anticipates, in this regard, a different and much later psychological theory, that of the Freudian "family romance," which explains why as children so many of us believe we are too special to be related to our folks.[2]

Up until I read Plato (I hadn't yet read Freud), I'd been worried that my longing for something more spoke to something missing in myself. Plato reframed this longing as that which made me insightful, rather than confused.

Plato also describes why our experience of life might feel confused. Take, for example, another famous passage, this one from Plato's *Republic*, in which Socrates explains life on earth in terms of the allegory of the cave.[3] Here on earth, most of us sit in a cave facing a wall with a fire behind us, so that the life we witness is just shadows passing before us on the wall. Most of us go through life happy with these shadows though never recognizing them as such. A very few of us suspect that what we see may be shadows, and so we try to leave the cave to see a version of life that is more direct. Some of us may be involuntarily ejected. Some of us may be carried out of the cave by force.

- This means that "Emily" here on earth is either a shadow of some ideal Emily-form or a prisoner in a cave watching shadow-forms on a wall, or she is both. But "Emily" cannot be all encompassing, since the specificity of any earthly manifestation implies a lack.
- "Forms" for processing a divorce in California include, among others, a FL-115, a FL-100, and a FL-141. The FL-165 is particularly important, for a reason I forget. FL-180, the judgment of dissolution, comes toward the end. The FL-190, the notice of entry of judgment, comes last. These final forms are collaborative, their correctness confirmed by seals and stamps.

When it comes to paperwork, I don't think Plato would have been particularly interested in forms. I find them oddly satisfying, from time to time. Forms organize uncertainty; forms break up bigger projects into smaller tasks. Forms fit emotions into tiny boxes; forms paper over any work or unhappiness that comes before. Forms suggest that one can finish something and that I can do this something right.

As I discovered in middle age, however, forms also offer opportunities to make mistakes. In Los Angeles, where marital separations tend to be the stuff of mediators, multiple lawyers, and high-end transactional fees, I TurboTaxed my divorce. Inspired by a variety of financial, geographic, and emotional limitations, this adult attempt to fill out legal forms without professional assistance uncovered an ongoing potential to mix up documents, check incorrect boxes, and submit something like an initial Marriage Settlement Agreement (called, I now know, an "MSA") utterly lacking in legal terms, albeit written in full paragraphs and eloquent sentences, with good transition words and a narrative arc. Such forms, I learned, afforded the opportunity to be submitted in person, only days later to be returned. Such forms supported an exercise that could have been farcical, except for the sense of castigation courthouses include with any form that they reject.

Still, Plato acknowledges that we should be eased into enlightenment. He tells us to experience shadows as shadows long before we try to look into the sun. "There would be need of habituation," he advises, otherwise, "do you not think it would be painful . . . when [s]he came out into the light?"[4] How else does one convert feelings into assets? How does one marry bureaucracy to grief? One can always fill out new forms, drive back to the courthouse, and study template MSAs. One can memorize the directions and the parking and the check-in procedures and the rooms. One can pass corrected forms under a plexiglass barrier, into that special region at the courthouse just for them. Perfection, Plato teaches us, can emerge as the result of trial and error.

The only problem with this concept is that if attaining perfection involves a process, then I want this process to be aligned with speed. Six months, California stipulates, must elapse before even the most perfect paperwork can be authorized by a judge. I know I've run stop signs with adverse consequences. I know going too fast can mean or make you fail. Occasionally, I've rushed to complete a form and gotten something wrong. There were jack o' lantern decals affixed to the courthouse plexiglass when I made my first venture, then cornucopias, and then faded Christmas trees. The finalized paperwork was mailed to me in March. Somewhere, a plexiglass barrier flaunted a lucky shamrock, a pot of gold.

Plato is also a good author to read when you want to learn about love. The funny thing about that statement (that is, apart from the statement itself) is that as a colloquial phrase "platonic love" doesn't mean romantic love but has come to mean a love absent of any sexual pull. A close relationship between roommates, a long-time connection between childhood friends: these might be explained by one or more of the participants as "platonic" to indicate that the bonds forged between the partners are strong, meaningful, yet not founded upon libidinal desire. Platonic love means this because Plato is usually read as celebrating a development or progression in love from erotic or carnal attraction toward a more generalized love of mind, soul, beauty, truth. The source of this phrase comes from Plato's work *The Symposium*, an extended Socratic dialogue on the nature of love and how we love in different ways.[5] I first read this particular work of Plato in high school. I dumped my first boyfriend soon after, since I didn't like him as much as I loved writing papers and the pursuit of truth.

As a senior in high school, I also already knew the basic narrative conventions of such intellectual contests, in which one or more people take a stab at a concept and then the philosopher/expert/detective closes with a response we all recognize as perfect, or correct. In *The Symposium*, Socrates does this by quoting lessons he learned from a wise woman named Diotima, and he has mostly finished his speech when the party is interrupted by the drunkard Alcibiades at the end. But the speech I found most resonant wasn't Socrates's penultimate presentation but the one given earlier by the playwright Aristophanes, which, because of its narrative positioning, we are later supposed to discount. My philosopher-colleague agrees that this is the speech most students like the best. Aristophanes spins what is meant to be a comic tale about how humans were at one time two people conjoined, except this initial human pairing was seen as threatening to the gods. So, Zeus cut everyone in half, and these halves subsequently wander around earth searching for their missing part. Since some humans were initially male-male dyads, some female-female, and some male-female, this Zeus-inflicted fission also accounts for sexual orientation, down the road (if you were originally half of a same-sex hybrid, you are drawn, libidinally, toward a partner of your same sex). Critics underline the presentation of Aristophanes as consciously ironic, an element that in high school I certainly missed. My main memory was his punch line, which I read straight: "love is the name for our pursuit of wholeness," for our desire to be complete.[6]

To this day, and even though Diotima-Socrates later contradicts him, I can't help feeling that Aristophanes is right.

These philosophers also taught me that love wasn't just a question of how I felt about the tables and dogs and people I encountered but how I felt about the artistic renditions of the same. What did Plato think of these? Artists and philosophers are divided in their response, but divisions can be interesting when they aren't about marital assets or a Zeus-inflicted cut.

My redacted adolescent understanding of this divided response, as taken from my college philosophy course, went as follows:

- You either read the artistic representation of the object as one step even further removed from the Platonic ideal and so lesser in every sense as a result (less worthy of attention or study or the time spent in composition);
- Or, you read the artistic representation as expressive of the human desire to attain the Platonic form that we intuitively know exists and can't quite reach. These human attempts are yet imperfect, but the impulse is honorable, and the artistic product improves upon the real-world table or dog that I am saddled with in life. The poet or painter has the ability to pare away some of the earth's doggy imperfections and give my readers and myself a product closer to the airy Platonic form that floats forever beyond my grasp.

Plato came down on the first side of the debate, which is one reason that he banished the poets from his Republic. Aristotle and later critics such as Sir Philip Sidney and Percy Shelley came down in defense of the arts. As a teenager, I was in this second camp, old enough to be in love with words, too young to believe that my love needed no defense. But I didn't like their theories because I liked art and wanted to be told that my liking had a moral or ethical use. I liked their theories because the concept of art as that which improved upon the world rang true. Reading Plato and Aristotle, I could understand my loves as stemming from a subconscious knowledge that my world was in fact lesser and that my pull toward writing was a homing instinct to draw me upward and to make me and the world around me better, brighter, clean. Aristotle explained the childhood moments when I'd be overtaken by what I could at the time merely call "strong feelings" and had to sit in the basement to write a poem. He explained a longing—to look at imperfections aesthetically, as a way to improve upon the world—that felt otherwise contradictory or confused.

Here's one of my early Aristotelian attempts to make my world a better place:

GRAY

Gray is a gray building
With gray pebbles by the door;
Gray are gray-ish seashells
Scattered on the moor;
Gray are gray-ish raindrops
That look like little stars
And a gray street,
Not yet full of cars.

—EMILY, AGE 7

"Emily" was a funny child, but I still like the movement of the poem from building, to beach, to street. While the images are lonely ones, the loneliness is beautiful to me, something that other people will overlook.

How rarely do we stare straight up into raindrops to see them sparkle. How rarely do we pause to look at an empty street.

The final step in a California divorce procedure involves a packet of many forms. It needs to be copied in triplicate, and each packet needs to be punched through with a double hole punch at the top. I'd seen the reason for this requirement on prior visits to the courthouse, as the clerks take the finished packet and insert it into a folder with those dagger-like bendable clips at the top. No holes, and the papers can't be foldered and bound and passed along to the judge. No holes, and the packet is not complete. Funny, that papers must be bound together so that individuals can be divided. Funny, how in *The Symposium*, Aristophanes says Zeus cut conjoined humans in two like "two parts of a fish."[7] Piscine wholeness, I should have told the clerk: that's what I miss.

I didn't own a hole punch, much less a double one. But the copy room at school did, which I knew since for weeks I'd done all my legal paperwork in this room, hiding my documents, like my divorce, from any colleagues who happened to come in. Before these necessities, my classroom Xeroxes would always miss a margin, and my paper cutting would leave pages crooked or uncut. Hole punching, especially, had been my nemesis: it never worked out well. Still, on that last day in the courthouse, I held my papers, knowing that I had the correct number of forms in the correct order, that I had made the correct number of copies, and most of all that I had lined up the pages of each packet perfectly and punched them hard enough for the hole punches, those double ones at the top, to go all the way through. I knew this because I could stare down through these holes to the floor beneath me, and I took turns squinting through one hole and then the other to prove this to myself. The floor was gray, I think.

I ask myself now, looking back at that courthouse Emily, how my desire for perfection has affected my relationships to others. I wonder how it has affected my relationship to myself. Those are good questions, and I don't know how Socrates would answer on my behalf. I just know that when I finally got to the front of the courthouse line and readied myself for my exchange, I was prepared to show the clerk that I'd succeeded. I had my forms, punched, no less, with a double hole punch at the top.

But did you know that double hole punches come in different scales or ranges, so that some produce parallel holes at a spacing of roughly three inches and some at less? The hole punch used by the courthouse, and the one I used at school, were not the same.

I do know now, in a way, that flaws and foibles make our life more textured. I know that my idiosyncrasies can make me charming, and I know that I can be more forgiving of myself and of my friends. And still: don't we all wish, from time to time, for a perfect experience here on earth? Because, you see, it turns out that there was a hole punch, the perfect kind, and it was sitting on the courthouse counter to the right of me, just beyond my grasp. I could stretch for it. With just a modicum of effort, I could strain my way to a place that would set things right.

I looked up for the first time since I had entered the building; I stared at that other woman behind the plastic partition, a Christmas decal casting a shadow on her desk.

"The hole punch," she said, locking eyes with me and sounding in that moment like Socrates—sounding in that moment like God—"the hole punch cannot be moved."

8

(AN ASIDE)

Shakespeare

I have that within which passeth show . . .
—William Shakespeare, *Hamlet*, 1.2.88

What are the first words Hamlet speaks? It's a good Trivial Pursuit–style question, one that reminds me of a trivia question we were once asked in junior high (what are the opening lines of *Moby-Dick*?). Opening lines set the tone, or the stage (as it were), for the rest of the work. But in Hamlet's case, I want to know if his words set the stage for life. He grates on me, these days, stuck in a misery that I need to know can change. I'm worried that he is responsible in some degree for his own isolation. I'm worried that many of these tendencies are fixed in him from the beginning of the play.

Shakespeare rewards such attention, since he is famous for being strategic about his openings, full stop. In *Hamlet*, for example, the first words of the play ("Who's there," spoken by Bernardo) give us a frame of reference for all that is to come. Think of how applicable those words are to the play's general mood (uncertainty: is it a damned ghost or his father's spirit we have seen?) and how applicable they are to so many subsequent scenes. (Who's there, lurking behind the arras in Gertrude's room? Who's there, Hamlet, that you do bend your eye on vacancy, and with the incorporeal air do hold discourse? Who's there, you, dressed in black, lurking amongst the other attendants at Claudius's court?) At the same time, despite the prescient quality of the play's first words, they also serve as something of a "soft launch": they set up an initial scene that provides some backstory but defers the appearance of those who will be the main characters in the play. (Shakespeare does this a lot. Think *The Tempest*, or *King Lear*, or again, *Hamlet*, in whose first scene no Hamlet appears.) And there's a reason that Shakespeare (also Hamlet) tends to dabble in delay. The technique builds our expectations; it forces us to "see" these characters first through another's eyes. By the time we finally meet Hamlet, we've worked up a good deal of anticipation (especially given that the play is called *Hamlet* and that Horatio and Marcellus and Bernardo have set off, after seeing the ghost in scene 1, explicitly to find him and tell him what they've seen), and once we get to see him, we are definitely waiting to hear him speak.

What, then, are Hamlet's first words? Given Shakespeare's strategy of deferral, Hamlet's grand entrance feels anticlimactic, to say the least. He's been onstage since the beginning of scene 2, but Claudius has been doing all the talking (for lines and lines and lines), so that Hamlet is there but not properly introduced. And then, finally, Claudius turns to his nephew with the following cue: "But now, my cousin Hamlet, and my son,—" Except, his isn't a proper cue in a conversational sense, because Claudius doesn't finish his sentence until his next line, which is a question ("How is it that the clouds still hang on you?") that finally pushes Hamlet into direct address ("Not so, my lord; I am too much i' the sun"). And yet even here, Hamlet's answer to Claudius's question is not the first time that Hamlet speaks, because his true first words come *between* his answer to Claudius and the first part of Claudius's sentence (the part that modern editors always break off with an em-dash, to show that here Hamlet interjects).

Another trivia tidbit: in Shakespeare's time, actors were almost never in possession of the complete play. Instead, the actor playing Hamlet would have been given only his part in the script (consisting of a roll of paper, transcribed with only his own lines), plus cue lines interspersed (the last words spoken by another character just before the character in possession of this roll is meant to speak).[1] In this scene, the actor playing Hamlet would have seen something like "my cousin Hamlet, and my son" as his prompt. He would have at this point finally uttered his first lines of the play, a statement marked by most modern editors as an [Aside]:

("A little more than kin, and less than kind").[2]

There's a respite, I realize, while thinking about *Hamlet*, for those who get to stay offstage. Sometimes I find it easier to wait until tomorrow, or next weekend, or never, to engage with people and just send an email with my regrets. But writing to decline takes effort. (Did I say that only to myself?)

Why do you think the first words Hamlet utters in Shakespeare's play are an aside? An aside makes the utterance resemble a mini-soliloquy, a statement meant for Hamlet's (and our) ears alone. A very few select productions have had Hamlet uttering his first statement so that other people onstage can hear, but most of the time we, the theater audience, are the only ones besides Hamlet to know that he speaks up to be critical of the man about to call him out.

Soliloquy, used for the first time by the fourth-century theologian Saint Augustine, comes from the Latin words *solus* and *loqui*, giving it the etymological meaning of "alone speak"; it eventually popped up in the English language in 1613 (probably about eight years after the composition of *Hamlet*) as meaning "private talk." Theatrical productions and scholarship vary, however, as to whether soliloquy onstage is meant to be actual "talk" or the verbalization of thoughts: a technique of rendering audible, to audiences, what is going on within a character's mind. Increasingly the stage has depicted soliloquy as the latter, since with the rise of secularism and the decline of rituals like prayer, audiences and directors have challenged the realism of characters strutting about talking to themselves. (But why? I talk to myself all the time.) One need not be physically alone, I tell my students, to utter a soliloquy onstage. The scholar James Hirsch defines the theatrical soliloquy as lines spoken by a single actor when the character portrayed by that actor does not intend for the words to be overheard.[3]

The paradigm shift to soliloquy as a representation of thought rather than speech and the privacy associated with the expression account for the emergent assumption that soliloquy gives us privileged access to a character's mind. Soliloquy, especially when considered as self-addressed speech rather than interior monologue, can actually serve a variety of functions, and early critics of Shakespearean soliloquy note that his monologues "serv[e] a number of purposes which have little or nothing to do with 'self-expression.'"[4] These alternative purposes include soliloquy as a device of exposition, as a means of linking scenes together, and as a way to identify other characters; soliloquy as a revelation of thought and feeling is only one function among many. But this latter function of soliloquy quickly overwhelms others in the audience's imagination. Objections to the realism of soliloquy as speech, stemming from the fact that many observers found it improbable for a man in words to "lay open his heart, and speak boldly of his most secret thoughts," also reinforced the assumption that soliloquy, whether spoken or thought, does exactly this.[5] The eighteenth-century philosopher Moses Mendelssohn describes the soliloquy as an outpouring of the soul; the early-nineteenth-century playwright Joanna Baillie defines it as "those overflowings of the perturbed soul, in which it unburthens itself of those thoughts which it cannot communicate to others."[6] Hamlet's most celebrated soliloquy, his "to be or not to be," is often summoned as exemplary of this effect. The critic Morris Arnold states that "when Hamlet muses, 'to be or not to be' . . . our whole attention is vibrantly sympathetic with the workings of his brain and the feelings of his heart."[7] As the figuration of thought and emotion, soliloquy, like Momus's glass, lets us see inside a character's mind and soul.

And yet, even without soliloquy, I always imagine there are some things about another person one should just be able to intuit. What a relief it can be to have someone else see within—even if what shows up are but black and grainèd spots—still, what a relief to have someone else hold up the glass. Why must the introverts among us always do the work? Why is Hamlet still so sad? Well, really, Claudius. Why do you think?

Hamlet will ultimately speak seven soliloquies over the course of the play, more than any other character Shakespeare scripts. If Hamlet talks to lots of people, he also, like Augustine, talks a lot to himself. His first words set up a character who enjoys "alone speak": a character who perhaps prefers his own company to that of others or who maybe believes he can trust only himself. Maybe he's grown up with few companions; maybe he is lonely; maybe he just likes to blurt out what comes into his head. Or maybe he is tired of having his words to others go unacknowledged, and maybe, with the clouds still hanging on him, he chooses to circumvent the experience of effacement by making himself the audience for what he says.

These are Hamlet's seven soliloquies throughout the play:

"O that this too, too sullied flesh would melt . . ."
"O, all you host of heaven . . ." (I always imagine the ghost as his audience for this address, though perhaps one definition of aloneness is being listened to by a ghost)
"O, What a rogue and peasant slave am I . . ."
"To be or not to be . . ." (his most famous, a soliloquy so well known that the actor Richard Burton complained his audience "settled down for a nice old nap the minute the fatal first words start")[8]
"Tis now the very witching time of night . . ."
"Now might I do it . . ." (while watching Claudius at prayer)
And, finally, "How all occasions do inform against me, and spur my dull revenge . . ."

These soliloquies all range in length, but a deeper dive into any of them would reveal his "private talk" to be a substantial meditation on a problem or question that needs parsing out. In all of these, you can see Hamlet in dialogue with himself, posing questions and trying out answers as he goes along.

(Why don't I have more social invitations?
Why do people only come so close?)

Note, however, that Hamlet's first words don't appear in my list of seven soliloquies. Soliloquy and aside, though they share the quality of "private talk," also emerge as serving different functions within the play. Aside for Hamlet tends to be more of a one-off, a confident if private observation, a criticism, a secret joke, a dig. (For Polonius, asides tend to be self-affirming; for Claudius, secret laments.) Hamlet's opening lines aren't a meditation on the existential conundrums of life but a snarky comment, what my kids might call a "burn." I'm way too closely related to you, he says to Claudius (but under his breath), yet I'm not *like* you, I'm not your "kind." I'm smarter than you, as well; just look at the way I can play with words. You are not kind, my kin king; I am the kinder man, your kin who should be king. And I am the kind of man who should be king, because I'm kind, and kin.

Except . . . am I kingly, because would a kingly man lurk on the sidelines, making jokes in kind?

(I just have so much trouble even *meeting* eligible straight men, I complain on the phone to my brother, while packing for a trip to a gay tourist site in Mexico with three of my single, gay male friends.)

Like soliloquy, Hamlet's aside has the effect of externalizing for us (and us alone) the anger and felt superiority that he yet keeps within. His lines are a way of talking without talking, of putting into space a critique he won't yet own. Until the very end of the play, he never directly tells Claudius that he is mad at him ("thou incestuous, murderous, damned Dane"), or that he thinks he, Hamlet, is the better man.

In the context of his first lines, Hamlet's mode of engagement, or nonengagement, makes a kind of sense. He is standing, after all, amid multiple courtiers in the pomp and circumstance of Claudius's court. We might say he is silenced by the power structures that surround him, or that his is a coping strategy adopted by a man who suspects he lives among hypocrites and villains. And he's right. To out himself in this setting and at this particular moment wouldn't be politic or safe. But his aside isn't an inevitable, or the only, strategy of engagement in the play. Hamlet's opening lines contrast most obviously with the responses of Laertes, a parallel for Hamlet in that he too is the son of a dead father, a son hell-bent on revenge. "That drop of blood that's calm proclaims me bastard," Laertes later yells at Claudius, one of my favorite lines of the play, when he comes home from France to learn of his father's death. He is in Claudius's face from the moment of his return. No quiet lurking and strategizing, no word play, no "alone speak" for him; my father is dead and I am going to *rage*. What kind of son would I be if I were calm?

Hamlet, by contrast, takes shots at others from the periphery, when they don't even know he is shooting at them and when they can't see to shoot him back (think of Hamlet's use of the "Mousetrap" play; think Polonius; think Ophelia; think the play's reliance on voyeurism, lying, disguise). Time and again Hamlet takes refuge in a supercilious cleverness that he flaunts from the margins, as if being smarter than everyone else could right his wrongs, as if intellectual superiority alone could place him upon the throne.

But intellectual superiority is not emotion, Hamlet, and what does it matter if you can work yourself up into a frenzy if no one else is around to see or know? No one is saying that you should act impulsively, but why don't you articulate more frequently to others your grief, your anger, your remorse? "I loved Ophelia," you say, but only once she is lying in the grave. And even to Horatio, your heart's core, your heart of hearts, you generalize

("give me that man") then back away ("something too much of this"). Why keep it as always, always as, "within"?
    Are you a coward? A strategist? A villain?
    I think you are ashamed.

But for what in the play should Hamlet be ashamed?

Hamlet's aside, in both form and content, is what I would define as "passive aggressive," and as such, it seems to mock more direct forms of aggression expressed by other characters in the play. Fortinbras, Laertes: these are characters, and approaches, that Hamlet dubs as rash, impulsive, indiscreet. And yet he envies them ("even for an eggshell!" "for Hecuba!"), with an envy and criticism that must be linked ("our indiscretion sometimes serves us well"). These characters do what Hamlet cannot bring himself to do.

    In a psychoanalytic reading, it is these forthright characters who should feel shame. Aggression, especially of sons toward father figures, can code as a manifestation of Freud's castration complex, a symptom of a love predicated on sexual competition and desire. You, father (the castration complex goes), have what I want: my mother's bed and the key to power, and if I don't emasculate you now, you will forever usurp me. Aggression toward the father becomes a source of shame, since to embrace it is also to give in to these illicit desires, and a Freudian reading of Laertes and Fortinbras might suggest that they can rage at their father-killers because they no longer have to suppress their own deeply buried desire to supplant the father who has now been killed. (It may help, too, that neither Laertes nor Fortinbras have mothers who are actively on scene.) But their aggressive approach also, I think, shows characters less tortured by the

Oedipal desires that, as Freud would have it, grip us all. To act on this aggression shows characters who aren't hiding from a primal urge, whether or not they fully process it as such. They suit the action to the word and the word to the action. There is a kind of integrity in Laertes's rage.

But, as Hamlet shows us, not all characters fight like this or have such a direct alignment between feeling and deed. Claudius, too, is another character who acts from the sidelines, who smiles and smiles and then stabs his brother in the back (or, pours poison in his ear). He even kills his brother while his brother is sleeping, so that old King Hamlet never has a chance to see or respond to what his brother does (kind of like stabbing a man behind an arras, a man hidden from your sight). In this manner and others, Hamlet and Claudius become uncomfortably alike.

See Ernest Jones, Freud's colleague, on the play: "[Hamlet] of course detests [Claudius], but it is the jealous detestation of one evil-doer towards his successful fellow. Much as he hates him, he can never denounce him . . . for the more vigorously he denounces his uncle the more powerfully does he stimulate to activity his own unconscious and 'repressed' complexes . . . in reality his uncle incorporates the deepest and most buried part of his own personality, so he cannot kill him without also killing himself."[9] And indeed this is what Hamlet finally does, stabbing his uncle with the sword poisoned by his uncle, the same sword that has already given Hamlet his own death wound.

In his sideline punches, his prancing asides, Hamlet, smarter than most, may be trying to dodge the Oedipal desires that he perhaps sees more clearly than other sons. Or maybe the digs and jabs—embraced by both Claudius and Hamlet—become a way to defuse aggression, a way to disguise uncomfortable desires under a search for certainty or self-protection. (If Old Hamlet can't see who killed him, maybe Claudius doesn't have to see it, either.) But I also find the approach exhausting and insincere. If you are ashamed of loving your mom and hating your father, Hamlet, I think you are also ashamed of how you engage. You rationalize a mode of encounter that lets you off the hook; you never truly acknowledge how the jabs you make at others can land and hurt; you are too weak to stand in public behind your words. Look at Ophelia, look at Polonius. Why don't you ever face those who oppose you? Even at the end, you stab an unarmed Claudius in a fight that is ostensibly with another man.

But the king, the king has always been to blame. By indirections find directions out.

If an aside is nonengagement, then what is its converse?

Dear Hamlet:
I have known you all already, known you all.
I have known you to complain about being on the sidelines, as if you have never also embraced all the sidelines have to offer. I have known you to hide the querulous nature of your position, as if the clouds that hang upon you could hide from you the very nature of your grief. I have known you to evade your evasions, as if you didn't actually know what was implied by an aside (you, the very master of them; you, who use them time and again). I have known you to feint and parry, as if in your own pain you didn't also want to hurt.
For I am like you, Hamlet, kin, and kind.
I have known you, then, to the extent someone can know another who introduces himself thus—

(Because an aside is talking without talking, all preamble and prefatory and white noise that none but you can share. Because what if we use asides to prepare ourselves for the simple declarative sentence, the act of direct engagement that forces us into the spotlight, limelight, floodlights, footlights, that makes us seen and heard and finally, finally ready to act? Because, Hamlet, what if the pathos of your situation is that all our preparation and fear and hiding-masked-as-thinking, what if all of that merely readies us for—and the readiness is all—that one sentence, that one act of engagement from whose bourn no traveler returns? Would it have been worth it? Would it have been worth it, after all?)

The rest is silence.

9

THE ONE AND ONLY JANE
Jane Austen

Four years ago today found me sitting, à la Louisa Musgrove, in a precarious place. I know this because Facebook reminded me it was the anniversary of my "most liked" post: not a funny picture or a popular meme but a lengthy narrative about an attempt to leave my son's soccer practice that had ended with me stuck atop a chain-link fence.[1]

I'd been rushing to get to student-teacher conferences; the gates to the field, despite practice being held as scheduled, had been locked. As a family we'd scaled them to get in, but egress was proving harder; I'd been both terrified to jump down and, as I soon realized, tethered in place by the back of my shorts. (My release would depend upon the shorts tearing; the underwear I was wearing that day was blue.) I'd described all of these details online: my children, laughing at me from the sidewalk; the other parents, starting to notice a forty-something-year-old woman awkwardly perched; my vertigo, the fence links pressing into my thigh, the expanse of leg that now showed more prominently than when I was standing, clothed as I then thought appropriately in running shorts. But how to explain the teleology of these incidents, the life events that had led me to such a pass? Apparently, I'd turned to Jane Austen to make sense and comedy of my fate. "I lack a Wentworth!" I had joked, in a catch-all explanation, referring to the lover of Louisa Musgrove in Austen's novel *Persuasion*, who promises to catch her when she jumps.[2]

I think I had Jane Austen's novels read to me for the first time when I was about ten years old, part of the evening bedtime ritual with my father, which in this case began at *Northanger Abbey* and went on to feature all Jane's subsequent works. As a young and sometimes sleepy listener, I could become fuzzy on the details of my nighttime stories, and I know that with Austen, characters and plot lines became especially tangled in my head. Knightleys overlapped with Darcys; Pemberleys and Highburys all seemed the same. Lizzy Bennet, the heroine of Austen's self-described "light, bright, and sparkling" novel *Pride and Prejudice*, for me blurred into Emma, the protagonist of the one novel named after its titular character and a character distinguished emphatically from Lizzy by her author: not sparkling but "a heroine whom no-one but myself will much like."[3]

I find it interesting that I'd see such similarities in characters that Austen contrasts. Even now, with multiple rereadings under my belt; my own love of detail; and the conscientious study of her letters, fragments, juvenilia, and the like, I'll find her characters and plots bleeding together, blurring, turning fuzzy in my head. I'm saved from full-on fears of senility by the fact that my much younger students suffer from these Austen confusions, too. My reading quizzes reveal to me that one courtship plot or protagonist feels to them very much like another, a reaction that confirms my own initial experience of her work. Maybe, I think, instead of naïve reading or weakening neural synapses, these confusions reflect something about life, love, and Austen's analytical concerns.

Specifically, I see a purposefulness in how Austen plays with character fungibility within the marriage plot.[4] The very plot that encourages us to root for soulmates and one-of-a-kind pairings itself works formulaically, suggesting that pairings produce patterns we can track. While reading *Emma* I can wish, along with her, that she and only she will be the fit partner for Mr. Knightley. But I can simultaneously confuse her life-changing events with those of Elizabeth Bennet and see Emma's story as roughly equivalent to that of every other female protagonist in Austen's work.

As my Facebook post indicates, I'm also encouraged to track equivalences between their courtship experiences and my own. Austen's most successful protagonists achieve their ultimate desires through a process of becoming better known to their suitors and to themselves. Such a statement may sound like a generic summary of the bildungsroman, but Austen's protagonists aren't maturing or "coming of age" so much as learning how to be less hidden from others and themselves.[5] In her early work Austen conveys this development rather literally, by having Catherine Morland move from her tiny village into the larger sphere of Bath, where "she was now seen by many young men who had not been near her before."[6] The process of becoming visible starts geographically, it seems. Or, in contemporary parlance, by "putting yourself out there," wherever "there" may be.

Nowadays, "there" often means the amorphous space of the internet, where aspirational dating profiles collide against each other like atoms and rebound. The new ease with which one can emerge from the shadows—a step now possible for anyone with an internet connection or a phone, a step less labored than a pilgrimage to Bath—makes this process seemingly more deliberate than the chance reappearance of a prior lover or the gradual shift in feelings of a brother-figure or old family friend. The volitional quality of these acts of self-revelation, however, also makes these profiles feel like carefully curated self-narratives, easily exchangeable, designed to reflect back to the individual sharing them a sense of who he or she wants to be.

And yet maybe I'm being too hard on Austen, on myself. There remains something to be said for that first step, in Austen or today, of articulating the desire to be desired. Maybe sharing a curated self-presentation is sharing, of a sort. Maybe by positioning ourselves against the background of formulaic prompts and poses, certain idiosyncrasies may emerge. Maybe in "putting ourselves out there" with everyone else in the world, we take the first step in letting ourselves be known.

Novels have long been celebrated as a literary form that offers readers unique access to that illusory and intoxicating kind of "knowing" not otherwise possible in real life. In classical mythology, this desire was emblematized through the character of Momus, possessed of a "glass" in his breast through which one could peer into his soul. Our longing for this access and ability is strong. "If the fixture of Momus's-glass in the human breast . . . had taken place," speaks the protagonist of Laurence Sterne's novel *Tristram Shandy*, "nothing more would have been wanting, in order to have taken a man's character, but to have taken a chair and gone softly . . . and looked in."[7] The novel gives us, narratively, this impossible access. Characters unburden their souls to us; omniscient narrators excavate for us the most hidden recesses of a heart.

Austen follows in this tradition, to a point. She is famous for her detailed character vignettes, her ironic and detached narrator, and for the narrative style known as "free indirect discourse" that makes it unclear if the thoughts being shared emanate directly to us from the character's mind or are somewhat subjective assessments of the character's thoughts given to us omnisciently by the narrator herself.[8] Either way, she's celebrated for the personalities she develops. The readers that love her love her protagonists as role models, friends.

Yet I'm not so sure Austen is invested in the Momus approach. For all her novelistic play with psychological access, for all the pleasure in empathy and projection that Austen's novels are said to offer up (which Austen character are YOU, demands of me a Facebook quiz),[9] her novels offer equally purposeful exercises in disidentification: experiments in what pushes us away from another character or person or what makes another person hard to know.

I'm not just talking here about Austen's unlikeable characters, which in her novels are not hard to find. *Not* liking certain Austen characters is as easy as cathecting onto others, and the Freudian in me often wonders why the sympathetic protagonists don't spend more time worrying about the fact that they share a gene pool with the folks we dislike. ("All women become like their mothers," states Oscar Wilde; how is it Lizzy Bennet never seems anxious about this claim?)[10] But I'm also thinking about a character like Jane Fairfax, who has all the trappings necessary for adulation and who is presented within *Emma* as a fit counterpart for Emma herself. "She would be such a delightful companion for Emma!" announces Emma's sister, sensing the scarcity of acquaintance that characterizes Highbury and leaves Emma to associate, Pygmalion style, with the lower-class Harriet Smith. "One knows Jane Fairfax to be so very accomplished and superior—and exactly Emma's age." A brunette foil to Emma's blonde (in cinematic depictions at least), Jane should be the experiment in character fungibility par excellence.[11]

So why are these the two characters I'm never in danger of mixing up? "I wish Jane Fairfax very well, but she tires me to death," states Emma, in an early assessment of her character, though why Emma so dislikes Jane remains hard to explain: "'she could never get acquainted with her: she did not know how it was, but there was such coldness and reserve—such apparent indifference whether she pleased or not . . . and it had been always imagined that they were to be so intimate—because their ages were the same, everybody had supposed they must be so fond of each other.' These were her reasons—she had no better."[12] My hunch is that Austen thinks these are quite good reasons, and they inform my own dislike of Jane. I don't like her because I don't know her, and I don't know her well enough to confuse her with anyone else. Her closest parallel for me is that other Jane, Jane Bennet in *Pride and Prejudice*, likewise a protagonist whom characters aside from her sister struggle to read and who almost loses her prospective husband as a result. These types of exceptionalism feel sad, as sad perhaps as the status attributed to yet another Jane: the author who according to the critic D. A. Miller uses her novels to achieve a unique and "absolute impersonality" that allows her to float, godlike and omniscient, above the fray of human life.[13] She's the author whose loves and losses remain shrouded in mystery, whose novels tell us everything about humanity but nothing about her.

Maybe Austen is coaching me, then, with all those other details and formulae and mannerisms, all those shared narrative excursions that cause me or my students to mix up her characters and plots. Maybe the lesson of Jane and Jane and Jane is that we don't need a window in our chests to be known to others. Maybe we just have to let ourselves participate in these social formulae, accept that the most momentous experience for one person fits into a narrative trajectory experienced by us all. Maybe we have to let ourselves be common in order to be unique.

These lessons are—I admit—hard for me to swallow. I've spent most of my life as a Jane. I always interpreted my reserve as stemming from humility, privacy, or shyness; often, I felt it as a sign of pain or suffering that I thought others could track. It's hard to read my behavior from the other angle, as something designed to keep intimacy at bay, or worse—as a supercilious gesture meant to shut out others and something at which others would take offense. Those of us who fear emerging from our Jane-dom fear being common, being misread; we fear the risk of exposure (an expanse of thigh, a sudden vertigo, a partner's affair).

Fortunately, Austen also understands these fears. She sketches them through *Persuasion*'s Anne Elliot, a character who blends something of an Emma with the benefits of a Jane. Anne needs to learn to express her feelings to those she cares for, yet Austen also distinguishes her from the indiscriminate "oversharer" represented by Louisa, who for some of the novel is a potential competitor with Anne for Captain Wentworth's affections and the alternative model of self-presentation against which Anne's reserve is placed. I feel relieved to track in Anne's happy ending a more mature trajectory of second chances, of measured judgment, and a uniqueness bred of being willing once more, on the basis of this judgment, to speak her mind.

And so: soccer practice that afternoon. "You were *literally* on the fence," a friend later exclaimed, an idiom made real that for all my aspirations to wit I had failed to note.[14] In *Persuasion*, when Louisa finds herself atop the steep stairs that line the harbor wall at Lyme, she flings herself forward before Wentworth is ready with his catch. As a result, she hits her head, knocks herself unconscious, and subsequently falls in love with someone else; her loves and lovers are as interchangeable as whims. But Louisa leaps because she assumes someone will be there to catch her, an assumption Anne, watching from the shadows, can no longer make. I feel for Anne, for myself, for all the Janes. Like Louisa, I sat on top of my chain-link fence, but like Anne, I didn't jump. I didn't move at all, in fact, until a random dad finally approached me, placed his hands on my waist, and helped me down.

10

OF PAIN, PARALYSIS, AND PURSUIT

Samuel Beckett, Mary Shelley

I was running when the stranger leaned in, in the final six hundred meters of a cross-country race on my home course. He was yelling at the woman with whom I'd been in staggered lockstep for two and a half miles and who had just now pulled two steps ahead. I'd been dazing, dreaming, falling away. "You'll remember this moment for the rest of your life!" he screamed, leaning toward the competitor whom for the sake of superstition I referred to by her initials alone. Such a clichéd phrase, I thought, even in the moment. How embarrassing to prove him right.[1]

There's a parallel scene in Mary Shelley's novel *Frankenstein*, a book we focus on as a creation story gone awry. Victor Frankenstein, after his creature's series of crimes, has vowed to follow his creation north until they meet in "mortal conflict"; the creature, throughout the months that follow, remains ever just out of reach. I've always found the asymptotic quality of their chase chilling—this game designed, by definition, to continue for as long as Victor and his creation remain alive.

My situation shared something with this experience. On this particular day, I had been racing "out of my head," as one expression goes: racing well beyond a level of exertion I'd ever experienced and despite any rational evidence that what I was doing made sense. My head tilt, always present, now canted far to the left; my right foot kept coming in to knock the inside of my left calf; my bladder gave with every stride. Every runner, in every race, experiences something called a "stopping moment"—a moment when you imagine how nice it would be just to walk off the track or course. (I think every writer feels this, too.) I was reaching mine. This was enough because it was too much.

When have we hit the lowest point we can attain? And is pain something we can remember, much less share? I think about these questions when the distances imposed among us feel painful and the stasis required by isolation feels, often, like too much. I think, too, about how literature meditates on these conundrums and how my own transitions between running and writing have always felt seamless: from aspiring professional runner to English professor, from thinking as I run to writing down my run-on thoughts.

On paper, however, these pursuits seem so opposed—running, of the body; writing, of the mind. Pain, too, can feel both isolating and communal, something that draws me inward and also something that, in the context of running, helped dissipate my shyness and bring me friends. My closest prior relationships, I realized once I started running, had been with fictional protagonists, figures who could love me as a reflection of my mind. Twenty-four years later, when our cross-country course record (my rival's) finally fell, I'd tell a newspaper reporter as much: "to race [her] was to race myself."[2]

Victor Frankenstein knows something about this kind of pursuit. In *Frankenstein*, a focus on movement pervades the novel, with the creation first pursuing the scientist throughout his apartments, the scientist on the run. And yet, even in these scenes it's as if the thing Victor flees is also an anchor that will only let him range so far, in a daemonic corruption of the compass conceit employed by John Donne. Frankenstein, "unable to endure the aspect of the being [he] had created," rushes out of his laboratory but only to his bedchamber and, after a bit of pacing, settles down for a nap. He is soon interrupted by the creature, and in response he moves, but again only partially, "taking refuge in the courtyard belonging to the house which [he] inhabited," where he will pass the night tracing a radius around the scene and creature he wishes to forget. When, at dawn, the porter lets him out onto the streets, he exits but continues to circle the scene of the crime, such that he can soon stumble into his best friend from childhood, Clerval, and return with him to the scene of creation, his lab.[3]

I make a joke of these behaviors when I teach Shelley, though I'm also sympathetic to Victor, here. As a long-time track competitor, I appreciate the irony of running for miles and miles in a circle, finishing quite literally at the place I began. Nowadays, hampered by old running injuries, I pace through my mornings on a backyard elliptical machine, watching replays from my favorite Olympic track events. Yet I've moved forward somehow, staying still. My machine running reminds me of my laps in the pool with my kids on deck; the track sessions that replaced my long runs when single motherhood meant that to run miles I had to orbit the infield where my children ranged; or the cross-country running, cheered on by my family, that I did so frequently as a young adult. Even there, I'd cover miles and miles to end up at my starting point. I always ran toward some consciousness of others; I always ran to come back home.

The other book I can't stop thinking about these days feels, at first blush, like the polar opposite of the pursuit scene from

Frankenstein or the memory of race day that keeps running through my head. "I'm trapped in a Beckett play," I keep repeating to friends. My set is minimalist, my days indistinguishable, and the sun rises and sets (it keeps doing that, at least) while little shifts. "Pancakes?" I'll say one morning to my boys; "Cheerios?!" I'll announce gamely, for variety and with great inflection, on the next. They seem relatively peaceful about the stasis; my dog, too, stares at me calmly from her chair. But while I'm trying to find the novelty in small changes, my Zen-like focus is disturbed by the hope that our situation is temporary and I needn't leave my remembered reality completely behind. I'm not living so much as waiting, and waiting jars painfully with my desire for movement, progress, pursuit.

Samuel Beckett's *Waiting for Godot* has also been described as "a threnody of hope." Featuring two protagonists who spend their time fixed nearly in place, their actions and purpose governed by an external figure who never appears, the play frames its titular "waiting" as a product of "hope deceived and deferred" but never fully quenched.[4] When I reread the play recently, the celebratory message in this description felt misplaced. Hope seems torturous to these two men—something that they'd be better off not having, something that blinds and binds them to their current status of neglect. Instead of models of human resilience, Vladimir and Estragon seem dupes who set themselves up to be overlooked. Hope doesn't keep them moving forward; it prevents them from moving on.

I'm not alone in my prickly response. When *Waiting for Godot* was first performed in the 1950s, it created confusion, even ire. American viewers, less familiar than their European counterparts with the theater of the absurd, believed they had been subject to a "hoax." "The play concerns two tramps who inform each other and the audience at the outset that they smell," wrote the American critic Marya Mannes. "It takes place in what appears to be the town dump, with a blasted tree rising out of a welter of rusting junk including plumbing parts. They talk gibberish to each other and to two 'symbolic' maniacs for several hours, their dialogue punctuated every few minutes by such remarks as 'What are we waiting for?' 'Nothing is happening,' and 'Let's hang ourselves.' The last was a good suggestion, unhappily discarded."[5] Billed somewhat unfortunately in the United States as "the laugh sensation of two continents," the play inspired a "mass exodus" in Miami soon after the curtain rose.[6] Attendance had apparently come to feel like duress. Why wait around, like Vladimir and Estragon, to get the joke?

Rereading the story of these early failures makes me think about why we do sit still to read a book, watch a movie, watch a play—why a runner like me is equally happy to sit for hours and write. It also makes me consider why not all the early productions of *Waiting for Godot* failed. Indeed, a 1957 performance of the play at San Quentin fixed inmates to their seats. As one reviewer describes it, the watching prisoners, initially disgruntled, "listened and looked two minutes too long—and stayed. Left at the end. All shook." Rick Cluchey, an inmate too dangerous to be released from his cell to see the production, and one who merely heard the play broadcast, recalls, "The thing that everyone in San Quentin understood about Beckett, while the rest of the world had trouble catching up, was what it meant to be in the face of it." In the words of Cluchey, the play "caused [a] stirring." In the face of captivity, suffering, stasis, something within the inmates—moved.[7]

To feel powerless, with time and agency stripped away: my children understand Beckett, too. "Time feels interminable when you are a child," a friend reminded me, and the way children spend their time is often dictated from on high. To fill their few unscripted hours, children will make meaning out of space; I've seen mine find entertainment in boxes, blank paper, each other, air. And yet: "I've been here for so long," said my six-year old the other day, after half an hour in the park. "Shall we go?" I asked, twitching, ready. They do not move.

Children have trouble with empathy also, a fact that makes me wonder how much childhood hurts. "Hurts! He wants to know if it hurts!" Estragon objects at the beginning of Beckett's play. "No one ever suffers but you," Vladimir responds. "I don't count." Victor Frankenstein is similarly self-absorbed, spending the novel asserting that his misery outweighs that experienced by others. All the protagonists considered here are childish in this regard. "How would you feel if . . . !" I often mutter fiercely at my youngest, in response to some injury he has inflicted on his brother, trying to get him with words to enter an altered feeling state. His ability to answer my question is always hampered by some prior wrong, physical or emotional, that has been inflicted upon him. All he knows are those infinite realms of what he feels now.[8]

And yet. I have two boys, just as there are two protagonists in *Waiting for Godot*, who circle each other like Frankenstein and his creature, their radius stretching just more tightly than the one that carries Victor north. "*He draws him after him,*" states one Beckett stage direction. "We can still part, if you think it would be better," suggests Vladimir; "it's not worth while now," Estragon responds.[9] I've seen my oldest make himself a "private room," only to design a sign inviting his brother in. I've seen my youngest curled under the crook of the other's arm. They hurt each other constantly: wrestling, hitting, yelling, tears. They appear to me often to be physically linked.

Do we chase each other in the hope that we are not alone?

I ran, I think, for the same reasons that I read. If lonely children tend to be avid readers, distance runners are a similar breed. We are creatures of introversion, experts in delayed gratification, fantasy, endurance. Like Frankenstein, we substitute physical pain for mental anguish, a sleight of hand that keeps our inner demons at bay. The "loneliness of the long-distance runner" notwithstanding, I wonder if the condition preempts the cause: if lonely people seek out running to reframe a preexisting struggle as a choice. And yet, some of my strongest friendships have been forged over running, just as they have been forged over books.

In the aftermath of my race, when friends and teammates applauded, I would feel slightly abashed. "You looked so strong!" they said. But I knew for much of the race I had been running automatically, drawn beyond a pace I wanted to be running because I felt connected to the woman whom I chased. I remember my surge, when it came, as feeling beyond my control, something perhaps mandated by that stranger on the sidelines and something that I was fighting with every fiber of my thinking mind. I remember feeling almost angry as I watched myself close the space between myself and my competitor, from two steps, to one step, until I pulled ahead.

The only way I can explain my reaction is that the stranger reminded me I wasn't the only one suffering out there; the stranger took me out of my own head. How little in some ways I knew her; how vivid she remains. All that remained before me now was a stretch of grass. "What do you do when you fall far from help?" Vladimir asks the interloping tramp Pozzo. "We wait until we can get up," he answers. "Then we go on."[10] But I could hear her just behind me, hurting, pushing me as she had pulled me before. We can never really outrun the presence of others; we are always, in some sense, going on. I told myself that once I finished, I could stop.

III

LOVING

11

SHADOW WORK

J. M. Barrie, Toni Morrison, Mark Twain

> *Show his eyes and grieve his heart*
> *Come like shadows, so depart.*
> —Shakespeare, *Macbeth*, 4.1.125–26

There is a moment I remember vividly from the beginning of J. M. Barrie's childhood classic *Peter Pan*, when Peter reenters the nursery of Wendy and Michael and John. He's searching for his shadow, lost there on a previous visit. More precisely, his shadow, lagging behind the body that was trying to flee, has been severed from that body the night before by a falling window sash. Given my particular reading background, the scene always reminds me of the tragicomic moment in Laurence Sterne's novel *Tristram Shandy* when a window sash similarly goes rogue. In that case, the young Tristram is relieving himself out the window when the sash falls; the narrator reassures us that only a fortuitous circumcision results. In *Peter Pan*, the sash severs something equally intimate: boy escapes, shadow remains.[1]

Peter's story has a happy ending in the main. Whereas Tristram spends his novel fleeing death, Peter always gets to return to Neverland, where boys like him never age. The loss of his shadow, however, tethers him temporarily to our world—he apparently can't subsist in Neverland without it—and the quest to retrieve his shadow is not without its perils.

Peter and Tinkerbell return to the nursery the next night, and Tinkerbell locates the shadow for him, rolled up like laundry in the children's dresser drawer. But Peter's initial delight at recovering his possession is short-lived: "If he thought at all, but I don't believe he ever thought, it was that he and his shadow, when brought near each other, would join like drops of water, and when they did not he was appalled. He tried to stick it on with soap from the bathroom, but that also failed. A shudder passed through Peter, and he sat on the floor and cried."[2] His tears wake Wendy, who offers a solution to his plight: "'It must be sewn on,' she said . . . .'I shall sew it on for you, my little man' . . . and she got out her housewife [sewing bag], and sewed the shadow on to Peter's foot." Wendy's procedure works, and soon Peter is dancing about the room with his shadow again following his every move, just as shadows should.[3]

Peter's joy, Peter's tears, show how important shadows are to children—think flashlights in tents and ghost stories or shadow puppets made at sleepovers, the hands that in silhouette become butterflies or dogs. "I have a little shadow that goes in and out with me," writes the poet Robert Louis Stevenson, "and what can be the use of him is more than I can see."[4] But their lack of efficacy lends to their appeal. The shadow is that faux person who can grow and shrink and change; it can travel in crevasses and over substances a small person cannot reach; it is something a child can move. I used to play a game of "shadow tag" with my father, inspired by the observation that certain angles of the sun could make my shadow oh-so-tall. I joked that stomping on my father's shadow would cause him pain, and when he tagged mine, I'd groan, then make it slip away. Stretching away across the grass, my shadow was fluid, feisty. It couldn't be contained or hurt.

"I shan't cry," says Peter, when Wendy proposes to sew his shadow on, and as I read I remember the almost visceral sensation of needle and thread passing through my feet.[5] Wendy's procedure seemed draconian and Peter's shadow recalcitrant in its refusal to reattach like water droplets or with soap. But Wendy's procedure also emphasized to me something about the nature of bodies and shadows—that they are different enough from each other to require some kind of external intervention, or labor, if they are to rejoin. Wendy needs to work to reattach them; Peter needs to suffer, a bit, to get his shadow back.

Peter Pan feels less innocent to me when I reread it. I'd forgotten the emphasis on Tinkerbell's curvaceous figure; I'd forgotten all the domestic duties that Wendy must necessarily assume. I'd forgotten most of the bits with Tiger Lily and the "redskins"; I'd forgotten the descriptions of Tiger Lily as a "dusky Diana," full stop. I knew nothing, as a child, about Barrie's friendships with the orphaned Llewellyn Davis boys who inspired the story—the fact that Peter Llewellyn Davies, mourned as "Peter Pan," would throw himself under a train in his sixties or that Michael Llewellyn Davies would die in his twenties of an ambiguous drowning, clasped to a friend or maybe a homosexual lover, in what could have been a suicide pact. It hurts my heart to read this, to see a seemingly idyllic childhood as the foundation for adult pain.[6]

My eyes work differently now that, like Wendy, I'm all grown up. Authors such as Barrie make much of the fact that children can see what is missing to adults (fairies, innate goodness, an imaginary world), but to be an adult rereader means, often, to see that the friend and guardian you worshipped as heroic can do bad things. It means, even, to realize that together you took pleasure in sharing activities you now recognize as bad. What do we do with those memories of enjoyment? If you go back to Neverland, it never looks the same.

I'm also not sure how Neverland originally looked. Is childhood innocence ever real? "Yes," says a friend, who has just finished rewriting a different children's book from another character's point of view. Or, he has rewritten a book, *The Adventures of Huckleberry Finn*, that I first read as a child. Frozen in childhood, Huck is his own kind of Peter Pan, and I remember loving Twain's novel, as a child.[7] "Why did he keep talking about that kid's story," the protagonist of Ralph Ellison's novel *Invisible Man* wonders at one point about Twain's novel, though Everett insists that *Huck Finn* isn't a book for kids.[8] I'm sure he's right, and after reading his novel, I'll never read the character of Jim, or James, the same. But children can repackage the unimaginable as mere obstacle to adventure, such as the descriptions of Huck's beatings and encounters with his alcoholic dad. Since Huck was telling me the story, I knew he'd be OK. Similarly, I have a frozen memory of Huck and Jim together on the river. Like Huck, I had a murky understanding of the conflicts. I had felt, as a child, that they were friends.[9]

"Show his eyes and grieve his heart / Come like Shadows so depart": so speak Shakespeare's witches to the tortured Macbeth, as they summon up for him a vision of Banquo's descendants, the heirs who will be born to populate Macbeth's tainted throne.[10] "Shadows" in this case aren't Peter's playful doppelganger but ghosts or spirits, ephemeral visions that are shadow-like in their insubstantial nature and also in their ability to come and go. ("He sometimes gets so little that there's none of him at all," states

Stevenson's child.) Adult phantoms, their childish origins buried deep, they exhibit to their viewer the biological necessity that a new generation will grow to efface the one that came before.

I'm intrigued by ghosts and shadows because I feel like them in this regard: not sure if I am really there. This shifting sense of self is hard. Macbeth feels crazy when Banquo's ghost comes to supper and no one else reacts, but we don't consider how it might feel to be Banquo here. My feet ached in sympathy with Peter's, but maybe his shadow—rolled up like laundry, stuffed away, darned into place—had feelings of its own. Maybe that game of shadow tag I played with my father wasn't completely innocent, or kind.

Like me, Shakespeare is obsessed with these insubstantial beings. They are all examples of absent presence caught in a "now you see it, now you don't" way of life. Sometimes it seems these spirits choose to hide, and I can imagine Banquo enjoying himself at that dinner, just as I see in Peter's untethered shadow moments of pure joy. Still, their agency is an exception. Sensing this fact, I feel for these shadows as much as I do for the people they haunt or serve.

Take, for example, Old Hamlet's ghost. His fluctuating appearance marks him as what Marjorie Garber calls the Freudian neurotic, trapped in a kind of repetition compulsion between haunting and spying, cajoling and command.[11] Like Stevenson's shadow, he's inefficacious: even his strongest imperatives are predicated on the ability of others to witness him, and even this ability waxes and wanes. Is he bothered in act 3 when Gertrude doesn't see him? Is he lurking in the graveyard when Hamlet is holding forth over Yorick's skull? If my shadow took pleasure in slipping out from under my father's foot, Old Hamlet finds his incorporeal nature to work against his goals. A shape without a body, the shadow of his like-named son, he must rely on others to act and do. And while I loved the fluidity of my shadow, I felt sadness at how it slid across the world. It never left a mark.

There's another sadness to how the potency of a shadow—that ability stretch and range—remains linked to servitude, tethered to the body it may seem to overshadow or outdo. Shakespeare is interested in this tension, too. Take Ariel, from *The Tempest*—if not a ghost, then a similarly airy form, joined to a master who controls his every move, albeit a form who is also, like Peter's shadow, occasionally able to float free. Or, we imagine as much. Prospero tells him that once Ariel gives all mariners safe passage back to Milan, "then to the elements" he may "be free . . . !"[12] But we never see this happen in the play. Perhaps the separation is too hard, dependent as it is on a guillotine, a window sash, a sudden cut. "I shall miss thee," states Prospero to Ariel, toward the end.[13]

And yet, Prospero is a cruel master, one who takes credit for much of the labor his dainty spirit exerts. Unlike Hamlet's ghost, who relies on living bodies to enact his commands, Ariel, as Prospero's shadow, accomplishes almost every action in the play. There are many opportunistic things about Ariel, as a result, that Prospero will miss. Shadow as servant manifests via a precise physiological debasement, an action that creates parallels with the attachment of the shadow in *Peter Pan*. "I'll swear myself thy subject," states Caliban, the other minion of the play, "I'll kiss thy foot."[14]

In this regard, Caliban's relationship to Prospero makes him the companion not of dainty Ariel but of other invisible figures in literature who are (like Caliban) substantial, made up of flesh and blood. These figures are invisible because others don't see them—because they are difficult, in the sense of painful or disturbing, to see. They have a hypervisibility that renders them unnoticeable, unless, like Peter's detached shadow, they behave in an independent way. The attendants in *Peter Pan*, who accompany Tiger Lily, are described as "shadows."[15] Mary Shelley's eight-foot-tall creation, who hides successfully from rustic peasants for months on end—who is able, later in the novel, to slip a locket, undetected, into a servant girl's dress—is called, while the peasants don't see him, a spirit for the physical labor he performs.[16] "I am invisible, understand," explains Ralph Ellison's protagonist, as nameless as Shelley's creation and sprung from a history of slave labor that he and these other books confront, "simply because people refuse to see me"—because to look at him puts pressure on the American conscience, because moral blindness is easier than acknowledging his predicament, their responsibility, his pain.[17] "Not only didn't they see me, but they couldn't see me," Everett's version of Twain's Jim explains, of potential observers who pass their raft on a steamboat in the night.[18] He's trying to get back to his family so he can buy his wife and children out of slavery and set them free. "I felt sad," states Ellison's nameless protagonist, decades and decades later, "and utterly alone."[19]

What, then, am I to do with Prospero's missing? I think that, in his tangled mind somewhere, he and Ariel are friends. But I think Prospero is the shadow, with Ariel the one who gives him shape and form. Prospero is the interloper on this enchanted island, his own version of Neverland, where he can exist with Ariel outside of time. As with Tristram, as with Peter, the loss of Ariel seems tied for him to the onset of death. "And thence retire me to my Milan," he laments, on the verge of leaving his spirit behind, "where / every third thought shall be my grave."[20] Their bond, once severed, won't be reforged.

These days, we often give shadows a negative connotation, as things that impede our clarity or as interchangeable commodities to be passed over, shoved in a drawer, analyzed away. We think of severed shadows as a development, as a helpful paring down. In Jungian psychology, the shadow indicates those aspects of one's personality, frequently the least desirable ones, of which one is least aware.[21]

Yet there are reasons to retain attachments to our shadow selves. When Toni Morrison was asked, on the occasion of Princeton University's 2017 naming of Morrison Hall, what she thought of the recent push to take down Confederate statues, she had a blunt reply. "I don't believe in erasure," she said.[22] She feels the same way about the teaching, in schools, of *Huckleberry Finn*. To remove the book from curricula represents, for her, "a purist yet elementary kind of censorship designed to appease adults."[23] She advocates instead for an open discussion of all that is disturbing about the book. "Too often," Ellison writes in the 1960s on what he believes to be the condition of his contemporaneous Black writers, "they fear to leave the uneasy sanctuary of race to take their chances in a world of art." He frames his own autobiographical essays as "an embodiment of a conscious attempt to confront, to peer into, the shadow of my past."[24]

One impulse behind the other gesture is that seeing can become akin to celebrating, and at my own institution, USC, we've unnamed buildings and taken down honorific photos of past deans. The hope is that other names and faces will take their place. But not-seeing also lets the present generation off the hook. There is a failure, in these compensatory gestures, to address underlying causes that cannot be corrected by mere inclusion. Or, as my friend put it, "the absence of antiracism is worse than the erasure of a Black text."[25] Inclusion without a direct engagement in antiracism can become its own kind of smokescreen, its own kind of shadow. In seventeenth-century England, for example, politicians passed something called the "Act of Oblivion," which stated that the intervening years of Civil War upheaval had simply been excised from memory, and from time. The gesture was as explicit, and as violent, as a window sash falling, or a sudden cut.

Here's another way to think through the implications of pretending we can't see that which by definition we actually ignore. In developmental psychology there is a stage known as "object permanence," which understanding very young children have not yet developed and which adults, supposedly, have.[26] The idea is that as adults we understand that an object doesn't cease to exist once we stop seeing it; the idea inverted means that we understand we need not be seen by others in order, ourselves, to be. The lack of this understanding explains why a baby cries when she leaves her mother; the presence of this understanding explains why adults or older children can better sustain, as temporary, such goodbyes. The lack also explains why very young children demand an audience for their activities; the presence explains why older children and adults can theoretically work more comfortably by themselves.

Erasure, however, speaks to a very infantile understanding, and I wonder how many of us have developed fully beyond this state.

To hide a shadow, as Wendy's mom does to Peter's, does violence to both the shadow and those who remain. "Begone!" shouts Frankenstein's creator, forced into confrontation with the creation he wishes to ignore. "Relieve me from the sight of your detested form." "Thus I relieve thee, my creator," states the creation, as he places his hands over his creator's eyes, "thus I take from thee a sight which you abhor."[27] The gesture is young and solipsistic, with a solipsism that goes both ways. The creation loses the reifying power of his creator's witnessing; the creator, blinded, loses the reifying power of knowing he is seen. If we know ourselves relationally, using books and people to reflect back to us who we are, then erasing others makes us disappear.

I imagine the adult Prospero, lonely, realizing that the bond he'd had with Ariel was self-created; I imagine Frankenstein's creation, when he realizes his dead creator is the only friend that he may have. I imagine him floating, lonely, without another traveling companion, on his ice raft toward the north.

"But think about how the child accepts Mary Shelley's creature," my friend says on the phone, referencing the book he knows I often teach. There is a protectiveness to his statement that I see also in his book. "They don't," I say, after cross-checking my own memory of the two children he could mean in the novel, once I get back home. The only character who accepts the creation is a blind man, though in the movie version of Shelley's novel, the one made in 1932 by James Whale, the now-inarticulate creature and a rustic girl play with flowers, briefly, on a bank. It is an interesting revision, since Shelley, unlike Whale, knew that her creation was articulate, knew that children could be mirrors of their guardians' prejudice, knew that children could be cruel. After all, the creation is himself chronologically a child for most of the novel and commits, as a child, the most shocking crimes. But the most shocking revelation is that he will at the end of the tale even approach another human or will, after all his miseries, still seek love.

Shelley herself was little more than a child when she wrote this novel, though she'd already lost babies, suffered heartbreak, and killed her own mother in the process of being born. "Perhaps Shelley is saying that love doesn't necessarily reside in innocence," my friend responds. Perhaps she is saying that children have a capacity for shadow work, and shadow play, that we have lost.

As Peter learns, to lose a shadow isn't liberating but unsettling, and we feel the ache from shadows that have been pulled off or reattached. "I shall miss thee," I knew, when I set one particular shadow free, and a chance expression on the face of my eldest son can still create in me a physical pain. My shadow, I think, as I watch him sleep, curled on anxious nights into the side of the bed where his father used to be. He's growing into the photographs I've thrown away. Those stitches hold, hurt.

And on hard days, I'll also feel a throbbing around my heels, a reminder of old surgeries that ended a much-loved competitive running career. A reminder, too, of the practice that necessitated those surgeries, which I embraced as I did that other shadow, with a love that was fervent and masochistic, both. Those physical scars are almost invisible now, the ridges gone flesh colored and smooth. Still, I wish that shadow had been faster. I wish we had escaped the knife.

I've been bred to interpret these pains as judgments for impulsive decisions, compulsive behaviors, poor choices in life. And I've been conditioned to experience them as incisions, evidence of things taken from me, my physical and emotional limitations, loss.

But perhaps what I'm feeling instead are signs of attachment. Perhaps these throbbings trace inevitable comings and goings, the necessary interventions in life's traumas, a childlike need.

Perhaps all I'm feeling are the outline of tiny sewing holes, the reminder of Wendy's care.

12

ANIMAL LOVE

Miguel de Cervantes, Jilly Cooper, Laurence Sterne

It was not seemly that the horse of so famous a knight, and a steed so intrinsically excellent, should not have a worthy name... and so, after many names that he shaped and discarded, subtracted from and added to, unmade and made in his memory and imagination, he finally decided to call the horse Rocinante.

—Miguel de Cervantes, *Don Quixote*

Horses breed fantasy, in every sense. Miguel de Cervantes's novel *Don Quixote*, that case study of fantasy and fantasizing par excellence, features in its opening pages a horse. Don Quixote is the aging gentleman whose overzealous reading of romances causes him to imagine himself a knight; Rosinante is the broken-down old nag who accompanies him on his quests and whom Don Quixote sees as "first and foremost" of all the horses in the world. Before Don Quixote even encounters the infamous Sancho Panza, and as he sets out in pursuit of his beloved Dulcinea, Rosinante is his sidekick, his better half. Quixote's relationship to his steed proves that even though not all horses are Black Beauties, a horse of any color remains an invitation to fantasy and a conduit to romance.[1]

Laurence Sterne's novel *Tristram Shandy* also features a horse: "a lean, sorry, jack-ass of a horse, value about one pound fifteen shillings; who, to shorten all description of him, was full brother to *Rosinante*, as far as similitude congenial could make him; for he answered his description to a hair-breadth in every thing,—except that I do not remember 'tis any where said, that *Rosinante* was broken-winded; and that, moreover, *Rosinante*, as is the happiness of most *Spanish* horses, fat or lean,—was undoubtedly a horse at all points."[2]

This horse is ridden by Sterne's country parson, Yorick, and Sterne makes the comparison because both horses are beautiful only to their owners and physically unprepossessing to all else. Anyone who has owned or loved a horse can agree: high withers, splayed feet, muddy coats, a balding tail—none of these are visible to an equestrian who is in love. But Sterne gives Rosinante a few physical advantages over his parson's horse that go beyond what one can see. Whereas most male horses used for riding are castrated, or gelded, Rosinante is apparently still a stallion: he was "undoubtedly a horse at all points."

From horse fantasy to sexual fantasy is a small leap, and Sterne's emphasis on Rosinante's sexual capabilities becomes a mirror for his insistence upon his protagonist's own. If Rosinante in Cervantes's novel exhibits a "chaste deportment," Sterne explains that this deportment arises not from inability "but from the temperance and orderly current of his blood." Just so, Tristram reassures us throughout the novel of his own libidinal capabilities; that, despite an accident with forceps during his birth, his "nose" remains fully functional and intact. This insistence on Tristram's sexual potency becomes the novel's "hobby horse," a term Sterne draws from the children's toy (horse head on a stick) that a child will mount and imagine as a steed but redefined by him here as a foible of character. A "hobby horse" for Sterne becomes that idiosyncrasy or verbal tic that defines an individual, that topic on which he or she ruminates or, more appropriately, rides. Tristram has several "hobby horses," but fantasizing about his sexual performance is one of his most loved.[3]

An ex-boyfriend reintroduced me to horses.

I'd grown up with horses, though not our own. Baby pictures feature me held in place on the back of a friendly pony, or naked in a field, reaching toward an animal whose head and my body seem roughly the same size. As a child I'd ridden, taking lessons at one barn after school and in the summers at a different spot just down the road from my grandparents' house. I'd played with the plastic ponies, read the children's books, memorized the different breeds. One summer I got to go to horse camp; one summer I even got to lease a horse. Then we moved houses, and horses faded into the background for a time.

Decades later, in Los Angeles and newly single, I started dating a guy who mentioned his daughter wanted to ride. He'd done some investigating and found a horse for her to meet; I offered to do the recon on horse and owner, both. A foray into the attic to find my old gear, a trip up to Topanga for a test ride, and I fell instantly, obsessively back in love.

So in love, that when the guy disappeared, the horse stayed.

On Loves That Come and Go

My mom was the true equestrian. Family stories of her riding proliferate, and we have pictures of her on horseback—yellowed pictures in tarnished frames—scattered throughout the house.

The pictures are disorienting because she looks so much like me: her hair then the same shade of blonde, then worn in a similar cut. Our posture on horseback is similar, too, the line of her shoulders, the tilt of her chin. And those plastic ponies I played with, the books I paged through: those were all hers, well loved and handed down. She'd ridden all throughout college and her early marriage. As I understood it, she rode regularly up until she had me.

If I'm right, that means horses were still figuring in among her lab work, her residencies, her nights on call. She's the modern equivalent of Sterne's midwife, the one in his novel who lives far away and for whom the townsfolks must always in a panic fetch by galloping off on the parson's borrowed horse. (Incidentally, this is why the parson finally chooses to ride only a rundown nag: all his nice horses have been ruined over the years by lending them out.) She's never not been able to do a million things; all my energy, I get from her. Had she had to choose, finally, between horses and kids? I was never sure.

Another ex-boyfriend introduced me to Jilly Cooper. Well, not Jilly exactly, but her books.

Erotica plus horses, he'd explained; how do you not know? "Sex and horses!" similarly announced one of the blurbs for her novel *Riders*, "who could ask for more?" Maybe I'd missed the books because I was too young in the eighties for their salacious content; maybe because I wasn't British; maybe because I'd spent my teens being an aspirational academic, reading all the "important" books. (Though *Tristram* and *Don Quixote* are plenty salacious, just perhaps fancier about it.) Or maybe because it was that as I stopped riding, I'd stopped some of the riding fantasizing that went along with it, too.

Fantasy feels different, now. I need something in addition to filial, or Platonic, love. "But the back cover tells me it is one of your 'nation's most beloved novels!'" I announce to another British friend, who had told me that while at Cambridge she wouldn't have been caught dead with a Jilly Cooper in her hands. I determine, singlehandedly, to dismantle the barrier between high and low culture that had inspired another friend to wonder if her magazine should commission a Cooper piece. But when *Riders* arrives from Amazon, an eight-hundred-plus-page tome, my sons are the ones to unwrap it. "This is for you, mom!" announces my six-year old, responding to the cover image of a woman's ass sheathed in white jodhpurs and cupped gently by a tan, masculine hand. "Is he sculpting?" my ten-year old inquires. I submit my Amazon receipt to the business office for reimbursement, the same image figuring prominently on my expense report. The reimbursement is approved.[4]

On Intimacy

His name is Rio, and he is a twenty-year-old Appaloosa gelding. I've been around horses off and on over the past few decades, but he's the first horse I've ridden, repeatedly and for real, in almost twenty years. He's the first one I've taken out of turnout, currycombed, bathed, and lunged. He is the first one in years to lip at my ponytail and leave white hairs on my vest; in return, I run my hands down his legs and brush out his tail. As his part-time partner, I have the chance, three days a week, to spend time with him: to work on my riding but also to get to know him—how to take care of him and what he likes. I learn that he likes pears, that he is food aggressive, and that he coughs three times at the beginning of every ride. He has a floaty trot, and he is good on trails. His owner has had him since he was five, and she loves him with all her heart.

About a month into our new partnership, his owner takes out a bottle of "Excalibur" and shows me how to clean his sheath. (For people not familiar with horses, the male horse, stallion or gelding, spends most of his time with his penis retracted into a pouch, and he usually only extends the organ to pee or mate. Sheath cleaning therefore requires gloves and following the retracted penis backward and up.) He stands ground tied, shifting just a bit from the water and never lifting a leg. Afterward, though, he's extra mouthy, tossing away his fly mask, grabbing at my sleeve. He acts a bit like a stallion in this regard. "I think he was cut late," his owner explains.

Sterne believes Rosinante to be a stallion because of an episode Cervantes describes when, breaking character, he "took a fancy to disport himself" with some mares. In his defense, Rosinante's behavior is most likely dictated by the mares being in heat, as even a gelding will lose his mind when such pheromones are around. The mares, however, don't return his interest but "received him with their heels and teeth to such effect that they soon broke his girths and left him naked without a saddle."[5] Rosinante, in exposing his most primal desires, is left physically exposed, an anthropomorphic vulnerability that would resonate with his humans, though not with him. (No horse ever requires a saddle or blanket to feel well dressed.)

I find it easy to be physically naked. I like the line of my biceps, the arc of my hipbone, the skin tag that grew after pregnancy under my left breast. I've always attributed this comfort to my athletic upbringing, since we all spent so much time together in locker rooms and gyms. I still laugh about the time in college that I chinned myself on the wall of an adjoining changing room (though why were we even in changing rooms?), to yell something to my roommate down below. "I'm peeking!" I cackled, only to see a horrified stranger cowering in the corner while my roommate shouted something from the stall beyond. None of us cared. I had a college nickname based upon the size of my breasts, and the majority of the men's cross-country team had nicknames describing their dicks . . . Golf T, Tiny Guy, Porn Star, the Hog. I knew my teammates' bathroom habits, menstrual cycles, and their sexual preferences and escapades, too. After all, everything we did was related to physical performance. As runners, the main thing that stood out to any of us was if someone got too thin.

As an adult, however, I've developed stage fright around bathroom behaviors. I can be shy about admitting to a new partner if I have to pee, and it has been years since I've had to choreograph my morning post-coffee rituals with having someone stay the night. Horses, on the other hand, share these behaviors with abandon and with relief. "He's pooping!" my trainer will say, in case I hadn't noticed, to explain the slowdown as he canters out of the corner or to account for the back muscles that arch up into my seat. A horse can technically poop on the go ("if he were being chased by a lion right now," my trainer yells, "he'd be running!"), though they like to take the opportunity to slow down or stop. Peeing, on the other hand, requires isolated focus, and if mounted a rider should rise up off the horse's kidneys to give him or her freedom to urinate on the stretch. A horse while peeing is "parked out": hind legs planted back, front legs moved up.

Horses will poop with some regularity in the cross ties during grooming (one I ride always accompanies these evacuations with such a self-satisfied grunt and groan I feel the need to look away), but ideally horses will wait to pee until they are in their stall or at least the ring. Another horse I ride, however, times his urinations for the instant I clip him up. Even if I walk him first or put him in a holding stall, he waits till I'm about to untack him and then, just when I have my arms full of saddle, parks out, goes up on his rear toes, and drops his cock. (For Jilly, it is always a "cock.") All I can do is sprint around kicking tack boxes and spare bags out of the way; watching a horse pee is like waiting for a fire hose to shut off. He always spends a few moments afterward with his penis dangling, a sure sign that he is relaxed.

"Why do they keep their penises up there, anyway?" asks my six-year-old, in the aftermath of one of these productions. He's astounded, impressed.

My trainer happens to be walking by. (Poor Rosinante, spurned by those mares.) "They're shy," she says.

On Love and Conversation

"Writing is . . . but a different name for conversation," says Sterne, and I agree, though conversations managed across text give one the ability to hide shyness or to control the pace of a response.[6] When I was an adolescent waiting to hit a (very late) puberty, I left my mother a letter in her top dresser drawer asking if she would buy me a bra. When I was dating the same man who reintroduced me to horses, he broke up with me by taping a handwritten letter to my front door. When I have a difficult colleague to engage, I'd rather hide behind an email exchange, so that I can decide when and if I will answer and use fancy vocabulary and feel self-righteous all at once.

As a single woman in a house with two growing boys, I recognize that I have many conversations forthcoming about sexuality and physical development that will take me into topics we may find embarrassing and physical experiences I have never had.

"I've announced that we are skipping male puberty at my house," I repeat to friends, who always just roll their eyes. I know it is a joke, but I'm nervous about how to relate to my boys during these dialogues, and my gut tells me sharing references to Freud's castration complex or the Lacanian idea of the phallus is not the way to go. I've already scarred at least one of them with literature, I'm convinced, as a result of some early-stage multitasking that involved breastfeeding while reading aloud to him from my teaching assignment for the following day. "It is true that in their dreams a lot of men have slept with their own mothers," I read to my youngest, then an infantile man-child gumming at my breast.

Both the boys are much older now, and we are just starting to tip over into the adolescent world. My first forays into these types of sexualized conversations have gone only OK. "My baseball coach tells us that all of us need to wear a cup," my older one shares, beginning to experience for himself the physicality of the athletic world. I never had a penis to protect, so I find myself typing words into Amazon, ordering something appropriate that is "youth" but also "one size fits all" and staring in bemusement at the oddly shaped neon-green piece of plastic that arrives and is somehow meant to fit into his pants. I don't have anyone to talk me through these conversations. But just as I've started to Google instructions on YouTube (something that spices up my internet suggestions for the next few days), another single mother friend with an older boy arrives. She provides an explanation, and my son, slim and wiry, goes around the corner to change. "Mom?" I hear him say, not yet venturing out, and when he comes forward, he is staring downward at the substantial bulge highlighted in his crotch. The effect is rendered grotesque by the hallway light and the silhouette of him that now stretches across the floor. "No, don't worry," my friend says. "That is the way it is supposed to look."

The story should end there, except that we spend the rest of the evening chasing his younger brother, the one who nursed his way through *Oedipus*, who steals his brother's accoutrement and shoves it in his pants. It lodges there in his pajama bottoms like a gigantic codpiece, and he spends hours jump-scaring the rest of us with invitations to "hit him in the nuts." He goes to bed still wearing it. I remove it from his bunk bed once he is asleep.[7]

A year into my renewed love affair, I decide to buy my first saddle. The saddle rep is a thirty-something French Basque, heavily accented and tattooed, an equestrian but also a semipro footballer in a past life. He speaks with animation about the construction of his saddles, the position of my pelvis, the angle of my hip. He examines my sacrum, the bend of my knee; he jots down notes and speaks French into his cell. At one point he places his hands on the small of my back.

Sterne's parson Yorick also has a thing for fancy tack. His saddle is "quilted on the seat with green plush, garnished with a double row of silver-headed studs, and a noble pair of shining brass stirrups, with a housing altogether suitable, of grey superfine cloth, with an edging of black lace, terminating in a deep, black, silk fringe."[8] The one I finally purchase isn't nearly as ornate: a used 2017 model, 17″ seat, 1A flap, in full calf. It comes with a fleece-lined saddle cover, but I get my own stirrup leathers and irons. Still, it has that deep dark French leather, well conditioned and maintained. For the first month I don't even keep it at the barn but drive it back and forth between the barn and my house. I clean it at home in my living room, and at night I sleep with it next to my bed.

Other reasons that horses and erotica make a natural pairing:

First, there is the English hunt seat wardrobe, featuring skin-tight pants (breeches or jodhpurs, depending), high black leather boots, spurs, crops. (Walking around Carmel in her riding gear after a show, my trainer got multiple socialite inquiries as to where one could purchase her boots.) Next, there is the descriptive terminology required. "Let yourself drape around him," my trainer often says. "Wow, he feels so much wider between my legs," I announce, shifting rides from a narrow thoroughbred to a draft horse cross. "I really feel as if I am riding a teenage boy!" I say loudly to a horse friend on the phone, while people standing nearby turn to stare. Finally, there is the riding motion itself, especially at the canter. Shoulders like a nun; hips like a whore. "Imagine you are making love to the saddle," a watching ranch hand once volunteered. "Hump it," a girlfriend similarly, if more crudely, advised. "Now don't let Satan, my dear girl . . . take advantage of any one spot of rising ground to get astride of your imagination," writes Sterne, setting up another erotic metaphor tour de force. "Or if he is so nimble as to slip on—let me beg of you, like an unback'd filly, *to frisk it, to squirt it, to jump it, to rear it, to bound it—and to kick it, with long kicks and short kicks*, till, like *Tickletoby's* mare, you break a strap or a crupper and throw his worship into the dirt." ("Tickletoby" here is eighteenth-century slang for dick.) No wonder that mounting one's "hobby horse" remains the key metaphor in Sterne's sexually explicit novel. The horse-rider relationship is by turns one of domination (from either partner) or symbiosis. Sending riding videos to my gay male friends always results in their unabashed celebrations of my ass.[9]

On Obsession

Many people agree that horses are beautiful, but some folks are horse obsessed. It seems a genetic trait, one that is passed down to some and one that passes others by. The horse obsessed can spend hours just watching other people ride; they stop by the barn for a quick visit and stay for the day; their skin is covered with a patina of alfalfa, oats, manure, and sweat. The horse obsessed can muck a stall, shove a bit barehanded into horse's mouth, and eat a sandwich with no need for personal hygiene in between. The horse obsessed can watch jumping rounds on repeat, counting strides and analyzing turns. "Shit!" I mutter while folding laundry, the volume on my laptop turned down low. "Ah, rail down?" my ten-year-old sympathizes, without seeing what I am watching, without even turning his head.

In Jilly, as in Cervantes and Sterne, horse obsession is a backdrop for erotic obsession writ large. The hero takes the virginity of his soon-to-be-wife in a horse stall; the wealthy soon-to-be-wife thanks him by buying him his first horse. The characters in her novel are stereotypical, their relationships titillating rather than deep—fed upon scandal, alcohol, money, sex. What emotional connections there are exist instead between the riders and their equestrian mounts. I forget the antihero's numerous orgies and affairs (as does the antihero himself), but the anger he feels toward the horse Macaulay, after his own poorly ridden round—that emotion is long remembered by horse and reader alike. And when the Rosinante-style stallion Sailor—the laughingstock gray who charms audiences with his athleticism and heart—dies of a heart attack after an ill-advised and muddy jump off, after pushing himself beyond his physical limits all because he loves and trusts the man who steers him around the course: that moment hurts.

Why can these characters feel more deeply for their horses than for one another, themselves? Maybe with horses it is different because they don't ask for anything and don't expect a rider to be other than how that rider rides. Maybe it is different because horses can't talk (Sancho Panza's donkey "let[s] himself be kissed and caressed . . . without answering a word"), because they are (most of them) pretty forgiving, because they don't anticipate or dwell. Maybe most of all it is different because they can't lie. I rode a horse for a while that my mom dubbed as "not quite honest," but all she meant was that, given the opportunity to duck out of work, or a jump, he would. He wasn't lying about it. If anything, he was showing me when I'd gotten lazy and stopped paying attention to him.

On the Absence of Desire

With horses, I never feel that unrequited longing that pulls me into flirtations or keeps me up all night trying to finish a book. ("Narrative desire," the literary critic Peter Brooks terms it, that thing that keeps us reading forward—that thing that Sterne stymies at every turn.) Horses, on the other hand, give me what I want, even when they misbehave. Even after a hard ride, I always leave them feeling calm.[10]

"They are called 'stables' for a reason," quips a friend, though I persist on calling my place a barn.

I start live-texting updates on my erotic reading to my academic friends, usually written while I'm working out:

The affluent multi-hyphenated-names anti-hero who just took a green stallion named "Satan" over a six-foot jump is possibly pairing up romantically with naive American anti-hunt heroine; said anti-hero comes from a broken home, and his wealth only thinly masks psychic traumas of which he is unaware, but which she intuits . . .

The hero and anti-hero have now met, as both are riding for the British national team, as selected by the militaristic and perceptive chef d'equipe, who sees the potential in our hero and also promises to function as the longed for father figure of the same. It turns out the hero and anti-hero were boyhood classmates at school, where our multi-names anti-hero loomed large in personality and wealth, and our half-gypsy hero attended by virtue of his mother's employment (she was the school cook). Boyhood traumas and competitions—expressed via horsemanship and erotic pursuits—now re-surface as they confront each other in the schooling ring. . . .

[A] lot of ink being spilled today over the masculine curve of our anti-hero's thigh, barely contained by his skin-tight breeches, as it contrasts to the lithe physique of our gypsy hero, who is slight yet powerful in his movement. Over here, I'm also working on keeping the toned musculature of my thighs intact so that the smooth curve of my riding breeches provides a silhouette suggestive at once of power and primal femininity.

My friends respond with appropriate expressions of mock horror and references to narrative theory of the sort that only English professors can provide.

On Love and Danger

Are horses scary? Rarely on purpose. They are prey animals who prioritize their own safety, and they use speed (first) and self-defense (second) to escape threats. Granted, there's a learning curve to what a horse considers to be a threat. Take, for example, the garbage truck unloading a dumpster—that one makes sense, and I ride toward it cautiously, deep in my seat. The rainbow-colored umbrella standing upright in a field? That one catches me unawares. In fact, I don't even see it until my 1,200-pound partner jogs out of his paddock to take refuge behind my 5′3″ frame. He plants his feet and snorts repeatedly, telling either me or the umbrella to beware. But they are big, powerful animals, and a scared horse can unintentionally do a lot of harm. I tell my children to treat them like the ocean: beautiful, but never something to take for granted. Never turn your back.

Horse stories often come from their unexpected behaviors, and my mom has many. First there was Sontag, the quarter-horse gelding whom we boarded in our apple orchard for a summer, and Smokey, the neighbor pony who taught Petunia (another mare) and Sontag the fine art of pasture escape. There was Daisy, the Shetland-Welsh cross with one brown eye and one blue, who taught all the kids to ride but used her blue eye to tell you when she was about to buck you off. Fat Pony was the horse my mom trained in college for endurance rides and who, after many gallops up their mountain road, soon thinned out of his name. He was also the one who could walk calmly through active construction zones during the day but would panic at night when those same machines were still. Pumpkin and Crocus were two other escape artists and master jumpers (the two skills connect). A family friend once bet his father that he could jump Pumpkin bareback over a 5′2″ panel fence, and he won the bet with ease.

Then there was the young filly my mom was schooling in college, whose name I don't remember, who slipped on ice outside the schooling ring, dropped her shoulder, and sent my mother over to the side. When my mom looked up from the ground the mare was still falling, and one hoof would come down on my mom's collar bone with all the weight of a falling horse. (This is very unusual: a horse will do almost anything in his or her power to avoid stepping on a rider. Only when the horse is also out of control or in danger do such accidents occur.) I grew up thinking that all moms were made with bony knobs along their clavicles, the result of a fracture that never had any possibility of being set. Similarly, there was the incident with May Queen, the three-year-old mare who, during a schooling ride with my mom, panicked and tried to outrun a train. "I'd kicked off my stirrups and was ready to bail," my mom said, as it was touch and go as to whether the mare would bolt in front of the engine; the conductor could only watch. At the last minute, my mom pulled so hard she got May Queen to turn right, and they galloped another mile straight up a hill before the mare stopped, quivering and covered in sweat. My mom had pulled so hard that she'd yanked the bridle off center—yanked the bit completely out of May Queen's mouth.

My own stories are much more tame. I tend to fall off in the training ring, my reflexes rusty, my leg not yet in place. One horse gets excited after a jump and bucks me off; another pulls me through a line, head down, and I tumble to the side; yet another spooks at a nearby pony and scoots left, leaving me behind. I do have one scarier experience, a last-minute jump refusal at a faster speed, and this time I don't immediately fall but find myself thrust forward and am reluctant to give way. Yet I lose my balance while attempting to push myself back in the saddle, and suddenly I've slung myself underneath the horse's neck, hanging there like a baby monkey, like a tired child. He's galloping, and all I can do is hang—because why would I drop to the ground while he is running and I'm in front of his legs? (In the future, the trainer tells me, better to let go.) I end up pulling him off balance, and we both fall, me underneath and him on top, a horse and rider role reversal, a Jilly Cooper faux-erotic fling. He scrambles up and away with his reins flapping and a skinned knee. I lie still for a bit thinking about what happened and what hurts.

How do we love those who can put us in such danger? How do we not?

I move on to writing Jilly Cooper parodies on my phone during my morning workouts:

> As they galloped down the backstretch, the outside world melted away, obscured by the dueling sound of pounding hooves and her own pumping heart. Two obstacles remained, a final outside line that most competitors had been covering in six, and she could feel her mount straining forward, convincing her that five of his massive strides would cover the distance with ease. She collected him gently into her hands, experiencing the familiar rush as 1,200 pounds of muscular horse flesh responded to her slightest touch. From ringside, she appeared an almost magical figure, communicating her desires to her partner with movements that were imperceptible to any but the most practiced eye. Her arms, evenly tanned from hours in the outdoor practice ring, rested delicately on the reins, the map of veins covering her forearms the only hint of the muscles that rippled underneath. A single strand of blonde hair escaped from her helmet as the two hurtled forward, and then, with a tremendous thrust from his hocks, the chestnut was over, clearing the final obstacle by a foot. She rested easily in the saddle, crouched over his neck, those supple hands following his head through the apex of their flight, until, wondrously, they landed, and she instantly regained control.
>
> A woman who could ride like that, he thought, could be capable of anything . . .

"M-Mrs. Anderson?" He stammered, uncharacteristically bashful as he stared up at her astride her chestnut mount.

"Dr." She corrected automatically, "not to mention I'm unmarried." She flicked an invisible speck of dirt off her well-worn dress boots with a violent twitch from her crop. "What do you want? I come here to be alone."

"This type of writing seems to come to you too easily," the ex-boyfriend says.

On Infatuation Versus Love

Jilly characters and readers thrive on the charge of potential, of new affairs. I, too, find myself cycling through romantic possibilities, the anticipatory buildup intoxicating if brief. Much like Tristram or Don Quixote, I keep suspense alive by finding new quests, new digressions, new stories to craft. At the barn, I'm always excited to meet the new horse.

I'm also angry, though, every time I start again.

A few months ago, I come home from the barn to tell the boys about a new quarter horse two-year-old who has arrived. She is a tiny bay, ears tipped with black, miniature little nose, sweet. I show them pictures; the next day we all go say hi. Maybe because she is closer to them in size, maybe because the barn is also to her (as to them) still a little scary, they find her dear.

We go back together a week later, on a Sunday afternoon. A horse dentist is here, going stall to stall, checking teeth. At some point we hear a loud thump, as if a horse has gotten angry and kicked out. At least, that's what I think for the moment, though a second later every horse on the property reacts. Mine in the cross ties, far from the source of the noise, joins the conversation, his whinny urgent. As they settle, a girl comes running toward us in tears.

The horses didn't need to see to know. It turns out that when the dentist went to check on the new mare, the very sight of the sedative injection needle, long before it reached her, sent the pony into a panic and she reared up. She reared at such an angle that she hit her head on the top of her stall and fell back, dead.

For some folks at the barn, this is all in a (bad) day's work. Others have never seen a horse die. I'm in that camp. I know we have to walk past her stall on our way to the car, so I give the boys a general explanation for what occurred. Still, it is a shock to see her stretched out. She'd been such a little pony; dead, she is vast. I still have the videos of her on my phone. "Say hi to baby Penelope!" I crow. "Cute little two-year-old baby mare!"

Then this morning, at the barn, a friend asks me if I've heard the news. That tiny bump they discovered on her horse's side last year, the one we thought was an abscess from an insect bite?—well, they did an ultrasound, and it is a tumor, malignant, albeit slow growing. I look at his side in the sunlight, for the first time in a while, and I see it there swelling under his coat, maybe now the size of half a cantaloupe, smooth and perfect and just behind where the saddle flap will lie. They trimmed his coat for the ultrasound, so he has a lighter square of short hair there, as if he is showing it off. It doesn't interfere as of yet with his tack, and she says it doesn't seem to cause him any pain. He's happy; he's been great; if anything, he's mellowed in the last year . . . perhaps because his energy is less? All of us are guessing. Friends gather around to pet his nose, but he's standing in the sun this morning, nibbling at her sleeve. That trailer ride up north, the word "tumor," all mean nothing to him. He can't even see the bump growing on his side.

Driving home, I find myself accelerating out of freeway ramps as if I am on a jumps course. "Ride *forward* out of the turn," I mutter to myself.

On Love and Loss

I finish the Jilly Cooper novel just as that particular romantic relationship is winding down. Both the novel and the relationship fade quickly, and, if I'm honest, I never expected either to last. Still, I find giving up on the relationship more painful than putting away the book. It's a short-term relationship, friends tell me; a crush; an infatuation; a fantasy; a (not horse related) fling. But what is the difference between love and eroticism, if both can end?

Sterne, tortured in his relationships, also had trouble putting away his book. He wrote while dying of tuberculosis, and every volume he completes is a testament to his continued life. But every volume he writes also reminds him that time is passing and that the life he loves is slipping away:

> Time wastes too fast: every letter I trace tells me with what rapidity Life follows my pen; the days and hours of it, more precious, my dear Jenny! than the rubies about thy neck, are flying over our heads like light clouds of a windy day, never to return more——everything presses on—— whilst thou art twisting that lock,——see! it grows grey; and every time I kiss thy hand to bid adieu, and every absence which follows it, are preludes to that eternal separation which we are shortly to *make*.——
>
> ——Heaven have mercy upon us both![11]

His dashes—they break my heart as they halt the flood of language and also press it on; they are grammatical separations that Sterne manufactures, inflicts, (sur)mounts. And that "dear Jenny" whom he addresses? She stands in for his real-life love affairs and also his love affair with life itself. Except "a jenny" is also an idiom for a donkey, a female ass. When Sancho Panza loses his donkey Dapple, he makes his head hurt with weeping; when they are reunited, he kisses and caresses the donkey as if he were a human being.

Why do small endings (a school drop off, an airport hug) feel so momentous, why do I struggle so with my goodbyes——except that they remind us of all the other endings we've experienced and will yet endure.——

13

PIONEER GIRL

Laura Ingalls Wilder

I'm a longtime Laura Ingalls Wilder fan. My parents first introduced me to the books, and since there are eight of them, they kept us company for a while. But when I say I am a fan, I mean that the reading experience didn't end there. My family lamented that they weren't sure I'd ever read anything new, since my ritual of mooning around the house asking for reading material would almost always end with me in front of my bookshelf, looking at favorite titles and then choosing something well worn, much read, and, thanks to its familiarity, easy on the eyes and heart. Much of the time this would be a Laura Ingalls Wilder book.

It is funny in some ways to think that I found these books easy on the heart. Laura's life wasn't easy, and those other fans out there will remember the plague of locusts, Mary's blindness, the hard farm chores and winter storms. Or you might remember the more universal childhood hardships: the fights with Nellie Olsen, Laura's standoff with her schoolteacher Eliza Wilder, and her jealousy of her sister Mary. But mainly, if you were a fan, you'll probably remember Laura as a tough little firecracker of a girl, that little "half pint of sweet cider half drunk up," who was not only undaunted by anything life could throw at her but who was happy with the life she had.[1]

I think this is why I found the books so comforting and why as an adult I still reread them, especially when I'm at odds in some way with the life I lead. Returning to my parents' home as a middle-aged woman with two kids is an exercise in regression, especially now that I don't have a romantic partner to remind my parents that I am not a child. I've found myself on these visits adopting adolescent behaviors that range from expecting my mom to do my laundry to picking up the books and reading habits I cultivated as a kid. Downstairs, in our little house, I can still find the bookshelves stacked with all of my and my brother's childhood books, including the copies of the Laura books that I read when I was young, and two summers ago, on a particularly difficult trip home, I reread all eight. Except this time, once I returned to Los Angeles, I threw myself down a Laura Ingalls Wilder rabbit hole full force. I got the annotated posthumously published draft manuscripts; I read the Caroline Fraser biography, *Prairie Fires*, multiple times.[2] "This is *such* a good biography," I gushed, mid-infatuation, to a friend. "You must read it. I am so in my happy place." "Emily," she said to me a few weeks later, "this is perhaps the most depressing book I've ever read. And I'm French."

Granted, the biography does expose a darker side to the life that Laura, in the fictionalized *Little House* books, sought to validate and reclaim. And yet the biography was as happiness-making for me as the novels that she wrote. Our lives weren't that different, I kept telling myself, while reading about early-twentieth-century pioneer life from my position as a twenty-first-century Los Angeles–based mom. Reading about Laura, in either fact or fiction, I felt that I wasn't crazy to struggle, that my family was somewhat normal, and that everything at the end of the day would be OK. I was a pioneer girl, and if Laura could find joy and beauty in this life, then I could too. If I was doing it like Laura, I must be right.

Pioneer Girl is the title of a draft manuscript written by Laura Ingalls Wilder in the spring of 1930. It consists of her first-person memories of childhood, handwritten straight through in number 2 lead pencil on six spiral-bound tablets without page numbers or section breaks. She would share this manuscript with her daughter, the author and journalist Rose Wilder Lane, asking for her opinion and editorial advice, and their collaboration would ultimately produce the eight beloved *Little House on the Prairie* books published during Wilder's life. At the time Wilder wrote her first draft of her first book, she was sixty-three years old.[3]

The volumes would grow to be beloved and controversial, both—for their attitude toward settler colonialism, their depiction of native peoples, and their slippery accounts of both personal and political events. Though nowhere mentioned on the cover, Rose Wilder Lane was actively involved in editing her mother's writing, and critics still discuss how much was written by Wilder and how much in the books was written or changed by Rose. Wilder, and Rose, also played fast and loose with fact and fiction. Finally narrated in the third person and embraced for their celebration of self-reliance and privation, the books were marketed as novels but read as autobiographies, and the sense that they told Laura's own life story helped her readers navigate everything from the Great Depression to national hardship after World War II.

The books, however, were acts of revisionist history: rationalizations of hardships sometimes inflicted, sometimes sought out.

I've found in this regard the biographies and annotated editions of Laura's manuscripts as fascinating as the final work. The paper trail she leaves behind shows the hidden labor behind publication: the extended process she and her daughter went through to reshape these stories, the initial stages of rejection they endured, and the physical effort involved in writing out by hand and then typing and editing her drafts. So too do they reveal what Wilder embellished about her life and what she chose to hide. None of the published books would mention the death of her infant brother or acknowledge her father's ongoing struggles with debt. None of the books indicate the influence of her daughter on their final framing and composition, and gone for good was the first-person "I."

Nor would any of the published books bear the title Laura affixed to her first draft. Instead, the "pioneer girl" is supplanted in her titles by a focus on houses, and spots of time, and the locations of her homes.

Like Laura's father, Charles Ingalls, driven by a desire for independence, a love of nature, and the promise of wide-open plains, my family seemed always to want to "get away." We were peripatetic throughout my childhood, a family unit moving in search of new opportunities or in response to parental, professional opportunities that hadn't manifested or been only temporary from the start. Like Laura's, many of my childhood memories involve snapshots of space: spaces that we loved and were hard to leave or spaces that we abandoned and were happy to forget. An apple orchard in Connecticut, a horse pasture overflowing with blossoms and birds; a large front yard in Georgia, dogwoods and magnolias in bloom; an apartment complex in North Carolina, its cement courtyard limning stalks of old bamboo; a house in New Hampshire, homemade flowerboxes against vinyl siding in an effort, an attempt.

In between, there was the twentieth-century version of the covered wagon: the moving truck, the boxes, the crowded back seat of a car.

"The wagon was home, we had lived in it so long . . ." For pioneers like Laura, the covered wagon emblematized a way of life. It was a conduit to new land and opportunities and the symbol of a more general push toward expansion achieved via the individual, dogged persistence lauded in Laura's books. This persistence was requisite given the mode of transport, as the wagons could be unwieldy and dangerous, productive of poor hygiene and nutrition, while the characteristics of what one pioneer called "irregular living" produced in many travelers "gastric fever," or, quite simply, the shits. Privacy was hard to come by, and such conditions were not temporary but endured. The wagons were heavy and slow, and families like the Ingalls traveled in them for months, over miles and miles.[4]

And yet the scenes Laura paints while she's in theirs, while she's in transit, are some of her most heartfelt. One of her earliest memories, recorded in *Pioneer Girl*, is of looking through the "opening in the wagon cover" at her parents sitting by a campfire "with the stars shining down on the great, flat land where no one lived." "They watched the clouds in the sky and the wind blowing the grass over the prairie and were as happy as they could be," Laura later writes in her original draft of *Little House on the Prairie*, describing herself and her sister Mary resting in the shade of the wagon before they've reached the site for their next little house. "Perhaps it was because the world was so big and everything was so sweet. The very wind smelled good . . . never before had they camped in such a wild beautiful place as this." When not camping outdoors, they are tucked into the wagon itself, along with most of their possessions, on a special bed in the back. Everything one might need is within reach, and Ma is good at making corncakes and coffee on the go. Indeed, the Garth Williams cover illustration for the 1953 reissued *Little House on the Prairie* features the wagon, not the little house, emphasizing how Laura remembers the covered wagon as one of her many homes. "In all that space of land and sky stood the lonely, small, covered wagon," Laura writes of her time in transit on the prairie, but she's describing a loneliness that sounds more like love. As home is portable, transitions for her become times of freedom, beauty, adventure, space.[5]

For us, by contrast, the in-between times, the process of traveling from one spot to another, were never part of the fun. My memories of transition feature dim scenes of packing and unpacking, set against the chaos of trying to compress then reconstitute the materials of a life. Home was never something we took with us but something we had to find or leave behind.

Laura Ingalls Wilder settled down later in her life. She and her husband, Almanzo, were longtime residents of Mansfield, Missouri, where she drafted *Pioneer Girl* in the elaborate "Rock House," a fieldstone English cottage gifted to her by Rose that included conveniences unknown to other neighbors at the time (a refrigerator, brass plumbing, steel-casement windows, hot and cold running water, a garage for their car). Surrounded finally by comfort and stability, Wilder chose to take on another hardship after a life of toil. She returned to her memoir and developed it into eight standalone books; she committed to her readers early on that she'd complete the series; she bound the next years of her life to that pressure, that promise, that goad.

I've fallen prey to the writing compulsion often myself. I've been known to stop between the end of a run and the beginning of a shower to jot down "just a phrase"; I've been known while writing to let a pot boil over; I've been known, I must admit, to yell at the inconveniently hungry dog. Laura, once immersed in this project, would similarly spend her days writing, just as once she'd spent her days on household chores or in the fields. She tried to pause in the evenings, as she told her daughter if she wrote too late at night the memories would keep her up. Still, sometimes memories would awaken her, and she'd sit down again to write.

Laura's end-of-life writing urge was also specific. She wasn't writing an essay "On Ambition" of the kind she wrote while still in school and later quotes in full in the final book she published during her lifetime, *These Happy Golden Years*. She's narrating instead the stories from her childhood that featured the people she remembered and the experiences she held dear. Hers is a common late-in-life desire to reminiscence, but there's something deeper than nostalgia in her pages, something more like an urge to explain what could not, for a child, have been easily understood. Why was money always so hard to come by? Why did the grasshoppers eat their wheat? Why did Mary have to lose her sight? Here, she tells her child readers, this is how parents-as-protectors can't always guard you from the hardships of life. This is how one single life can encompass such vast quantities of space and time. This is how unimaginable circumstances—the death of a child, crippling illness, loss of food—can be sustained and held in tandem with the joyful, the banal, the everyday.

And also, she tells them again and again, this is how home can be such a fluid concept and simultaneously such a defining need.

Does writing itself produce a kind of home? A lonely child, I offset transience with writing, first drafting poems on what I considered to be adult topics (a description of the moon, an aubade to morning, a meditation on silence, a patriotic paean to the United States) and later writing a forty-two-page novel about a court stenographer who'd been fired from his job. (I had just learned the word "stenographer" and must have been trying to show it off.) I usually wrote at a small desk in the back corner of our basement, next to the laundry room on one side and a bookshelf on the other. Everything I needed was within reach. One ceiling light shone, dentist-office-style, directly overhead.

Laura started her writing career as a newspaper columnist for the *Missouri Ruralist*, while living in the grand house made for her by Rose, and many of her early *Pioneer Girl* drafts show this journalistic start. She's word-efficient in her early memoirs, sparse in detail, to the point. As a farm columnist, she wrote on topics pertinent to her profession: the economics of farming, techniques for raising chickens, the advantages (or disadvantages) of time-saving devices to help with chores. Her topics were generalized, though personal anecdotes increasingly crept in. While in Rock House, she may have used the dining room table for her work. Later, when she and Almanzo had moved back into the nearby cottage also on their property, she wrote in a small room reserved for the purpose with two windows and a table and a desk. (Ironically, though Laura is the better remembered writer, it was Rose—novelist, journalist, biographer, and at one point one of the highest-paid American women writers—who would purchase for her family most of the property her parents had.) It also had a small fainting couch under one of the windows, and she'd rest there when awakened by memories during the night.

Home can look different, when you return. Big rooms can look smaller. A fancy object can have dulled. As a child, I knew Laura wanted to be an "Indian"; I remember her fascination with the dark eyes of the "papoose." Laura writes, in an early version of *Little House on the Prairie*, of her beloved expanse as a place with "no people. Only Indians. . . ." In *Little Town on the Prairie*, Pa dons blackface and puts on a minstrel show. Audiences and editors began calling Wilder's attention to such moments in the 1950s, and she responds to such pushback as a sign of changing times.[6] But Frederick Douglass had denounced blackface performance over a hundred years before. She chooses to keep such memories in her work. To see her father up on stage, to look deeply into a baby's eyes. I had loved that Laura. It can be lonely to go home and to find that home, or your view of home, has changed.

Descriptions of Laura's little houses are, alongside her descriptions of the wagon and prairies, some of the other most memorable scenes in her books. "The house was a comfortable house," writes Laura of her first little house in the big woods. "Upstairs there was a large attic, pleasant to play in when the rain drummed on the roof. Downstairs was the small bedroom, and the big room. The bedroom had a window that closed with a wooden shutter. The big room had two windows with glass in the panes, and it had two doors, a front door and a back door. All around the house was a crooked rail fence, to keep the bears and the deer away."[7] A similar level of detail embraces the series of houses and cabins and claim shanties that Pa goes on to build: some with logs and tarpaper roofs and blankets for partitions, some with proper windows and a door on hinges with a latch. There's the dugout they inherit too, on the banks of Plum Creek, which initially gives Ma pause yet which Laura loves for its warm, thick, whitewashed walls, its camouflage, its grassy roof. While a black-and-white photo of an actual dugout conveys the poverty associated with such a dwelling, the Williams cover illustration bursts with color correspondent to Laura's joy. He shows her frolicking among rooftop flowers while Ma can be seen through a window in the hillside, ironing, in the carved-out house under her daughter's feet.

The way Laura recounts all her dwellings and the particulars of their construction reminds me of my children's ongoing obsession with making forts. There's an autonomy, a security, I realize (as I watch my kids again rig up blankets over chairs), in making dwellings and in knowing how homes are made. "Come find me!" one child calls, from behind a wall of pillows; "check out my cozy corner," another invites, though I can fit only my head and shoulders through his makeshift door. No wonder Laura loved her little homes. One could go inside the dugout and be an almost invisible part of the landscape—just one more green hill.

We actually had a little house that we clung to throughout all our moving, a tiny cabin on top of a mountain surrounded by the big New Hampshire woods. My parents had purchased it long before having children, a second home before they had a first.

To be fair, it wasn't really a "little house" by the Ingalls's standards. My dad hadn't made it singlehandedly from logs, and we had indoor plumbing, plus windows made out of glass. It had an unfinished basement, two bedrooms on the main floor, plus a bathroom, a kitchen, a living room, and a porch. It also had an attic up top and, luxuriously, a second bathroom, though the bathroom in the attic we rarely used. It seemed an afterthought, convenient if someone needed privacy, but tucked into a section of the house that, like the basement, had never been fleshed out. In the winter the attic was too cold for habitation anyway, while in the summer it would bake. Battens of pink insulation, partially installed under rafters by my dad, hung down from where they'd come unstapled, and old bed frames plus boxes of memorabilia were stacked around: college notebooks, my mom's old saddle, an ancient set of dishes, an electric typewriter, a makeshift table made from two sawhorses and a plank of wood. There was pockmarked linoleum on most of the attic floor. In the summers, we'd play games up there, using the old china as treasure and weaving our way through the sections of pink fiberglass I'd been warned not to touch. The attic was its own kind of air conditioner, too. Fifteen minutes up there could make the rest of the house feel cold.

Our place may not have been a cabin by the Ingalls' standards, but it still had enough elements to pretend. We had our own well, and our water, while safe to drink, had the metallic tang that comes from excess iron and left rings of rust in the toilet basins when it sat. We had our own pump, which had to be reprimed and drained around every cold-weather visit, so we peed in snow banks upon arrival and emptied toilets with turkey basters when we left. We had no central heating or proper insulation, and in winters the downstairs bathroom remained so cold that my dad often rested his can of shaving cream on the woodstove in the mornings to thaw before he shaved. We carried wood for that stove up from the basement, where it rested in cords split and stacked during the summer months and where the smell of sap blended with a generalized basement odor of must and dirt. In the darkness, on the basement steps, I could hear the clicks of beetles as they chewed their way through logs.

Like Laura, I remember finding the comforts of our little house accentuated by the hardships it involved. A space by the woodstove always felt warmer in comparison to the cold air beyond its reach; a cold toilet was a luxury compared to the snow bank outside; a hot shower was an extra pleasure, since the water heater usually gave out. Summers at the cabin had their own trials, mostly involving humidity, lack of air conditioning, and mosquitoes, deer flies, black flies, ticks. In the sunlit months, we'd take cold showers at night and sleep on top of sheets made stiff by being hung outside, while a fan upstairs would circulate hot air.

But in the summers, our pilgrimages to the cabin also made more sense. We were traveling to a space of abundance, all trees and wildlife and flowers and birds. There was the pond to help us fight the heat, and there were salamanders and fish and fireflies to catch. We spent the weeks happily sunburned and bug-bitten, and we'd stay up late playing canasta, or flashlight tag, or making s'mores. Mornings we'd be awakened by the sound of rain on the rafters or the birds, always loudest in those pre-dawn hours. The days that followed were full of ice cream and hiking, and we'd go berry picking and get good at walking in bare feet.

The winters at the cabin were more puzzling to me, since fewer people visited, and our visits featured hardships that seemed not inflicted but sought out. To make the cabin liveable required stoking, priming, shoveling, and shopping, though even with these amenities "liveable" and "comfortable" never became quite the synonyms that we were taught. We'd visit for weekends, sandwiching the trip between the end of work or school on Friday evenings and the Monday morning beginning of the same, so that we were always getting ready for the trip or packing up. And just to get to the cabin in winters required its own adventure, perched as it was at the end of the dirt switchbacks that navigated the mountain's side. "It could be a bad drive tonight; we'll see if the caretaker has had a chance to sand the hill," one of my parents would announce, and with that, we'd fling ourselves into the blackness, toward the unpaved road that, while often graded and sanded to help with access, usually hadn't been tended to on snowy nights. When it would present to us Robert Frost style, an unbroken white expanse, we'd start a verbal negotiation as to how far we'd get before lack of friction, the pitch of the road, and spinning tires all did their work. And while the last and steepest section of the hill came after a small turnout area, we'd always attempt this final climb, my dad downshifting and focusing on some precise balance between acceleration and clutch. When, inevitably, the wheels would start to slip, he'd steer us backward down the hill, toward the turnout, toward the place where we probably always knew we would park.

Why did we drive north to the cabin even on weekends that we knew a heavy snowstorm was on its way? Why, given this familial penchant, did we always drive at night? Why did we never have cars with four-wheel drive? Why, given this mechanical reality, did we set off into blizzards with a sense of speculation, a white-knuckled determinism that also felt like a version of Russian roulette?

There's an episode in *Little House on the Prairie* when the Ingalls family almost gets swept away in their wagon by a quickly rising creek. "What do you think, Caroline?" Pa says, before they attempt the ford. "Whatever you say, Charles," she answers, and the family does make it safely across. But barely. Pa has his own account. "I never saw a creek rise so fast in my life . . . [the horses] wouldn't have made it if I hadn't helped them," he announces, once they are on the other side. Laura reinforces this assessment: "If Pa had not known what to do, or if Ma had been too frightened to drive, or if Laura and Mary had been naughty and bothered her, then they would have all been lost."[8] The family together is heroic, surmounting a difficulty that had been placed quite literally in their path. But Laura's list of contingencies leaves out a lot. What if they had taken a different route? What if they had chosen to camp for the night? What if they had quite simply chosen not to cross the creek?

Our winter trips to the cabin were never quite so fraught, but they did incite anxieties that seemed at once predictable and unsought. The conditions of the highways as we drove north could vary greatly; visibility and traffic created their own kind of familial stress. And every unsuccessful drive up the mountain meant that we'd have one last task. Packed to the roof like Laura's covered wagon, our stranded car needed to be emptied of any perishable possessions to carry with us for the evening, before we returned the next morning to retrieve the car. One year this task involved my pet guinea pig, whose cage posed a challenge as we got ready to unload and climb. Never daunted, we transferred her to someone's ski cap, and I tucked her inside the front of my parka as we walked. Once at the cabin, I made her a makeshift home out of a trashcan and some shredded paper, and I gave her, I think, the place of honor next to the stove. If she found the change disorienting, she never mentioned it. She spent the night warm enough.

During their hard winter in De Smet, South Dakota, the Ingallses almost starve. By the end of it, they are eating cakes made from seed wheat ground up in a coffee grinder and twisting sticks of hay to burn for warmth. They have had no supplies delivered to town for almost five months, and they only survive because Almanzo Wilder and Cap Garland venture out on the prairie between blizzards to bargain away extra seed wheat from a homesteader rumored to have some in storage, which they bring back to the inhabitants of De Smet for food. (This episode might not have happened; the historical record is unclear.) Blizzards come and last for days, producing whiteout conditions, and temperatures hover well below zero for weeks on end. The cold and claustrophobia make Laura feel dumb, and she has no appetite for their coarse bread even though it is all they have to eat. Laura titled her manuscript *The Hard Winter* in draft, though it was changed to *The Long Winter* by her publisher so as not to scare child readers away. A Garth Williams cover illustration features children in a snowball fight, as if the winter bit of her book was all good fun.

"When possible," Laura writes later in life of her parents, "they turned the bad into good. If not possible, they endured . . . they found their own way."⁹ Sometimes it makes sense to climb up a mountain, late at night, with a guinea pig in your shirt. Not everyone can just keep going like that, half frozen, no matter what.

But I've lived in Los Angeles now for almost two decades. My boys have never moved.

My folks live in the cabin year-round, these days. Actually, the original cabin was razed to the ground, and a proper four-season house now sits on roughly the same footprint, with radiant heat in the floorboards and a new water heater and all new appliances, too. It is still a funny house; my brother finds it large and echo-y, and with more square footage it somehow seems harder to find within it a place to hide. I miss the privacy of the old attic, with its pockmarked linoleum and working typewriter, though the top room of the house remains my dad's study, a wide room in which one can sit and write. We still store firewood in the basement, and every winter my parents keep us posted on how many months they can go without turning on the heat.

My kids are the latest generation to make the trek to the cabin, though until recently they only visited in the summer months. My two winter visits with them, so far, have seemed tame compared to my memories of winter growing up. An all-wheel drive Subaru Outback now zooms us up the hill; a backup generator kicks in if and when the power dies. My boys shovel the driveway as a novelty and play king-of-the-mountain in the plow pile at the end of the road. They have the same friends they've known since kindergarten, a home and anchor in LA. They don't know about our little house.

And yet: they have seen the bit of wall from the old cabin that's still in our front mudroom, the bit we use to mark the heights of all the pioneer children to come through her doors. And they've taken their turn standing against it, chins down, in stocking feet. My oldest is now the height I was, back then, when I was his age. That wall is the first thing you see when you come in, if you look for it, with handwriting that goes back to prior owners of the cabin and names of children that I have never met. The names and dates stretch back for decades, and the pen or pencil has had to press hard to make an imprint in the boards. The wall reminds me of Laura, sitting down in Rocky Ridge, with her spiral-bound tablets, and her pencils, and her fainting couch. How we work, in writing, to recreate a safe haven; how we can be so haunted by the memories we also love. So many children, so many houses, so many names.

14

THE EFFICIENCY EXPERT

William Wordsworth, Frank and Ernestine Gilbreth

"Dad thought the best way to deal with sickness in the family was simply to ignore it," the narrators of the 1940s childhood memoir *Cheaper by the Dozen* pronounce. Growing up, I'd read this book, coauthored by two of the Gilbreth siblings, who'd grown up in a family of twelve, maybe forty times. The family outings in the Pierce Arrow and Bill honking the horn while Dad tried to fix the overheated car, Jackie belching at the dinner table and blaming it on a guest, the girls convincing their dad to let them bob their hair—I could tell these stories as if they were my own. In real life, I had only the one younger brother, but in large families, another child could slip in unawares. And in large families, I was also told, everything goes well. "We don't have time for such nonsense," the father proclaims. "There are too many of us. A sick person drags down the performance of the entire group. You children come from sound pioneer stock. You've been given health, and it's your job to keep it. I don't want any excuses. I want you to stay well."[1]

This patriarchal edict to stay healthy was issued by a man of forceful will, indeed. Spoken by the real-life, upper-class industrial engineer Frank Bunker Gilbreth from the seat of his 1920s

New Jersey family estate, the sentiment builds consciously on a couple of traditions from a rather different time and place. First, it develops the idea that an old-fashioned pioneer lifestyle would both require and be productive of good health, cue the "sound pioneer stock" from which the Gilbreths are said to descend. But it also activates a more implicit association, that being from such pioneer stock means having the large family that makes illness, in Frank Gilbreth's view, the inconvenience he asserts. In reality, while manual labor rarely waits for recuperation, and while human illness never comes at a good time, the logic of the large pioneer family provided a safety net for sickness: more bodies in times of hardship to cover the hard physical labor of farming life.

The Gilbreths, however, were anything but famers. Frank and Lillian Gilbreth were both industrial engineers who initiated the field now known as "motion study," and Lillian Gilbreth was a psychologist, too. Together they paired the study of factory efficiency with the psychology of management, and together they were hired by major companies around the world to help those companies speed up production and increase profits as a result. Speed was key, in the Gilbreth's self-invented industry, with the goal being to eliminate all wasted motions, a wasted motion defined as a physical movement that didn't further, or didn't further in the most efficient manner, the task at hand.

Frank Gilbreth, who got his start as a bricklayer and general contractor, was a self-proclaimed and self-educated "efficiency expert," and his work philosophies and life philosophies went hand in hand. His own biography attests to a man who pursued his professional and personal goals with a clear purpose and then attained them at a good clip. Beginning as a manual laborer, he climbed the class ladder very much on his own steam, and "by the time he was twenty-seven, he had offices in New York, Boston, and London" and a yacht and cigars to boot.[2] Lillian was from a well-to-do, large family in Oakland, California, and their courtship also proceeded apace. Famously, perhaps apocryphally, the couple determined on their honeymoon to have twelve children, six boys and six girls. Over the course of the next seventeen years, they did just that.[3]

Large families also figure in a famous poem by William Wordsworth, a poet beloved by my dad.[4] A nameless traveler encounters a young girl and asks how many children are in her family, counting her. There are seven of us, she answers, this little girl just eight years old. But when she extrapolates, she reveals that two of her siblings are dead. So, are there five children, or seven? The girl and the traveler disagree. Either way, it is a small number compared to the Gilbreths' twelve. Either way, it is a funny question to ask of a child so independent, so on her own. Wordsworth claims he got the idea for the poem during a 1793 walking tour across England, in the course of which he met and conversed with such a girl.

In the pioneer ethos of reproduction, large families become a testament to the health and vitality of the parents, as well as the children they produce. Note how Frank and Lillian coordinate the production of their family with seeming efficiency and ease: all the children are single births (apparently to the father's mild chagrin, as not the most efficient way of having twelve), but every year to eighteen months sees the birth of another Gilbreth child. No fertility issues cloud the horizon, and while some of the deliveries are rapid, none of them are vexed. Lily has every child at home until her twelfth, and her children recall her as running the house up until the moment the baby started coming, then being inaccessible for about twenty-four hours. Her pregnancies never seem unpleasant, and she recovers from them with speed.

She aligns the reviewing of book proofs with the "unavoidable delay" of her child-bearing confinements, and she also ties hair ribbons and reads bedtime stories to her older children while convalescing from her latest birth. Frank, in turn, regularly brings children with him on business trips, stays in close touch with his children's teachers, and brags about his children whenever he is away. The only time his children remember him as sick, as temporarily out of commission, is when he voluntarily undergoes a tonsillectomy as an act of solidarity with his kids.

On the childhood side there are, granted, bouts with measles, whooping cough, and tonsillitis; such germs have a way of flouting the most stentorian patriarchal command. And yet, as a long-time rereader of the book, I remember the Gilbreth children as hearty individuals, recuperating quickly from the measles, recovering easily from tonsillectomies, and barely registering the bruises, cuts, and bangs that childhood inflicts. Maybe their strength resulted, after all, from their parents' example, good genetics, and their father's commandment to stay well; maybe it owed something to the communal aspect of their suffering and recovery, too. There's an irony, perhaps, to Martha's loneliness when, as the one Gilbreth not to contract the measles, she is exiled from the sickroom while her siblings recover above stairs. But even the father feels the loneliness and shows up in the sickroom one day with faux measles inked upon his face.

Wordsworth's little girl also never relinquishes the sense of community she feels with those siblings who are gone. She brings her sewing and knitting out to do by their gravesites; she sings them songs; she eats dinner there, with them, at night. Indeed, they are much closer to her now, a scant twelve steps from her mother's door, than those brothers and sisters who have grown up and moved away.

They stay with us, those friends and siblings from our past. Remember when Frank tries to teach Lillian how to swim, out on Nantucket, and all the children watch? Remember the birdbath that collapses? Remember the road trips with twelve different children who all have to go to the bathroom at different times?

In the true pioneer tradition of the large family, mortality lurks behind the appearance of vitality that multiple children set forth. Beyond the need to have many hands to help with physical labor, such families had many children because of the high probability that one or more would succumb to infant mortality, farm-related injuries, or childhood disease.

In the family and work model put forward by the Gilbreths, efficiency and economic calculation are intertwined. To keep a family or factory running smoothly requires money, while a smoothly running factory or family recoups the profits one lays out. Stories of visits back to Lillian's family home feature multiple servants, outbuildings, and limousines that zip the family from the train station to the family estate and back. The Gilbreth family home in New Jersey, though not quite as aristocratic as Lillian's, is yet described by the children as a veritable "Taj Mahal" of a house, complete with two servants, a grape arbor, a two-story barn, fruit trees, and rooms enough to accommodate the Gilbreth family brood. The Gilbreths summer in Nantucket, where the father buys two lighthouses that he moves to abut their cabin, so that the family has room to spread. The family attitudes toward race and servants are enfolded into class. Had I found the chapter on their Chinese cook funny, back when I read this book so many times as a child? I can't imagine my children, with their own Chinese background, as my audience, should I read those passages aloud. (Though my kids' dad, aunts, uncles, and cousins make their own jokes, and the family welcomed me to Hawaii by gifting me sunscreen and a copy of *Pidgin to Da Max*.)[5]

Class attitudes notwithstanding, the Gilbreth family vacations, albeit by choice, without running water. They seem aware of a more primitive life. The children are kept responsible for household chores and invited to put in bids to complete some of the more arduous household tasks. Little Lillian submits the lowest bid to paint a fence when she is just eight years old, the same age as the young girl in Wordsworth's poem. The task costs her ten days of labor and blistered hands. The family is conscious of the relationship between labor, income, and time.

This awareness of calculation begins from the title page. "Cheaper by the dozen" is the repeated family joke to explain Lillian and Frank's joint decision to have the number of children that they did. (The other family adage to explain the father's desire for a large family was that he knew whatever he and Lillian teamed up on would be a success.) When astonished bystanders comment on the family's size, Frank responds with the titular expression, implying that going in for lots of offspring was part of an economic computation and implying that children, like donuts, can be set out on counters to be bundled and selected at will. The idea that the Gilbreths would be able, unproblematically, to have exactly the number of children that they desired, and to have within that number an even pattern of boys and girls, is already a hubristic notion, but the fact that the familial plan manifests exactly as the honeymoon plan mapped out seems to endorse the idea that children are, in fact, akin to donuts: able to be voluntarily selected and grouped together, more affordable as you bundle them, and useful, in the long run, for the very efficiency experiments that Frank Gilbreth made his life's work.

"Life's work" here is key, as the Gilbreth children are constantly made aware that any time spent while conscious should be put to use. They listen to language records while in the bathtub; they practice Morse code on vacation; they learn multiplication tricks while at their meals. There's a beauty in their choreography, that synchronicity between child and child and task and task. There's joy and humor when it doesn't work. (Yoga, swimming, breakfast, shoes, I think every morning, in a series of aspirational pirouettes.) After all, in the factory model, the idea behind working efficiently is not just to finish a single task more quickly but to fit more completed tasks within the same amount of time. After all, in the factory model, a factory that stopped moving would be dead.

My children are learning these same lessons, as they sit through a speakerphone car ride on workplace compliance or wait in the backseat as I scribble shorthand notes from an editor friend on an envelope before we go into a store to get new shoes. ("Be quiet for just a second," the older one will announce to his brother, "this is important because this is about *how you publish a book*.") In everything aside from athletics, I seem to have gotten faster as I've aged. I pack for the airport quickly, respond to emails on my phone, and segue almost instantly from mom mode to work mode to anything in between. I love the variety that results from our rapidity, though there's an anxiety behind my responsiveness, too. I embrace to-do lists the way a professional tennis player confronts a rally, with every request a ball hit over the net that I need to return at lightning speed.

My kids, of course, stymie me at every turn. For the neophytes in my house, we've got two timers that help coordinate our morning rituals, but "put on your shoes" means "nerf gun battle," and "get your backpack" means "I've lost my water bottle and broken my shoelace and have just now decided that instead of shorts I'm going to put on pants." Still, they are pretty organized, for small kids. And I don't usually feel as if I am rushing us, more that I'm trying to keep our every minute full. As long as everything runs smoothly (the car starts, I can find my keys, and the youngest doesn't remember halfway to school that he was supposed to bring in an empty two-liter plastic bottle for science), my children and I can accomplish a lot.

Reading and writing seem like paradoxical loves in this respect. Writing is one of the few activities I enjoy that can't predictably be completed within a set amount of time. I can tell you to the minute how long it will take me to swim three thousand meters, but three hours can go by writing and I'll be left with fewer pages than when I began. Reading, too, keeps me off the clock. I've missed phone calls and pick-up times while in a book. Somehow the world has not collapsed. "Ah, stuck in your writing again?" the youngest will say, coming to find me in the garage. After I tuck them in, my boys read in bed with headlamps, a miniature camping lantern hung from the slats of the upper bunk. I never know how long they stay awake.

There's a breath of efficiency, too, in the Wordsworth poem.[6] The traveler channels the Gilbreth philosophy that anything unusable should no longer take up space. The young girl, by contrast, numbers her siblings as if none of them could ever be "used up." Who is right? It makes me wonder what Frank Gilbreth, the motion-study expert, would say to young Hamlet or to Old Hamlet's ghost. *Hamlet*, in Frank Gilbreth's hands, would likely become a one-act play.

But as a child, I loved the Gilbreths' book because it suggested there was a best, or correct, way to move through life.

The other implication behind large pioneer families was that the more children one had, the less the death of one might hurt. An "heir and a spare," the expression goes. Recall the anecdote in *Cheaper by the Dozen* when Lillian returns from a business trip and finds that Frank has in her absence mistaken one of the neighbor's children for their own and spanked him as a result. (Frank redeems himself when the family doctor mixes up the tonsillectomies of Martha and Ernestine, and Frank insists that he, at least, can tell which child is which.) There's a fungibility suggested by sheer numbers, a sense that if Frank Junior fails, Jack or Bill can step in. And in terms of farm labor, trench warfare, or monarchical succession, this ability bears out. Perhaps, too, in times of hard living and little medical care, one can in fact become desensitized to pain. Mary Wollstonecraft was suckled by puppies when the childbed fever that would finally kill her required doctors to remove Mary Shelley from her breast.[7] Mary Shelley herself had five pregnancies and only one living child. Even in life somehow people manage to survive childbirth, lose children, and keep on.

The Gilbreths never actually had twelve children living at the same time. Mary is the second Gilbreth born, after Anne, and she dies of diphtheria in 1912. At the time of her death, Anne is seven, Ernestine four, Martha three, and Frank Jr. one. In the sequel they wrote to *Cheaper by the Dozen*, Frank and Ernestine acknowledge Mary's death in a brief footnote at the beginning of the book. Throughout *Cheaper by the Dozen*, however, the narrators present the family as if they are twelve.

There are weird moments, such as when Anne, enduring the trials of female adolescence, laments being the oldest girl and names her sisters, leaving Mary out. Or when Mary is named multiple times in "The Latest Model" chapter without acknowledging any circumstances of her life. The narrators are basically hiding her, suggests one critic, in plain sight.

Hidden deeper: the fact that in 1915 Lillian Gilbreth gives birth, prematurely, to a stillborn baby girl. The birth was perhaps a result of Lillian's fall down some stairs. The baby is never named (neither was Mary Shelley's first). Eleven months later, Lillian gives birth to baby Frank.[8]

So: how many children are there? Five, seven? Eleven, twelve, thirteen? The Gilbreth family autobiography features what one writer calls an "endlessly wobbling number of kids."[9] And in large families, it is easy for a kid to get lost. (Remember when Frank Jr. gets left behind at a restaurant? Don't worry, he's in the kitchen, happy and safe.) But when it is your job, your passion, to tabulate numbers, the wobbling shows.

Counting becomes hard, I think, when time isn't working the way it should. "But two months dead; nay, not so much, not two," claims Hamlet, of his father's death. "My father died within these two hours," he later weeps. Grief makes time simultaneously speed up and slow down, a concept designed to wreak havoc on an efficiency expert's mind. "Nay, 'tis twice two months, my lord," Ophelia replies. So how long has it been? Two hours, one month, two months, four? We never know.[10]

The first Gilbreth family memoir ends with their father's death. He's been hiding a bad heart for years, we learn, and he drops dead from a heart attack en route to a business trip. He's fifty-five when he collapses; Anne, the oldest, is eighteen; the baby Jane is two. Many of his family efficiency experiments had been prescient, fueled by the knowledge that he may leave Lillian alone with their eleven, or thirteen, or twelve. A well-run family will offset the burden placed upon her by his absence, he reasons. When things run smoothly, who is to say that anything, or anyone, is even gone?

Counting is an act of the living, and efficiency is something you practice, Frank Gilbreth Sr. asserts, to make more time for love. "Someone once asked Dad," the narrators conclude, what he wanted to save all that time *for*. "For work, if you love that best," their Dad replies. "For education, for beauty, for art, for pleasure . . . for mumblety-peg, if that's where your heart lies."[11] For eating supper in a churchyard, I'd imagine. For knitting, for singing songs.

In yoga, you learn to pace your respirations, given the philosophy that every lifetime contains a set number of breaths. In swim workouts, you push the main interval so you can bank your rest. Maybe sometimes we go fast because grief is painful, and maybe we lose count when the things that matter are things we want to hide. But efficiency can also mean having to make fewer choices between love and obligation. Maybe sometimes, we rush through life so that when we need to, we can pause.

15

INVISIBLE LABOR, INVISIBLE HANDS

Adam Smith, Zadie Smith

Invisible labor is important to me because I feel engaged in a lot of it, and I suppose I retain a fair amount of resentment about this fact. Case in point: a friend once shared a review of one of my books with another friend, who observed that I "must have had a very good nanny to pull that off." My friend had answered no, to the contrary, but instead of feeling prouder of my accomplishment, I'd felt angry and confused. Had I been blind to the way the rest of the world was going about such activities? Didn't everyone get called away between sentences to wipe a butt that was not their own? Was the rest of the writing world leading lives with more support?[1]

Honestly, we never know what hurdles others have to overcome in their daily lives, and I'm usually happiest doing things the hard way around. I also know that my concept of "hard," in reference to the writing life, might sound, in the context of different professions, privileged and out of touch. I know that in my own life, when I'm scrubbing a toilet, or doing a postwork grocery run, or up at midnight with a feverish child, it certainly feels that way to me (and I am far from a Cinderella in this regard—let's just say my toilets aren't always clean). Still, I think writers love it when their books are published with a celebratory impulse directly proportional to what they experience as unseen gestational time and angst. And I think that learning to appreciate these efforts has made me more attuned to the unseen efforts that those around me are, in a variety of ways, constantly putting forth. When Jeanette Winterson writes that "a tough life needs a tough language," she's talking about why the work of literature is particularly important to the working class.[2] I've found that we don't always see this kind of labor, either because we don't think it is important or because skilled artists and workers can make their final product seem as if it required no work at all. I wonder if these laborers recognize the artistry, or effort, of obscuring effort. I wonder if any of them feel that their audience should know more about what went on behind the scenes. I want to tell the ballerina that I appreciate the ballet performance and also that I remember, on some level, her invisible, bloody feet.

So when it comes to invisible labor, I know that I'd like more of this preparatory work to be acknowledged, maybe through funds or better systems of regulation or, say, through a golf-handicap system that would account for what I feel to be my external challenges and rank my finished work more highly as a result. I can imagine that same book review, for instance, with an asterisk indicating that "the author wrote all this WITHOUT A NANNY," though upon reflection I'd want the asterisk to be revealed only retroactively, after my work had already towered over all the other, ostensibly nanny-supported books.

Upon reflection, I'll also admit that many of these desires reveal psychological baggage specific to me. To wit:

I have trouble saying no, and I would appreciate if institutional structures or supervisors, better seeing the whole picture of my work-life imbalance, said no to some efforts on my behalf.

I also have trouble acknowledging many of my own activities *as* work, and if I could see more clearly as work some of what I do, I'd feel better about my allocation of time, my end-of-day fatigue, my choices in life.

This is because, as the latter statement makes clear, I have trouble appreciating pleasure in a nontransactional context, since I've inherited a skewed life view in which work is the main purpose of existence, with pleasure earned as a result of work. Work I've done that is invisible even to myself thus robs me of extra joy, and extra rest, and for this reason especially, I'd appreciate if more of what I call my invisible labor would be seen, probably first and foremost by myself.

My final bit of psychological baggage is that I'm someone who believes that the answers to life's mysteries are to be found in books. As a result, I decided that the best way to address my struggles with invisible labor was to read some Adam Smith.[3]

Adam Smith is not someone I had read a lot of earlier in life. I spent most of my college and graduate school career reading novels and poetry and plays, not eighteenth-century Scottish philosophers who wrote big books that I found—and still find—somewhat dry. To this day I've never read all of Smith's most famous work, *The Wealth of Nations* (1776), though I did finally enjoy his *Theory of Moral Sentiments* (1759), or most of it, I think.[4]

I've more enjoyed getting to know Smith as a person, since he's a character, to say the least. He's the original "absentminded professor": someone who supposedly wandered miles through town in his nightgown while thinking, fell into a tanning pit while discussing free-trade economy, and put bread and butter into his teapot only to complain of the taste of his tea. He suffered from hypochondria and regularly talked to himself or to his imaginary, invisible friends. He is known today for his contributions to our current theory of a free-market economy, but he considered himself more of a philosopher than an economist.

He never married, and his closest heterosexual relationship was with his mom. He is also most well known for a phrase that is still used by current economists, the concept of "the invisible hand."[5]

In economic theory, the "invisible hand" stands in for the unseen forces that motivate a natural movement in prices and trade in our economy, as independent of any governmental control. When I first started expressing my interest in invisible labor, it was also the metaphor that many colleagues kept mentioning that I should pursue as relevant to my work. I found this curious, since, as I discovered, the concept of invisible labor wasn't defined until much later, by the sociologist Arlene Daniels, who in 1987 coined the term "invisible work." The date of Daniels's definition suggests that before 1987 "invisible labor" wasn't a known concept, although we'd spent the past two centuries seeing invisible hands.[6]

My point here is that regardless of my colleagues' recommendations, Adam Smith doesn't automatically equate invisible hands with invisible work. Really, Smith doesn't seem much interested in what I would intuitively define as invisible labor, at all. Reading Smith to learn more about the concept of invisible labor instead raised for me a whole new set of questions. Do invisible hands do invisible labor, or are they engaged in something else? Is invisible labor even done by invisible beings, or does labor become invisible by a different mechanism altogether? And if invisibility is not the key requirement for invisible labor, how and why does labor . . .

. . . disappear?

Let me start Platonic-dialogue style:
Can we have labor without invisibility?

Yes. We have many examples of this. The construction workers I saw this morning on my street, for example. The cashier who chatted with me as she rang up my groceries at Trader Joe's.

Can we have invisibility that does not involve labor?

Yes. Hide and Seek would otherwise not be a game. When I ask my kids what they'd choose as a superpower, flight or invisibility, the question isn't meant to be a thought experiment in productivity but in pleasure. Superheroes sometimes seem to use invisibility to advance their goals, but generally being an invisible superhero seems like fun.

Do we have any examples of invisible beings that do visible work?

Yes. Literary examples that come to my mind include the spirit Ariel from Shakespeare's play The Tempest, *who does many tasks for his master Prospero while invisible, and also the sylphs from Alexander Pope's mock epic "The Rape of the Lock," who basically work in the poem as invisible chambermaids, doing dress and makeup for the poem's heroine. One of the sylphs, not coincidentally, is named Ariel, too. Ralph Ellison's invisible man would also claim this title, though how well audiences see his labor remains in doubt.*

Do we have any examples of technically visible beings that do invisible work?

Yes. But this question is more complicated . . .

To define invisible labor, I need first to define labor itself.

Intuitively, I define labor as that which involves sweat, fatigue, and/or exertion. I also define labor as the opposite of pleasure or relaxation, even though, ironically, I'm usually happiest when I sweat. I define labor as compulsory, as opposed to voluntary: something I do because I have to do it and not because I seek it out. But labor in my mind begins with the idea of sweat, though

I'm not actually sweaty every time I work. I think the connection stems from my decades-long association of working with working out, and though I'm not doing jumping jacks every time I teach, I am a relatively sweaty lecturer, thanks to adrenaline, and I also not coincidentally do a lot of my teaching in yoga clothes—what my college friends used to call "my uniform" and what a current friend calls my "active wear." Back when I was a hard-working college student, my dad would try to send me email missives addressed "Hi, sweetie!" but had to insist upon this nomenclature because his computer spell-check would religiously change my name to "sweaty" instead. "The association is becoming powerful," he once wrote.

Interestingly, given the ideas that follow, my commonsense definitions of labor don't involve money, or value, or a wage.[7]

In *The Wealth of Nations*, Smith defines labor by contrast as "the exact measure of the real exchangeable value of all commodities."[8] Another way of putting this concept is that labor for Smith is that which creates tangible goods that can be bought, traded, or sold. To count as labor, exertion has to produce some tangible product, and that product has to be exchangeable for money. Working out wouldn't count as work for Smith. Nor would academic pursuits. Philosophy is not labor for Smith, because it produces no value and "must be considered economically 'unproductive,' along with the work of 'churchmen' and 'opera singers.'"[9] To be productive is to be *economically* productive. Churchmen and opera singers, take note.

The sociologist Arlene Daniels, the one who coined the term "invisible work," agrees that, thanks to Smith, we have long defined labor as something for which we get paid. Sometimes labor is skilled, and sometimes it is monotonous or backbreaking, but even if we enjoy the activity, it is work if we get paid for it. If it isn't paid, we don't recognize it as such. Daniels also argues that "the notion of work as something set apart from the rest of life is a peculiarly modern and Western idea."[10] Our Western association of salary, public systems of exchange, and definitions of labor has rendered many laborious activities—in my more general sense of the adjective—unseen.

A different Smith, but this one from the twenty-first century, returns to economic definitions of labor and adds in the category of time. Zadie Smith defines labor as "work done by the clock (and paid by it, too)." Given this fact, she, like Adam, distinguishes "the artist's labor" from "the work of truly laboring people," because she claims that artistic activities cannot be compensated by fitting them within a quantifiable component of time. "Art takes time and divides it up as art sees fit," this Smith declares, which makes it different from labor, since inspiration can't be put on a timeline or rushed (even though deadlines are the mother of invention, I always say).[11]

Her distinction almost makes me feel for the academic administrators, of which I am one, burdened with artists who are also employees—administrators who must carve out space in contracts for inspiration and recompense our employees at a calculable rate. Forty percent of your salary represents time for "research"; a semester or even year at some academic institutions can be set aside for an intellectual sabbatical with one's salary unchanged. Written down as opportunities, these calculations carry with them expectations, too. Have you used your research time "productively"? Have you done in this time what you are being paid to do?

Domestic and professional labor also remain, for me in these examples, confused. I understand that only one makes the laborer money, but what if—as is true for many writers—the artist works from home? Or, what would Smith or Smith say of domestic labor's effect on my productivity or prominence "at work"? I finished reading Zadie Smith's essays on writing and isolation just before her visit to our campus, an event that was to be preceded by a small, invite-only dinner I'd been anticipating enough to put into my calendar a week too soon. She's written so well about, and through, her own domestic- and professional-life juggle.[12] Maybe I'd thought we could even bond. So on the day of the faux-dinner I wrote to another colleague, to say I'd see him that night at dinner with Zadie Smith. "Oh," he wrote back, "I'm having dinner on campus with Zadie NEXT Wednesday." "Really?" I replied, "That's so cool she's coming to our campus TWICE."

But on the night of the actual dinner (or as I like to refer to it, the second dinner), I was too tired—this chapter—and shy— "The One and Only Jane"—to participate in a conversation that had come to feel like work. She was brilliant, and glamorous, and I may have been wearing someone's breakfast oatmeal on my shirt. Still, I guess the dinner wasn't a total loss. I do remember overhearing an interesting discussion about what it is like to travel these days when you don't own an iPhone (apparently Smith doesn't) and how it creates a unique kind of loneliness because in airports there is no one to meet your gaze since everyone is staring down at screens.

Whatever either Smith would say, I never feel tortured by the fact that I'm drawing a salary for the months that I'm writing, or supposed to be writing, a book. I feel tortured by the other sense of productivity, by the creative, artistic imperative to manifest what it is I am trying to say. The work that happens there happens internally, for a long time before any visible product can result. Such intellectual angst is a privilege, and that angst makes me feel that my salary is earned.

Based upon these definitions of labor, "invisible" labor would be work that one can't see. It is work that goes on behind the scenes, though it yields results that appear to have required but little labor at all. Think of the "improvisational" speech that disguises the hours spent in rehearsal; the dinner party, with its meals that seem to come together just so; the college seminar, its free-flowing conversation registering as unplanned. Invisible labor hides behind any final performance or project that seems to burst forth from the void, fully formed: that "perfect" painting, recital, athletic performance, book. And yet these final projects dazzle us because behind them lurks the knowledge of work that came before. We make much, while sitting on our couches, of the hours of athletic training that must have produced that world record. A quick trip to the kitchen reveals the dishes in the sink.

There are other products, though, for which the preparatory labor hides deeper, either because society won't recognize that certain activities require work or because society has rendered certain kinds of work uncomfortable to discuss. Female beauty is one such example, once and still predicated on its hidden creams, undergarments, and pomades. The long trade in sugar and cotton, dependent on its history of slave labor, is a darker other. As a culture we still don't see what we attempted for centuries to hide. The National Underground Railroad Freedom Center, in downtown Cincinnati, hosts a permanent museum exhibit titled "Invisible: Slavery Today." Centuries earlier, Adam Smith tried to expose the atrocities of chattel slavery, on moral but also economic grounds. He figured abolition would be better advanced if he could convince slave owners that slavery was an unprofitable way for owners to manage work.[13]

In our day and age, so many types of service work continue to be unseen. There's the Amazon delivery person who leaves me boxes, the DoorDash dinner that shows up magically on my stoop.

Parenting, I think, is my invisible labor, something that feels like labor acknowledged and unacknowledged both. But writing, in the moment, can also feel like invisible labor, most frequently when I'm stuck or between projects or just having a bad day.

On good days, of course, neither of these activities feels like work. But the hard days make me think. Labor that doesn't add up to one definitive product but is instead ongoing, unremitting, open-ended, never done—that, too, becomes a labor that can be very hard to show to others or to see.

Formal definitions of labor aside, where else does the term occur in our language, as an idiom or metaphor or phrase?

Note: when we say a "laborer," we tend to mean an unskilled worker.

A now archaic phrase, "the labours of the moon," refers to a lunar eclipse.

Labored breathing, we call it, when we must work to do something that typically requires no effort, no thought.

Labor is also the process of childbirth, an effort that is unpaid and involves sweat and labored breathing and doesn't require any particular skill.

A "labor of love," we call it, when we work hard at something for years despite competing demands and attention and for no compensation other than our ideological commitments or, contra Daniels, for the pleasure we receive from doing the work. A labor of love, by any definition, would then seem to be a contradiction, since love is our only recompense and since the term, the labor-ing of love, is one that disrupts the boundaries between public and private activity that Western culture has used to define the category of "work." A love of love, more like it, or a labor of labor—that is, until the result of love's labor bursts forth.

Take, for example, the experience of emotional labor, which often, though not always, falls to women and is kept in the shadows as an added and typically unrealized expectation of many kinds of public-facing work. Emotional labor is the need to smile and smile and keep up everyone else's morale. Emotional labor can look like the flight attendant who calms terrified passengers when an airplane engine fails, the parent who suppresses personal sadness to help a child, the friend who balances the death of a parent with teaching a classroom full of struggling young adults. Emotional labor doesn't usually qualify for financial compensation, though it lets its recipients borrow a strength from others that we can later, hopefully, pass on.[14]

Note: if, however, we can only see a labor of love after the fact, once the product has been produced, we also must consider how often we see—or fail to see—the process of labor, versus the product of it, from which we intuit the activity that has come before. If the product is invisible or never forthcoming, the work that came before will likely remain invisible, too. But even when the product is visible, we often miss seeing the laborer at work. How much do we really look at the workings of those around us? If a laborer works alone, who is to say that she can actually be seen? Does "labor" describe a theoretical construct, constructed only ever after the fact?

Is work always done by invisible hands?

Adam Smith developed the concept of the invisible hand by considering how hands function and then extrapolating the implications if these hands were unseen. The concept of the invisible hand is attributed to him, but it is important to note that he didn't invent it, in the same way that David Hume would say we didn't invent the Pegasus but created it by combining known ideas about horses with known ideas about wings. Smith, similarly, borrowed the invisible hand, combining an idea about hands and how they function with implications about what it would mean were these hands to be unseen.

People before Smith talked about invisible hands, too. As a phrase, it appears in Shakespeare's play *Macbeth*, when Macbeth calls upon night, "with thy bloody and invisible hand," to "cancel and tear to pieces the great bond that keeps me pale!" (The blood here is either also invisible, or Macbeth, who has already been tortured by the sight of a dagger suspended before him, held in place presumably by some invisible hand, is rehearsing a familiar horror.) Horace Walpole also uses the concept in *The Castle of Otranto* (1764) to describe a Macbeth-style supernatural experience of having a real (as it were) invisible hand frighten his heroine by closing a door. When hands become invisible, life can become scary or confusing as a result.[15]

But Smith actually used the phrase before Walpole, in his never-finished, never-published essay on the "History of Astronomy," written in the 1750s or thereabouts. Here, it describes how the motions of the cosmos confuse an uneducated observer, who can only attribute them superstitiously to the invisible hand of a pagan god. "Hence the origin of Polytheism," Smith asserts, "which ascribes all the irregular events of nature to the favors or displeasure of intelligent, though invisible, beings." So, the earthquake and the eclipse: since the earth should not shake independently or the moon just disappear, those who don't understand these motions create an external, non-natural mover to explain them. They believe, much like Walpole's superstitious characters, that an invisible hand must introduce motion from an outside source.[16]

Some unskilled observers, however, didn't make these supernatural attributions: nature contained many seeming miracles that most ancient people accepted without assuming they relied on an invisible cause. "Fire burns, and water refreshes; heavy bodies descend, and lighter substances fly upward . . . *nor* was the invisible hand of Jupiter ever apprehended to be employed in these matters," Smith explains. Regardless of our level of education or religious beliefs, we often experience the results of actions without seeing their causes, and we sometimes benefit and come to depend upon these actions occurring. By calling attention to such matters, Smith wants to make us aware that life involves many efforts that often pass unseen.[17]

Maybe the pagan observer should wonder more at the workings of gravity. Maybe we all regularly take credit for what are, as Alexander Pope would phrase them, labors "not our own."[18]

Why are we so convinced that the moon labors independently, covered as she is by the invisible hand of night?

Here are some other things that night can hide from public view:

- dirty dishes
- the small dead animal brought inside by a pet
- unfinished homework
- a cockroach (but only one)
- insomnia
- a crying baby
- a nightmare
- depression
- mice or rats
- stars (but only when there are clouds. The cosmos is most visible when the sky is dark.)

After using "the invisible hand" in his "History of Astronomy," Smith recycles the concept twice more.

First, he uses it again in 1759, in *The Theory of Moral Sentiments*. This time, instead of associating the invisible hand with a group of pagan observers from which we set ourselves apart, Smith attributes it to the workings of a divine providence from which we all benefit and in which we all believe. The invisible hand now describes why even the rich who mean to behave in a selfish and rapacious manner end up dividing their goods pretty equally with the poor. They all are led, Smith states, "by an invisible hand to make nearly the same distribution of the necessaries of life."[19]

Seventeen years later, Smith recycles the concept in *The Wealth of Nations* to explain how our free-market economy works. The individual who labors with only a thought to his personal gain in fact acts to benefit the larger economy, since he is "led by an invisible hand to promote an end which was no part of his intention." The reasoning is the same as that in *The Theory of Moral Sentiments*, but the end is now about financial profit or monetary gain.[20]

In these scenarios, Smith has shifted from depicting the "invisible hand" satirically, as something in which educated observers should not believe, to presenting it as a legitimate force in the workings of moral and economic life. In the process, he shifts from viewing his readers as educated observers who can see how less educated others might believe fallaciously in this concept to viewing them as educated observers who don't see the forces moving them, who don't even see that they are being moved.

But, Smith says, we are all being led in this manner. The invisible hand allows us to believe that we are acting in our own self-interest, and, fueled by this (mistaken) belief, we continue acting in the service of the greater good.

As an idiom in our language, "hand" stands in for the concept of activity, an invisible synecdoche affirming the able-bodied notion that hands are our prime movers, responsible for how we manage—that is, *handle*—the responsibilities of our days. We use our hands to build things, just as we use them to write and type. What one hand makes, another hand must grasp (since for Smith, labor had to produce a product you could touch). "Let me give you a hand," we say to someone struggling to complete a task, though Adam Smith obviously never juggled five bags of groceries while shutting a car door with his butt.

Making that laboring hand invisible doesn't necessarily take away its strength. When I was a child, invisible hands would lift me sleeping from my car seat and transport me into bed. Invisible hands hefted a ten-speed bike down my chimney one Christmas and placed it next to our tree.

Adam Smith wanted his hands to be pretty invisible, too. For all the attention he gets for this particular concept, he uses it but sparingly. Three brief mentions, in pages and pages and pages of work.

The more curious question is why he makes the idea visible, at all.

Look at all of you, Smith says, but only in passing. You are being guided; I am guiding you along. But don't look too closely, because our collective blind spots are necessary if this system is to work. It is just—sometimes I need for you to see what I have done. While I'm at it, can I have some tea?

The labors of the moon happen independently, in part because she is engaged in altruistic work. Still, she wouldn't mind some accolades from time to time. It is nice to be told that what you do has value. It is nice to believe that your invisibility supports the growth of others instead of being taken for granted or overlooked.

Adam Smith, as I mentioned, never married, and from the ages of forty-four to fifty-three, he lived with his mother, during which time he was writing *The Wealth of Nations*, explaining how our self-motivated actions are guided invisibly to serve some greater good. One assumes that during this time all his necessaries were taken care of, so that the proponent of the invisible hand was blind to the invisible hand that supports his needs. (The Swedish journalist Katrine Marçal has written thoughtfully on this topic.) It reminds me of the stories of women who used to type their husband's manuscripts, instead of writing up their own.[21]

Production is a result of labor, but you can't have labor without the level above. Does this higher-level management count as work? "Clean your room," I pronounce, to keep myself from being infantilized, to teach my children responsibility, to assert my position in the chain. Still, there are days I find myself crawling on their floor, and my children are just learning to feel guilty about that fact. When the invisible hand emerges, it can be molded in a gesture of reproach.

If I don't see what you do, it is because I believe you love me.

When I don't show you my hands, I love you more than I love myself.

16

NO ROOM OF ONE'S OWN

Homer, Virginia Woolf

During the course of the play the table collects this and that . . . by the end of the play the table has collected an inventory of objects.

—Tom Stoppard, *Arcadia*, 1.2, stage direction

Our dining-room table sits in the middle of our house, though to call it a dining-room table already endows it with an elegance it lacks. The "room" it occupies isn't truly a room but a causeway, a semi-independent space that connects our living room—which doubles as a foyer, which triples as a play area—to our kitchen, to the bathroom hallway, and beyond. It is a dining room because it is the house-space in which we dine; it is a dining-room table because it is the hard surface around which we gather to eat.[1]

Like many a good dining-room table, however, its functions vary. The coffee table, ten steps and one room away, holds toys, notebooks, cups; the built-in desk, sandwiched between the bookshelves on the other wall, supports a printer, folders, and, when I can find them, my sunglasses and keys. Our dining-room table serves as the receptacle for all else: a veritable shrine to abundance, the surface that catches the overflow of the overflow of life. This table is as I imagine Odysseus and Penelope's arboreal bedpost, rooted to the very foundations of our home, displaying accretions in lieu of rings: layers of spilled syrup, wayward marker, paint. It is where we do homework, draw pictures, read stories. It is where we eat pancakes and have Zoom meetings and pay bills. It is also where I often write.

> 10 March, Table: jug of maple syrup; 2 school photos, framed; breakfast plates; pencil sharpener and associated pencils and pens (loose); copy of *Peter Pan*; notepad, various to-do items; copy of *Hamlet*; copy of the collected verses of A. A. Milne; daily planner; vase of assorted roses, new and old; edited collection of scholarly essays (to be reviewed); manila folders and legal pad; child's camera; shoebox diorama; copy of the *New Yorker* (issue number obscured); magic wand (a piece); copy of Virginia Woolf's *A Room of One's Own*; printed essay, "Viva Voce"; essay on Virginia Woolf, "Penelope at Work"; dishtowel; baseball cap[2]

Virginia Woolf may have lamented for me this fact. "A woman must have money and a room of her own if she is to write fiction," Woolf asserts at the outset of her famous essay, an idea her narrator came to while sitting not in such a room but on a river's banks. Indeed, her narrator is subsequently barred from the library that might have furnished such a room, because in her time "ladies are only admitted to the library if accompanied by a [male] Fellow of the College."[3] Between the 1929 publication of this work and my own twenty-first century reflection on it, I see evidence of change: unlike Woolf's narrator, I have job security and a job that I feel pays me fairly for what I do. I have a library at school that admits me and an office at school into which I can go and close the door. I have, occasionally these days, a babysitter that I can hire and even a garage at home into which I can retreat. Still, at the end of the day I spend much of my intellectual life at our table, in a room that is not a room, in a space with no doors to close.

This fact makes me consider everything from the status of feminism to the nature of the writing process. "Women never have half an hour . . . that they can all their own," writes Woolf, quoting Florence Nightingale, describing me.[4] And yet I'm conscious today of a more general frenetic-ness, perhaps symptomatic of the technology and social media that make us all, regardless of gender, susceptible to interruption and distractions that we voluntarily seek out. Family structures are changing too, rendering the interruptions Woolf attributes to women's parenting and domestic duties more gender-neutral, more equally shared.

In frustrated moments as a writer, however, I feel Woolf's resentment of my state. If I were a man, I think, or, if I had more money, more room, more time . . . perhaps I would emerge as Woolf's cryptic Judith Shakespeare, my genius freed from the domestic labor of my life. I dream of that Platonic office—airy, sunlit, still—in which inspiration flourishes, and everything remains organized and neat. I crave more of the privacy that Woolf supports and that she feels women in particular have lacked.

---

12 March, Table: jug of maple syrup; 2 school photos, framed; associated pencils and pens (loose); copy of *Peter Pan*; notepad, blank; copy of *Hamlet*; copy of the collected verses of A. A. Milne; daily planner; vase of assorted roses, new and now very old; box

of pencils (Blackwing, very nice); copy of Virginia Woolf's *A Room of One's Own*; printed essay, "Viva Voce"; essay on Virginia Woolf, "Penelope at Work"; transformer toy; plastic candle; sunglasses; clothespin with paper face attached; coffee cup; iPhone; dish of salt

---

Interruption, Woolf asserts, has shaped the types of literature that women write. One of my favorite Woolf contentions is that interruption has pushed women more frequently toward the crafting of "prose and fiction" rather than poetry or plays, since when one is writing fiction, "less concentration is required."[5] Yet that women could craft even fiction under such conditions amazes Woolf, too. She describes Jane Austen as doing all her writing in sitting rooms, subject to casual interruptions, driven to hide her manuscript under blotting paper every time a visitor entered the room. Austen's contemporary Maria Edgeworth also wrote in this manner, surrounded by the siblings and half-siblings who made up her father's large brood (twenty-two children he had finally, by four different women, a man prolific in every sense). These women wrote through chaos, though Austen and Edgeworth, like Woolf, never had kids of their own. In my life, I've finished many a memo, reader's report, work email, lesson plan, and book review in similar manner, at the dining-room table, tilting my computer screen away from my boys. (This chapter, too, their activities and presence in its very warp and woof.)

Interestingly, my multitasking has not yet transformed me into an Austen, much less a poet. It has, however, moved me to consider how the condition of "interruption" that Woolf indicates as characteristic of a woman's life is not inimical to creativity, full-stop. Far from lamenting the narrative of chaos that surrounds them, women writers often mourn the isolating effects of the writing life: "I remember once . . . . I was just in the solitary, melancholy state you describe," Edgeworth writes to another woman-writer friend, "and I used to feel relieved and glad when the tea-urn came into the silent room, to give me a sensation by the sound of its boiling."[6] "Would *Pride and Prejudice* have been a better novel," Woolf muses, if Jane Austen had not had to do all her writing in a communal space? Interestingly, she feels that it would not.[7]

I have these musings about my own writing, too. For all my moments of resentment, I know I've wasted many an hour solo, in a room with a door that is tightly closed. I know, too, that I rarely feel more lonely than when I am uninspired. Writing is hard work, even when conditions are "perfect," and perfect conditions have a way of making me feel guilty when the work is hard. What does it mean for a writer when, given time and opportunity, the words still won't come? How much easier to attribute a lull in writing to external agency or another's needs: the fact that the washing machine has gone off, or a child is crying, or a cup has spilled.

---

13 March, Table: jug of maple syrup; 2 school photos, framed; copy of *Peter Pan*; notepad, blank; copy of *Hamlet*; vase of assorted roses, some dead; box of pencils (Blackwing, very nice); copy of Virginia Woolf's *A Room of One's Own*; printed essay, "Viva Voce"; essay on Virginia Woolf, "Penelope at Work"; coloring book and markers; catalogues: Athleta, REI; sight-word flashcards, scattered; clothespin with paper face attached; assorted bills (dentist office); rose petals; dish of salt

---

Interruptions, the very structure of Woolf's essay suggests, are not always occasions to be mourned. Poetry lovers may regret that Coleridge, writing "Kubla Khan" in a delirious, opium-induced haze, was interrupted midthought by "a person on business from Porlock" and never able afterward to complete the poem. Yet for every Coleridge there is a David Hume, who finds himself so tortured by an isolation-inspired "delirium" that he preaches the benefits of dinner, play, and backgammon for his philosophizing, not to mention his overall quality of life. Ludwig Wittgenstein, whose biography I read when myself in a flu-inspired, fever-induced state, would knock off at the end of the day to watch westerns and let his brain recharge for the next day's work. (Intriguingly, this is the main fact I remember about him, once my own delirium had passed.) Wordsworth toggled between wandering lonely as a cloud and the "joint labour" of his friendship with Coleridge, his bouts of writing interspersed with their famous, frequent walks.[8]

There can be something maddening, these examples suggest, about isolated focus—something maddening and also punitive about a room of one's own. Scan the headlines for the relationship between loneliness and mental illness. Recall the titular yellow wallpaper that haunts the protagonist of Charlotte Perkins Gilman's short story; recall the fits inspired in Jane by the Red Room in *Jane Eyre*. Consider Ramona, of the Beverly Cleary books, who finds herself tortured by the transition from a shared room with her sister to a bedroom meant for her alone. Why else does Frances the badger persistently sneak out of her bedroom in *Bedtime for Frances*, the childhood story designed to revive insomnia in adults? Why else do children ask to sleep with the door ajar? Mary Shelley cues us to find Victor Frankenstein's "workshop of filthy creation" suspect precisely because it is a "solitary chamber," isolated from all other apartments at the top of the house.[9]

The difference between Woolf's room and these examples, I reflect, is the same as the difference between Wordsworth's or

Wittgenstein's situation and my own: do we experience isolation (or its converse, interruption) by compulsion or by choice?

---

13 March, Table, night: jug of maple syrup; 2 school photos, framed; copy of *Peter Pan*; notepad, blank; copy of *Hamlet*; vase of assorted roses, dead ones now removed; box of pencils (Blackwing, very nice); copy of Virginia Woolf's *A Room of One's Own*; printed essay, "Viva Voce"; essay on Virginia Woolf, "Penelope at Work"; coloring book and markers; phonics worksheets (scattered, incomplete); iPhone headphones; fork and paper napkin; dishtowel; dish of salt

---

Writing, I think, writing these words while the boys are in the shower and bath, doesn't always require isolation so much as produce it.

---

14 March, Table: jug of maple syrup; 2 school photos, framed; copy of *Peter Pan*; notepad, blank; copy of *Hamlet*; empty vase; box of pencils (Blackwing, very nice); copy of Virginia Woolf's *A Room of One's Own*; printed essay, "Viva Voce"; essay on Virginia Woolf, "Penelope at Work"; coloring book and markers; one breakfast plate; copy of *Frankenstein*; Kleenex, lightly used; coffee cup; rose petals; dishtowel; dish of salt

---

I've finally read that dining-room-table essay on Virginia Woolf. I tracked it down for the subject matter and because it was written by someone I know. I also flagged it for its title: "Penelope at Work." What does Penelope, the heroine from Homer's classical epic *The Odyssey*, have to say about the twentieth-century conditions of feminism outlined in *A Room of One's Own*? One connection lies in the designation of women's labor. "Take up your own work, / the loom and the distaff," Penelope is twice told. Go back to those domestic tools of weaving and spinning, she is told by men, go back to that inner sanctum in which these works take place—though those tools also represent the key metaphors for the telling of tales.[10]

Penelope is of course famous for her weaving, or, more accurately, she is famous for tricking her suitors by undoing her weaving every night. I'll marry one of you, she tells them, once I've finished making my father-in-law a funeral shroud. And so for years, she weaves during the day and unpicks what she has done every night. By doing so she postpones the need to choose a husband; she also postpones, I've always thought, the threat of death.

The other connection to Woolf's essay is how the weaving and the trickery happen in some private room, so that Penelope, although following orders, isn't exactly banished or confined. Making—and unmaking—occur in her mysterious boudoir, in a manner that the common sitting rooms of Austen and Edgeworth could never support. She's trapped with her domestic labor, yet her domestic labor becomes the creative labor I now miss. Maybe, she tells me, I can reclaim the work I resent as material for my other work. Maybe I can reclaim as privacy, or for narrative inspiration, an isolation that would otherwise feel enforced.

In the contemporary essay on Woolf that I read, the movement of Penelope's weaving—two steps forward, two steps back—also finally becomes emblematic of "a woman's work which is never done." These days, as I juggle parenting with teaching my students, emailing my colleagues, and keeping my refrigerator stocked and my dishes mostly clean, the phrase hits especially hard. There is something in this idiom of the conditions of interruption, of Jane Austen's blotting paper, of how the work of domesticity takes precedence over the other "work" that a woman must hide. There is also something in this phrase of Woolf's lament, as if without the disruptions, the extra chores, the daily-ness of laundry, lunches, teaching, baths, something else might become complete. Yet there is something wonderful in this phrasing, too: something that captures the consistency of parenting or of devotion to one's art. Penelope's loom, hidden away in Woolf's interior, contains a movement of the ocean, with its waves that come and go and come again. The interruptions of life are as transient as its moments of isolation. If weaving is writing and writing is weaving, then how much more hopeful to say that it will be ongoing, without teleology, without morbidity, without end.[11]

---

16 March, Table, night: jug of maple syrup; 2 school photos, framed; daily planner; notepad, blank; vase of roses (pink) with branches of rosemary, intermixed; copy of Virginia Woolf's *A Room of One's Own*; 2 placemats, Star Wars, one ripped; copy of *Alice in Wonderland*; book on Lewis Carroll; copy of *Emma*, very old; coloring book and gel markers; sunglasses; potholder; dish of salt

---

NOTES

INTRODUCTION:
LONELINESS AND THE LITERARY LIFE

1. For the technique of using serial installments, Post-it notes or otherwise, to narrate in real-time a sequence of events, see authors such as Samuel Richardson, Charles Dickens, and Laurence Sterne.
2. Deidre Shauna Lynch, *Loving Literature: A Cultural History* (Chicago: University of Chicago Press, 2015), 4.
3. John Milton, *Paradise Lost*, ed. David Scott Kastan (Cambridge: Hackett, 2005), 12:648–49.
4. For some reflections on shifting reading habits during the pandemic, see my appearance on the podcast *Office Hours*, https://www.uscannenbergmedia.com/2021/03/30/office-hours-with-english-professor-emily-anderson/.
5. Zadie Smith, *Intimations: Six Essays* (New York: Penguin, 2020), 19–20.
6. I read the statistic on adult reading habits in a 2022 issue of *The Week, Junior*; it is also cited here: https://news.gallup.com/poll/388541/americans-reading-fewer-books-past.aspx.
7. For one example of how society questions the importance of the writing life, see Nathan Heller, "The End of the English Major," *New Yorker*, February 27, 2023, 28–39, https://www.newyorker.com/magazine/2023/03/06/the-end-of-the-english-major.
8. Toni Morrison, "The Site of Memory," in *Inventing the Truth: The Art and Craft of Memoir*, 2nd ed., ed. William Zinsser (Boston: Houghton Mifflin, 1995), 100–1.

9. The quotation from Ralph Ellison appears in his introduction to the essay collection *Shadow and Act* (New York: Vintage, 1995), xx.
10. Lewis Carroll, *Through the Looking Glass*, in *Alice in Wonderland*, ed. Donald J. Gray, 3rd ed. (New York: Norton, 2013), 124.
11. Carroll, *Through the Looking Glass*, 123.
12. Carroll, *Through the Looking Glass*, 108.
13. Carroll, *Through the Looking Glass*, 108.
14. The "carnal versus courtly" book lover reference is from Anne Fadiman, "Never Do That to a Book," in *Ex Libris: Confessions of a Common Reader* (New York: Farrar, Straus and Giroux, 1998), 37–44. My now-rumpled copy was gifted to me while I was teaching at boarding school by my Latin teacher friend MaryLiz. Her "words on a flyleaf" (another essay in the collection by Fadiman) describe me as "the fretful paper writer," a Homeric epithet that still applies.

1. THE SHADOW LIFE OF BOOKS: WILLIAM SHAKESPEARE, WILLIAM HAZLITT, ALEXANDER CHEE

1. This chapter first appeared under the title "Shadow Work: The Secret Life of Academic Books," *The Rambling*, issue 1, July 16, 2018, https://the-rambling.com/2018/07/16/shadow-work/. For context on the shadow as a literary trope, see the wonderful John Hollander, edited by the equally wonderful Kenneth Gross, *The Substance of Shadow: A Darkening Trope in Poetic History* (Chicago: University of Chicago Press, 2016). My epigraph is from Alexander Chee, "The Autobiography of My Novel," in *How to Write an Autobiographical Novel* (New York: Mariner, 2018), 217.
2. Emily Hodgson Anderson, *Shakespeare and the Legacy of Loss* (Ann Arbor: University of Michigan Press, 2018).
3. Alexander Pope, "An Epistle to Dr. Arbuthnot," in *Selected Poetry of Alexander Pope*, ed. Pat Rodgers (Oxford: Oxford University Press, 1998), 93–105.
4. See Laurence Sterne's dedication to *Tristram Shandy*, ed. Howard Anderson (New York: Norton, 1980). For more references to Sterne's life, see Wilbur Lucius Cross, *The Life and Times of Laurence Sterne* (New York: Macmillan, 1909).

1. THE SHADOW LIFE OF BOOKS ⌘ 225

5. See John Hemings and Henry Condell, "To the Great Variety of Readers," in *The Norton Facsimile: The First Folio of Shakespeare*, prep. Charlton Hinman (New York: Norton, 1996), 7.
6. See Ben Jonson, *Timber, or Discoveries Made Upon Men and Matter*, ed. Felix E. Schelling (Boston: Ginn & Co., 1892), 23.
7. For more on the Shakespearean authorship controversy, see James Shapiro, *Contested Will: Who Wrote Shakespeare?* (New York: Simon and Schuster, 2010). Adding to said controversy is the fact that the cover layout for Shapiro's book juxtaposes the question of the subtitle, "who wrote Shakespeare?," with the words "JAMES SHAPIRO" in large font.
8. Freud connects Shakespeare's grief on the death of his son to the composition of *Hamlet* in *The Interpretation of Dreams*, in *The Basic Writings of Sigmund Freud*, ed. and trans. A. A. Brill (New York: Random House, 1966). See too Stephen Greenblatt for one example of a critic who finds Shakespeare's autobiography in his work: "To understand who Shakespeare was, it is important to follow the verbal traces he left." Stephen Greenblatt, *Will in the World: How Shakespeare Became Shakespeare* (New York: Norton, 2004), 14.
9. The Aphra Behn quotation comes from the Dedication to *Oroonoko*, ed. Paul Salzman (Oxford: Oxford University Press, 1994).
10. For information on how academics address the writing process, see William Germano's *Getting It Published: A Guide for Scholars and Anyone Else Serious About Serious Books*, 3rd ed. (Chicago: University of Chicago Press, 2016); see too, now in its second edition, his *From Dissertation to Book* (Chicago: University of Chicago Press, 2013). These are wonderful resources, and I studied them both fastidiously. Unfortunately, neither saved me from the thinking and writing required to do what both advise. On the proliferation of MFA programs, see Mark McGurl, *The Program Era: Postwar Fiction and the Rise of Creative Writing* (Cambridge, MA: Harvard University Press, 2009).
11. See Chee, "How to Write an Autobiographical Novel," https://www.buzzfeed.com/alexanderchee/how-to-write-an-autobiographical-novel. He later revises the quoted sentence to read, "you **like** the child who believes they are invisible," suggesting that common slippage between affinity and affection: that we like what we are like. Chee, *How to Write an Autobiographical Novel*, 246; see too "Shaking Hands," chapter 4 in this volume.

12. The Wordsworth quotation is from the 1805 version of *The Prelude*, ed. Jonathan Wordsworth (New York: Norton, 1979), 1.645–47.
13. Jonson, *Timber*, 23. For reflections on Shakespearean duds, see Victoria Blake, "Shakespeare's Worst Line," in "On Writers and Writing," https://victoriablakewriter.wordpress.com/2016/01/08/shakespeares-worst-line/.
14. William Shakespeare, *The Winter's Tale*, ed. Frances E. Dolan (New York: Penguin, 2017), 3.3.64.
15. William Shakespeare, *King Lear*, ed. Stephen Orgel (New York: Penguin, 2000), 5.3.265.
16. Shakespeare, *King Lear*, 5.3.217.
17. For the interpretation of Odysseus's name, see Robert Fagles's translation of *The Odyssey* (New York: Penguin, 1996), 19.464. For the translation of Megapenthes, see D. S. Carne-Ross, "The Poem of Odysseus," in *The Odyssey*, trans. Robert Fitzgerald (New York: Farrar, Straus and Giroux, 1998), xv.
18. Blake's reflection on Milton is quoted in Leopold Damrosch, *Eternity's Sunrise: The Imaginative World of William Blake* (New Haven, CT: Yale University Press, 2015), 8. It originally appears in an 1800 letter he wrote to his friend John Flaxman.
19. William Hazlitt, "On Play-going and on Some of our Old Actors," in *Hazlitt on Theatre*, ed. William Archer and Robert Lowe (New York: Hill and Wang, 1895), 144–45.
20. William Hazlitt, "On Actors and Acting," in *Hazlitt on Theatre*, ed. William Archer and Robert Lowe (New York: Hill and Wang, 1895), 136.

2. READING TO A CHILD: ROALD DAHL, SHAKESPEARE, T. H. WHITE

1. This chapter originally appeared in the *Los Angeles Review of Books*, October 27, 2019, https://lareviewofbooks.org/article/reading-to-a-child/. I'm citing William Shakespeare, *King Lear*, ed. Stephen Orgel (New York: Penguin, 2000), in my epigraph. The Dahl quotation is from Roald Dahl, *The Witches* (New York: Random House, 2013), 7. For background on Dahl, I referenced Jeremy Treglown, *Roald Dahl:*

2. READING TO A CHILD ∽ 227

A Biography (New York: Houghton Mifflin, 1995), as well as Jenny Diski's review of this biography, "Stinker," in the *London Review of Books* 16, no. 8 (April 1994). I also read Roald Dahl, *Boy* (New York: Viking, 2010) and *Going Solo* (New York: Viking, 2010). On Dahl's adult writing, see David Ulin, "Roald Dahl's Twisted, Overlooked Stories for Adults," *New Yorker*, July 21, 2016), https://www.newyorker.com/books/page-turner/roald-dahls-twisted-overlooked-stories-for-adults.

2. Dahl, *The Witches*, 10.
3. Adam Gopnik, "Grim Fairy Tales," *New Yorker*, November 18, 1996, 96–102, https://www.newyorker.com/magazine/1996/11/18/grim-fairy-tales.
4. Roald Dahl, *Matilda* (New York: Random House, 2013).
5. Bruno Bettelheim, *The Uses of Enchantment: The Meaning and Importance of Fairy Tales* (New York: Vintage, 1989), 7.
6. "Chloe Wofford Talks About Toni Morrison," in *Toni Morrison: Conversations*, ed. Carolyn C. Denard (Jackson: University Press of Mississippi, 2008), 98–106. On making peace with the ugliness of the artists that one loves, see too Claire Dederer, *Monsters: A Fan's Dilemma* (New York: Knopf, 2023).
7. "Chloe Wofford Talks About Toni Morrison," 101.
8. Dahl, *The Witches*, 10.
9. Stanley Cavell, "The Avoidance of Love," in *Must We Mean What We Say?* (Cambridge: Cambridge University Press, 2002), 267–353. This is one of my favorite essays on *King Lear*.
10. T. H. White, *The Once and Future King* (New York: Ace, 2011), 253–54.
11. White, *The Once and Future King*, 256.
12. White, *The Once and Future King*, 263.
13. On the benefits and effects of rereading, see Patricia Meyer Spacks, *On Rereading* (Cambridge, MA: Harvard University Press, 2011). Other books on rereading that I read (and reread) include Vivian Gornick, *Unfinished Business: Notes of a Chronic Re-reader* (New York: Farrar, Straus and Giroux, 2020); Rebecca Mead, *The Road to Middlemarch: My Life with George Eliot* (New York: Granta, 2014); Laura Miller, *The Magician's Book: A Skeptic's Adventures in Narnia* (New

York: Little, Brown, 2008); and Anne Fadiman, ed., *Rereadings: Seventeen Writers Revisit Books They Love* (New York: Farrar, Straus and Giroux, 2006).

14. The professor is known particularly for his biography of Alexander Pope: Maynard Mack, *Alexander Pope: A Life* (New York: Norton, 1988); see also Maynard Mack, *Everybody's Shakespeare* (Lincoln: University of Nebraska Press, 1994). I was an early graduate student when I was reading to the professor, far from choosing any research specialty of my own, so it is only coincidence that I ended up working on the two topics of study—Shakespeare and eighteenth-century literature—for which the professor was revered. Any opportunity I had to learn from him about those topics was lost, since we only talked about how we enjoyed poems.

15. William Shakespeare, *King Lear*, ed. Stephen Orgel (New York: Penguin Random House, 2000), 1.1.160–61.

16. Wallace Stevens, "The Snow Man," https://www.poetryfoundation.org/poems/45235/the-snow-man-56d224a6d4e90.

17. Catherine Gallagher covers antinovel sentiment in *Nobody's Story: The Vanishing Act of Women Writers in the Marketplace, 1670–1820* (Berkeley: University of California Press, 1994).

18. Gallagher, *Nobody's Story*, 277.

19. For the background on reading to children, see Maria Tartar, *The Enchanted Hunters: The Power of Stories in Childhood* (New York: Norton, 2009). Tartar takes her title from *Lolita*, where it describes Humbert Humbert in what Tartar calls "a somewhat unsavory manner" (27). Tartar means to reclaim the term to describe child readers, though I keep getting sidetracked by the image of the story reader as Humbert Humbert. Seth Lerer, *Children's Literature: A Reader's History, from Aesop to Harry Potter* (Chicago: University of Chicago Press, 2009), is also very good on children's literature, and Laura Miller, *The Magician's Book: A Skeptic's Adventures in Narnia* (New York: Little, Brown, 2008), is terrific on the disorienting experience of revisiting a book you loved as a child.

20. Tartar, *The Enchanted Hunters*, 167.

21. Samuel Taylor Coleridge, "Frost at Midnight," in *The Complete Poems*, ed. William Keach (New York: Penguin, 1997), 231.

22. My dad's reading of the snowball as synecdoche appears in John A. Hodgson, *Coleridge, Shelley, and Transcendental Inquiry: Rhetoric*,

Argument, Metapsychology (Lincoln: University of Nebraska Press, 1989), xi. I informed him at the time of the book's writing that a title shouldn't contain more than two words of fourteen letters.

23. For transitional spaces and objects, see D. W. Winnicott, "Transitional Objects and Transitional Phenomena: A Study of the First Not-Me Possession," *International Journal of Psychoanalysis* 34 (1953): 89–97; see too Adam Phillips, *Winnicott* (New York: Penguin, 1988), 117–18.

3. THE DETECTIVE'S MIND: ARTHUR CONAN DOYLE

1. My epigraph comes from Sir Arthur Conan Doyle, "A Scandal in Bohemia," in *The Complete Sherlock Holmes*, 2 vols. (New York: Barnes & Noble Classics, 2003), 1:189. All quotations from the Sherlock Holmes stories will be from this edition.
2. Doyle, "The Musgrave Ritual," 1:461.
3. Doyle, "The Musgrave Ritual," 1:461; Doyle, *The Sign of the Four*, 1:100.
4. Doyle, "The Musgrave Ritual," 1:461.
5. For comparisons between the understanding and the eye, I consulted my father's annotated copy of John Locke, *Essay Concerning Human Understanding*, ed. Alexander Campbell Fraser, 2 vols. (New York: Dover, 1959), 1:8.
6. Doyle, "A Scandal in Bohemia," 1:189.
7. Doyle, "The Adventure of the Cardboard Box," 2:381.
8. Poe's detective Dupin performs this trick of "mind reading" in "The Murders in the Rue Morgue," in *The Collected Tales and Poems of Edgar Allan Poe* (New York: Modern Library, 1992).
9. For more on Poe's fascination with "secret writing," see John A. Hodgson, "Decoding Poe? Poe, W. B. Tyler, and Cryptography," *Journal of English and Germanic Philology*, 92, no. 4 (October 1993): 523–34.
10. Doyle, "The Musgrave Ritual," 1:462.
11. Doyle, "The Musgrave Ritual," 1:462.
12. For a brilliant reading of "The Musgrave Ritual," see Peter Brooks, *Reading for the Plot: Design and Intention in Narrative* (Cambridge, MA: Harvard University Press, 1992), 23–28.
13. Doyle, *Sign of the Four*, 1:100.

14. See Alfred, Lord Tennyson, "Ulysses," in *Tennyson's Poetry*, ed. Robert W. Hill Jr. (New York: Norton, 1999), 82.
15. Doyle, "The Adventure of the Abbey Grange," 2:191.
16. Note how cross-references create a feedback loop, so that the reading process need never end (see too "No Room of One's Own").
17. I teach my students from Malcolm Heath's translation of the *Poetics* (New York: Penguin, 1996). Heath, too, asserts in his introduction that "what we read today are notes . . . and are consequently very difficult to understand" (vii). I love the tone of many of Heath's annotations ("a perplexing statement . . . the text is in a hopeless muddle here" [57n83, 92]), but I think my favorite annotation is the simple declarative sentence: "No one knows what this paragraph means" (55n67). I think what I like is the action of using an endnote, usually reserved for scholarly pontificating, to announce, in a pontificating style, that the translator knows for certain that nobody knows.
18. I've read much of my father's work on Doyle, but the essay I'm specifically thinking of for this piece is his overview "Arthur Conan Doyle (1859–1930)," in *A Companion to Crime Fiction*, ed. Charles J. Rzepka and Lee Horsley (West Sussex: Blackwell, 2010), 390–402.
19. For thoughts on clues, vis-à-vis Holmes, see the brilliant Carlo Ginzburg, "Clues: Roots of an Evidential Paradigm," trans. John and Anne C. Tedeschi, in *Clues, Myths, and the Historical Method* (Baltimore, MD: Johns Hopkins University Press, 1986), 96–125.
20. My preferred copy of *Joseph Andrews* is a 1961 Riverside edition, edited by Martin C. Battestin, once owned by my dad.
21. All quotations from Doyle, *A Study in Scarlet*, 1:14–15.

4. SHAKING HANDS: LUDWIG WITTGENSTEIN, PERCIVAL EVERETT

1. Wittgenstein's idea of the language game appears in his *Philosophical Investigations*, which I read as translated by G. E. M Anscombe (Oxford: Blackwell, 2001).
2. *Sir Charles Grandison* did for a time exist in a paperback one-volume Oxford World's Classics edition, as edited by Jocelyn Harris. I currently own a three-volume edition of the novel, also edited by Jocelyn

Harris, and published in 1972 by Oxford University Press. A recent four-volume edition of the novel just came out with Cambridge University Press, in 2022. For more on the quest to obtain this novel, see Sarah Raff's recent review of the four-volume Cambridge edition, in *Eighteenth-Century Studies* 57, no. 2 (Winter 2024): 271–73.

3. Griffin's *Black Like Me* was first published in 1961 by Houghton-Mifflin. I'm quoting here from the updated version (San Antonio, TX: Wings, 2004), ix. The retrospective essay I mention is by Percival Everett, "Chemically Darkened Like Me" (or, as he remembers the title, "White Skin, Black Masks"), and it appears in *Oxford American: New South Journalism* 78 (Fall 2012): 132–33.

4. The Rita Felski reference to shock occurs in her *Uses of Literature* (Oxford: Wiley-Blackwell, 2008).

5. The beetle-in-the-box reference occurs again in Wittgenstein's *Philosophical Investigations*, as part of his discussion of "private language," or forms of language comprehensible by only a single individual. For a great biography of Wittgenstein, see Roy Monk, *Ludwig Wittgenstein: The Duty of Genius* (New York: Penguin, 1991). See too my thoughts on Wittgenstein in "No Room of One's Own," chapter 16 in this volume.

6. For some amazing meditations on living statues, see Kenneth Gross, *The Dream of the Moving Statue* (University Park: Pennsylvania State University Press, 1992).

7. For how mimicry becomes menace, see Homi K. Bhabha, "Of Mimicry and Man: The Ambivalence of Colonial Discourse," *Discipleship: A Special Issue on Psychoanalysis* 28 (Spring 1984): 125–33, later reprinted in his book *The Location of Culture* (New York: Routledge, 1994). The Derek Walcott quotation occurs in his play *Pantomime* and is included in *Crosswinds: An Anthology of Black Dramatists in the Diaspora*, ed. William B. Branch (Bloomington: Indiana University Press, 1993): 130–61.

8. For the history of the first Black actor to play Black parts, see William Torbert Leonard, *Masquerade in Black* (Metuchen, NJ: Scarecrow, 1986); and Bernth Lindfors, *Ira Aldridge: The Early Years, 1807–1833* (Rochester, NY: University of Rochester Press, 2011).

9. For the account of Booth wiping makeup off his face, see Philip H. Highfill Jr. et al., *A Biographical Dictionary of Actors, Actresses, Musicians,*

Dancers, Managers, and Other Stage Personnel in London, 1660–1800, 16 vols. (Carbondale: Southern Illinois University Press, 1973–93), 10:211–12. For the account of James Quin, see Francis Gentleman, *The Dramatic Censor: Or, Critical Companion* (London: J. Bell, 1770), 1:152. For other accounts of early modern performances of Black roles, see Virginia Mason Vaughn, *Performing Blackness on English Stages, 1500–1800* (Cambridge: Cambridge University Press, 2005).

10. For background on blackface performance in the States, see, among others, Eric Lott, *Love and Theft: Blackface Minstrelsy and the American Working Class* (1993; Oxford: Oxford University Press, 2013).
11. See https://exhibition.mixedmuseum.org.uk/museum/timeline/paul-robeson-and-peggy-ashcroft.
12. The interviews I was reading are included in Vladimir Nabokov, *Strong Opinions* (New York: Vintage, 1973).
13. Thanks to Sarah Kareem for the tip about manicures and loneliness.
14. Performative speech acts were first described by J. L. Austin, *How to Do Things with Words* (Cambridge, MA: Harvard University Press, 1975).

5. POOL OF TEARS: LEWIS CARROLL

1. See Sarah Hart's wonderful *Once Upon a Prime: The Wondrous Connections Between Mathematics and Literature* (New York: Flatiron, 2023) for more on the myriad points of contact between literature and math.
2. I am quoting here from Lewis Carroll, *Alice in Wonderland* and *Through the Looking Glass*, both in *Alice in Wonderland*, ed. Donald J. Gray, 3rd ed. (New York: Norton, 2013). Other books I consulted for this essay include Gillian Beer, *Alice in Space: The Sideways Victorian World of Lewis Carroll* (Chicago: University of Chicago Press, 2016); Jenny Woolf, *The Mystery of Lewis Carroll: Discovering the Whimsical, Thoughtful, and Sometimes Lonely Man Who Created "Alice in Wonderland"* (New York: St. Martin's Griffin, 2011); and Mark J. Davies, *Alice in Waterland: Lewis Carroll and the River Thames in Oxford* (Oxford: Signal, 2010). For thoughts on how a focus on trauma has affected the recent reading and writing of fiction, see Parul Sehgal, "The Case Against the Trauma Plot," *New Yorker*, December 27, 2021, https://www.newyorker.com/magazine/2022/01/03/the-case-against-the-trauma-plot.

5. POOL OF TEARS ∞ 233

3. Carroll, *Alice in Wonderland*, 8–9.
4. Carroll, *Alice in Wonderland*, 17.
5. Herman Melville, *Moby-Dick* (New York: Penguin, 1992), 452.
6. Melville, *Moby-Dick*, 452.
7. My copy of Samuel Taylor Coleridge's *The Rime of the Ancient Mariner* is an ancient edition (broken spine, mixed-up pages) edited by Martin Gardner, with illustrations by Gustave Doré (New York: Meridian, 1965). It contains my father's marginalia ("how? why?") and a Xeroxed copy of Baudelaire's poem "The Albatross" that I tucked inside the front cover when I was teaching both poems to high school students.
8. Carroll, *Alice in Wonderland*, 10.
9. See Stuart Dodgson Collingwood, *The Life and Letters of Lewis Carroll* (London: T. Fisher Unwin, 1898), 173.
10. William Shakespeare, *King Lear*, ed. Stephen Orgel (New York: Penguin Random House, 2000), 4.6.194–95.
11. For the full quotation, see Kenneth Grahame, *The Wind in the Willows* (New York: Charles Scribner and Sons, 1908), 4. I also consulted Inga Moore's illustrated and abridged version of Kenneth Grahame's *The Wind in the Willows* (Eastbourne: Gardners, 2000), gifted to my oldest son by Melissa Farman, who is also the Parisian friend I quote in "Pioneer Girl," chapter 13 in this volume.
12. The actual title is "I wandered lonely as a cloud . . .". William Wordsworth, https://www.poetryfoundation.org/poems/45521/i-wandered-lonely-as-a-cloud.
13. Carroll, *Through the Looking Glass*, 101. Also quoted in Davies, *Alice in Waterland*, 14.
14. Carroll, *Through the Looking Glass*, 153.
15. Mark Twain, *The Adventures of Huckleberry Finn* (New York: Sterling Children's Books, 2006), 122.
16. I used the "Pooh's Library" box set of four books (*Winnie-The-Pooh, The House at Pooh Corner, When We Were Very Young, Now We Are Six*) published by Dutton in 1988, which I purchased for my children to replace an older box set of my own copies left at my parents' house far away. The quotations are from *The House at Pooh Corner* (New York: Dutton, 1988), 92.

17. Twain, *Huckleberry Finn*, 122.
18. Ernest Hemmingway, *The Old Man and the Sea* (New York: Scribner, 1980), 28.
19. Milne, *House at Pooh Corner*, 92.
20. Edmund Spenser, "Amoretti LXXV," https://www.poetryfoundation.org/poems/45189/amoretti-lxxv-one-day-i-wrote-her-name.
21. I have many copies of *Tristram Shandy*, but I cite from my teaching copy for this essay, the old Norton critical edition edited by Howard Anderson (New York: Norton, 1980), 237.
22. William Shakespeare, *Hamlet*, ed. A. R. Braunmuller (New York: Penguin, 2001), 4.7.211–12.

6. OBEDIENCE TRAINING: JOHN MILTON, WILLIAM KOEHLER

1. This chapter originally appeared in the *Los Angeles Review of Books*, March 20, 2021, https://lareviewofbooks.org/article/obedience-training/.
2. For this chapter, I consulted David Scott Kastan's edition of John Milton, *Paradise Lost* (Cambridge: Hackett, 2005), which is in turn based upon the classic edition, *John Milton: Complete Poems and Major Prose*, ed. Merritt Y. Hughes (New York: Odyssey, 1957). These quotations come from 9.235–382.
3. The two William Koehler books I cite are *The Koehler Method of Dog Training: Certified Techniques by Movieland's Most Experienced Dog Trainer* (New York: Howell Book House, 1962) and *The Koehler Method of Open Obedience for Ring, Home, and Field* (New York: Howell Book House, 1970).
4. For the quotations, see https://www.koehlerdogtraining.com.
5. Koehler, *The Koehler Method of Dog Training*, 11.
6. Koehler, *The Koehler Method of Open Obedience*, 96.
7. Koehler, *The Koehler Method of Dog Training*, 36.
8. Milton, *Paradise Lost*, 3.117–19.
9. Milton, *Paradise Lost*, 3.99.
10. Milton, *Paradise Lost*, 9.26.
11. Milton, *Paradise Lost*, 3.41–42, 7.27.

7. PERFECTION AND PLATONIC LOVE: PLATO, ARISTOTLE

1. The Platonic theory of forms comes up in several different dialogues, among them *The Symposium*. My own first exposure to the relationship between artistic performance and the region of forms came via the Platonic dialogue *Ion*, perhaps not coincidentally the shortest of all the Platonic dialogues, which I read for the first time in Hazard Adams, *Critical Theory Since Plato* (New York: Harcourt Brace Jovanovich, 1971).
2. For the theory of the family romance, see Sigmund Freud, "Family Romances," in *The Standard Edition of the Complete Psychological Works of Sigmund Freud*, vol. 9, *1906–1909* (London: Hogarth, 1959), 235–42.
3. "The Allegory of the Cave" can be found lots of places; I referenced it in my epigraph as translated by Shawn Eyer (Plumbstone, 2016), https://scholar.harvard.edu/files/seyer/files/plato_republic_514b-518d_allegory-of-the-cave.pdf; and in the chapter as translated by Paul Shorey, in *Plato: Collected Dialogues*, ed. Edith Hamilton and Huntington Cairns (Princeton, NJ: Princeton University Press, 2005), 575–844.
4. Plato, *Republic*, 748.
5. For references to *The Symposium*, I used the Penguin Classics version translated and edited by Christopher Gill (London: Penguin, 1999).
6. The philosopher-colleague I cite is Edwin McCann. The quotation is from Plato, *Symposium*, 26.
7. Most translators read Aristophanes as explaining that we've been "cut in half like a flatfish," which is how Gill translates the line, with the sense that a flatfish or flounder looks like a whole fish that has been cut in half (*Symposium*, 24). "Hole-y love," my poet-friend David St. John called it; thanks to David for reading the whole of this work.

8. (AN ASIDE): SHAKESPEARE

1. For the tidbit about actors possessing only their part ("their roll") of the script, see Simon Palfrey and Tiffany Stern, *Shakespeare in Parts* (Oxford: Oxford University Press, 2007).

2. I'm quoting in this chapter from William Shakespeare, *Hamlet*, ed. A. R. Braunmuller (New York: Penguin, 2001).
3. For definitions of soliloquy, see "soliloquy," etymology and definitions 1 and 2, *OED*. See too Morris Arnold, *The Soliloquies of Shakespeare: A Study in Technic* (New York: Columbia University Press, 1911); Wolfgang Clemen, *Shakespeare's Soliloquies* (Cambridge: Cambridge University Press, 1964); and James Hirsch, *Shakespeare and the History of Soliloquies* (London: Associated University Presses, 2003). For connections between soliloquy and free indirect discourse, and to my own essay on Jane Austen ("The One and Only Jane"), I'm indebted to Brad Pasanek, "Staging Thought" (paper delivered at the annual meeting for the American Society of Eighteenth-Century Studies, San Antonio, TX, March 2012), and written remarks shared courtesy of the author. The French writer Jean-Francois Marmontel also claimed, "il est tout naturel de se parler à soi-même" (quoted in Arnold, *The Soliloquies of Shakespeare*, 19), so I am in good company when it comes to talking to myself.
4. Clemen, *Shakespeare's Soliloquies*, 3.
5. See Abbé d'Aubignac's "Practique du théâtre"; the English translation is quoted in Arnold, *Soliloquies of Shakespeare*, 18.
6. Qtd. in Arnold, *Soliloquies of Shakespeare*, 18, 19.
7. Arnold, *Soliloquies of Shakespeare*, 22.
8. Qtd. in Hirsh, *Shakespeare and the History of Soliloquies*, 429.
9. For the Ernest Jones quotation, see *A Psycho-Analytic Study of "Hamlet,"* in *Essays in Applied Psycho-Analysis* (London: International Psycho-Analytical Press, 1923), 57. For silent subtext, see T. S. Eliot, "The Love Song of J. Alfred Prufrock," first published in the June 1915 issue of *Poetry: A Magazine of Verse* and read aloud by me multiple days a week for two years to the professor (see "Reading to a Child," chapter 2 in this volume). Like Dahl, Eliot had many unsavory life views. As Claire Dederer has explored, and as I discuss in "Reading to a Child" and "Pioneer Girl" (chapter 13 in this volume), it is an uncomfortable fact that unsavory people can create moving art. Claire Dederer, *Monsters: A Fan's Dilemma* (New York: Knopf, 2023).

9. THE ONE AND ONLY JANE: JANE AUSTEN

1. This chapter initially appeared under the title "Can We Talk About How Austen's Characters Tend to Blur Together," *LitHub*, March 18,

2020, https://lithub.com/can-we-talk-about-how-austens-characters-tend-to-blur-together/.
2. I've read Jane Austen's novels in many different editions, often because I favor a particular editor, but in graduate school we used the Penguin editions in my Jane Austen class. Those tend to be the copies I reread most, I think because of their size and flexibility. I also find the cream-colored back covers and black spines of the Penguin editions comforting.
3. Qtd. in James Edward Austen-Leigh, *A Memoir of Jane Austen*, ed. R. W. Chapman (Oxford: Clarendon, 1967), 157.
4. For studies of the marriage plot, see Lisa O'Connell, *The Origins of the English Marriage Plot: Literature, Politics, and Religion in the Eighteenth Century* (Cambridge: Cambridge University Press, 2019); and Joseph Allen Boone, *Tradition Counter Tradition: Love and the Form of Fiction* (Chicago: University of Chicago Press, 1989). For a fun fictional take on the topic and some play with Derrida and Barthes, see Jeffrey Eugenides, *The Marriage Plot: A Novel* (New York: Farrar, Straus and Giroux, 2011).
5. For studies of the bildungsroman, see *A History of the Bildungsroman*, ed. Sarah Graham (Cambridge: Cambridge University Press, 2019).
6. Jane Austen, *Northanger Abbey*, ed. Marilyn Butler (New York: Penguin, 1995), 24.
7. Laurence Sterne, *Tristram Shandy*, ed. Howard Anderson (New York: Norton, 1980), 52–53.
8. Critics who study the novel, free indirect discourse, and psychological access include James Wood, *How Fiction Works* (New York: Farrar, Straus and Giroux, 2008); D. A. Miller, *Jane Austen, or The Secret of Style* (Princeton, NJ: Princeton University Press, 2003); and Daniel P. Gunn, "Free Indirect Discourse and Narrative Authority in *Emma*," *Narrative* 12, no. 1 (January, 2004): 35–54. For studies of how Jane Austen novels encourage association with the characters or their author, consider Claire Harman, *Jane's Fame: How Jane Austen Conquered the World* (New York: Henry Holt, 2010); Sarah Raff, *Jane Austen's Erotic Advice* (Oxford: Oxford University Press, 2014); Devoney Looser, *The Making of Jane Austen* (Baltimore, MD: Johns Hopkins University Press, 2017); Jenny Davidson, *Reading Jane Austen* (Cambridge: Cambridge University Press, 2017). Other excellent

critics on Jane Austen that I have been indebted to over the years include Claudia Johnson, Paula Byrne, Clara Tuite, and Marilyn Butler.
9. "Which Jane Austen Heroine Are You?," nametests.com, https://www.facebook.com/100064391721174/posts/1224797540869924/.
10. Oscar Wilde, *The Importance of Being Earnest* (Project Gutenberg, 1997), 26.
11. Jane Austen, *Emma*, ed. Fiona Stafford (New York: Penguin, 2003), 100.
12. Austen, *Emma*, 84, 156.
13. See Miller, *Jane Austen, or The Secret of Style*, 96.
14. Many thanks to Sarah Kareem for noting the links between Jane Bennet and Jane Fairfax and the observation that my literal predicament at soccer practice provided an apt idiom for my situation in life.

10. OF PAIN, PARALYSIS, AND PURSUIT: SAMUEL BECKETT, MARY SHELLEY

1. This chapter originally appeared in the *Los Angeles Review of Books* (blog), September 20, 2020, https://blog.lareviewofbooks.org/essays/pain-paralysis-pursuit/.
2. The very important account of my cross-country nonrecord being eclipsed, along with my interview quotation, can be found in "Phelps Happy as Her Old Running Record Falls," *Fosters Daily Democrat*, November 23, 2016, https://www.fosters.com/story/sports/columns/2016/11/23/whaley-phelps-happy-as-old-running-record-falls/24487227007/.
3. I have many copies of *Frankenstein*, but I'm most comfortable with my first edition of the Norton, edited by J. Paul Hunter (New York: Norton, 1996). I also prefer to teach from the first, 1818 version (which Norton reprints), for reasons I can discuss at length. I'm citing that edition here, and quotations appear on pages 34, 35. See too Carlo Ginzburg, "Clues: Roots of an Evidential Paradigm," trans. John and Anne C. Tedeschi, in *Clues, Myths, and the Historical Method* (Baltimore, MD: Johns Hopkins University Press, 1986), 96–125, on how the "hunting narrative" and "literary research" are interlinked. The John Donne compass conceit appears in "A Valediction Forbidding Mourning,"

https://www.poetryfoundation.org/poems/44131/a-valediction-forbidding-mourning.
4. I cite from Samuel Beckett, *Waiting for Godot* (New York: Grove, 1994), which prints the quotations from *The Times* (London) review on the back cover.
5. The Marya Mannes review appeared in the August 1955 edition of New York's *The Reporter*.
6. Alan Schneider describes how the play was billed as "the laugh sensation of two continents" in the *Chelsea Review*, 1958.
7. The description of the San Quentin production appeared in November 1957 in the *San Quentin News*. For the Rick Cluchey quotation, as well as an obituary of sorts, see Edward Helmore, "Beckett's Prison Protege: The Inmate Who Became a Top Interpreter of Writer's Work," *The Guardian*, January 3, 2016, https://www.theguardian.com/culture/2016/jan/03/samuel-beckett-prison-rick-cluchey-inmate.
8. For the infinite realms, see Emily Dickinson, "Pain—has an Element of Blank—." Her use of the em-dash means that the opening line of the poem at once describes and inflicts, something like a blend between the ekphrastic and performative speech act. Some online versions of the poem print it without the dashes, which hurts. See https://allpoetry.com/Pain--has-an-Element-of-Blank-- versus https://www.poemhunter.com/poem/pain-has-an-element-of-blank-2/.
9. Beckett, *Waiting for Godot*, 44.
10. Beckett, *Waiting for Godot*, 79.

11. SHADOW WORK: J. M. BARRIE, TONI MORRISON, MARK TWAIN

1. My epigraph is from William Shakespeare, *Macbeth*, ed. Stephen Orgel (New York: Penguin, 2000), 4.1.125–26. For this chapter, I was using a hardcover edition of J. M. Barrie's *Peter Pan* (published in its own time as *Peter and Wendy*) with the original 1911 illustrations (Greenwood, WI: Suzeteo Enterprises, 2019). For a Freudian reading of *Peter Pan* (along with some interesting context on the book's reception and publication history), see Jacqueline Rose, *The Case of Peter Pan, or The Impossibility of Children's Fiction* (Philadelphia: University of Pennsylvania Press, 1992).

2. Barrie, *Peter Pan*, 20.
3. Barrie, *Peter Pan*, 21.
4. The Robert Louis Stevenson poem "My Shadow" is contained in *A Child's Garden of Verses* (New York: Simon & Schuster, 1999), 24, which I was then reading from regularly, in the illustrated version by Tasha Tudor, to my kids.
5. Barrie, *Peter Pan*, 21.
6. For the biography of Barrie and the "real story" of Peter Pan, see Andrew Birkin, *J. M. Barrie and the Lost Boys: The Real Story of Peter Pan* (New Haven, CT: Yale University Press, 2003).
7. The novel by a friend I cite throughout this essay is *James* (New York: Doubleday, 2024), by Percival Everett; thanks to Percival for providing me with an advance copy of his book.
8. Ralph Ellison, *Invisible Man* (New York: Vintage, 1980), 188.
9. My copy of *The Adventures of Huckleberry Finn* is the Sterling Classics edition, definitely meant for children, illustrated by Scott McKowen (New York: Sterling Children's Books, 2006).
10. Shakespeare, *Macbeth*, 4.1.125–26.
11. Marjorie Garber discusses old Hamlet's Ghost as a Freudian neurotic in *Shakespeare's Ghost Writers: Literature as Uncanny Causality* (New York: Routledge, 2010).
12. William Shakespeare, *The Tempest*, ed. Peter Holland (New York: Penguin, 1999), 1.2.609.
13. Shakespeare, *The Tempest*, 5.1.105–06.
14. Shakespeare, *The Tempest*, 2.2.158.
15. Barrie, *Peter Pan*, 50.
16. My preferred version of Mary Shelley's *Frankenstein* is an old Norton edition, edited by J. Paul Hunter (New York: Norton, 1996).
17. Ellison, *Invisible Man*, 3. For context on how Mary Shelley's creation was appropriated in American culture to aid in racial critique, see Elizabeth Young, *Black Frankenstein: The Making of an American Metaphor* (New York: New York University Press, 2008). For the Shelleys' own involvement in the debate over abolition, see Jill Lepore, "The Strange and Twisted Life of *Frankenstein*," *New Yorker*, February 5, 2018, https://www.newyorker.com/magazine/2018/02/12/the-strange-and-twisted-life-of-frankenstein. For more of my thoughts

on *Frankenstein*, see "Of Pain, Paralysis, and Pursuit," chapter 10 in this volume.
18. Everett, *James*, 75.
19. Ellison, *Invisible Man*, 156.
20. Shakespeare, *The Tempest*, 5.1.358–59. On the racism of Shakespeare, see Farah Karim-Cooper, *The Great White Bard: How to Love Shakespeare While Talking About Race* (New York: Viking, 2023).
21. For some quick takes on Jung and the shadow, especially negative connotations of the shadow, see Christopher Perry, "The Shadow," Society of Analytical Psychology, https://www.thesap.org.uk/articles-on-jungian-psychology-2/about-analysis-and-therapy/the-shadow/; and Jack E. Othon, "Carl Jung and the Shadow: The Ultimate Guide to the Human Dark Side," *High Existence*, January 11, 2023, https://www.highexistence.com/carl-jung-shadow-guide-unconscious/. Jung's version of the shadow self has also yielded a plethora of self-help self-published therapy books on "shadow work," some with subtitles that rival those of any eighteenth-century novel (for example: "A Short and Powerful Guide to Make Peace with Your Hidden Dark Side and Illuminate the Hidden Power of Your True Self for Freedom and Lasting Happiness").
22. The Toni Morrison quotation appears in Namwali Serpell, "Morrison Hall," *New York Review of Books*, August 18, 2023, https://www.nybooks.com/online/2023/08/18/morrison-hall-toni-morrison-princeton/.
23. Morrison's statement on *Huckleberry Finn* appears in "This Amazing, Troubling Book," which she wrote as an introduction to *The Oxford Mark Twain: Adventures of Huckleberry Finn*, ed. Shelley Fisher Fishkin (New York: Oxford University Press, 1996), xxxi–xli. Everett reflects on concepts of "erasure" also, in his novel by the same name, *Erasure* (Minneapolis, MN: Graywolf, 2001), which forms the basis for the 2023 film *American Fiction*.
24. The Ralph Ellison quotations come from his introduction to *Shadow and Act* (New York: Vintage, 1995), xxii.
25. Conversation with Everett.
26. For the American Psychological Association's definition of "object permanence," see https://dictionary.apa.org/object-permanence. The phenomenon was first studied by the Swiss psychologist Jean Piaget,

and a discussion of this study can be found in, among other places, his *The Psychology of the Child* (New York: Basic Books, 1969), coauthored with his collaborator Barbel Inhelder. Attachment theory originated in the 1950s with the work of John Bowlby and Mary Ainsworth. For a comic take on attachment issues, see Tim Kreider, "The Strange Situation," in *I Wrote This Book Because I Love You* (New York: Simon & Schuster, 2018), 115–48. Kreider was a participant in the experiments of Ainsworth. Thanks to Sarah Kareem for the reading recommendation.

27. Shelley, *Frankenstein*, 67.

12. ANIMAL LOVE: MIGUEL DE CERVANTES, JILLY COOPER, LAURENCE STERNE

1. My epigraph is from Miguel de Cervantes, *Don Quixote*, trans. Edith Grossman (New York: Ecco, 2005), 22. My preferred copy of *Don Quixote* is Edith Grossman's 2005 translation, though I dip into many different translations when I read the book, including the one published in the eighteenth century by Tobias Smollett and reprinted still by Modern Library. For other writers who write on riding and the links between writing, riding, and love, see Halimah Marcus, ed., *Horse Girls: Recovering, Aspiring, and Devoted Riders Redefine the Iconic Bond* (New York: Harper Perennial, 2021). Rosinante can be spelled with a "c" or an "s" in translation. Grossman chooses the "c." I opt for the "s" in this chapter, as that is the spelling used by Laurence Sterne.
2. Laurence Sterne, *Tristram Shandy*, ed. Howard Anderson (New York: Norton, 1980), 11–12.
3. Sterne, *Tristram Shandy*, 12, 55.
4. I'm using Jilly Cooper's *Riders* (New York: Simon and Schuster, 1985). Do linger on the cover art. Sarah Kareem is the friend who wouldn't read Jilly Cooper while at Cambridge. The very well-done magazine review of Jilly, which was commissioned and which I quite enjoyed, is of Cooper's book *Mount!*, reviewed by Ian Patterson, "Miss Dior, Prodigally Applied," *London Review of Books*, May 18, 2017, https://www.lrb.co.uk/the-paper/v39/n10/ian-patterson/miss-dior-prodigally-applied. Big applause to Jilly for most effective use of punctuation in a title.

5. Miguel de Cervantes, *Don Quixote*, trans. John Ormsby (Digireads, 2015), 71.
6. Sterne, *Tristram Shandy*, 77.
7. On whether a codpiece can serve as a transitional object, see D. W. Winnicott, "Transitional Objects and Transitional Phenomena: A Study of the First Not-Me Possession," *International Journal of Psychoanalysis* 34 (1953): 89–97; and also maybe "The Detective's Mind," chapter 3 in this volume.
8. Sterne, *Tristram Shandy*, 12.
9. Sterne, *Tristram Shandy*, 164.
10. I highly recommend Peter Brooks, *Reading for the Plot: Design and Intention in Narrative* (Cambridge, MA: Harvard University Press, 1992), for far more than just his reading of Doyle.
11. Sterne, *Tristram Shandy*, 430. For more on endings, see Geoff Dyer, *The Last Days of Roger Federer: And Other Endings* (New York: Farrar, Straus, and Giroux, 2022).

13. PIONEER GIRL: LAURA INGALLS WILDER

1. On the comforts of rereading, see again Patricia Meyer Spacks, *On Re-Reading* (Cambridge, MA: Harvard University Press, 2011). My childhood copies of the Laura Ingalls Wilder books are the ones illustrated by Garth Williams and printed for Harper Collins. My copy of *Little House in the Big Woods* was published in 1971, but the reissued, reillustrated set first appeared in the fall of 1953 (the original editions had been illustrated by Helen Sewell). The description of Laura as a "half pint" appears for the first time on page 35. See too Caroline Fraser, *Prairie Fires: The American Dreams of Laura Ingalls Wilder* (New York: Henry Holt, 2017), on the publication history of the Little House books, esp. 475–79.
2. Fraser, *Prairie Fires*. I so recommend Fraser, who is very good on the politically problematic aspects of Wilder's work.
3. See *Pioneer Girl: The Annotated Autobiography*, ed. Pamela Smith Hill (Pierre: South Dakota Historical Society Press, 2014).
4. Qtd. in Fraser, *Prairie Fires*, 47.

5. Qtd. in Fraser, *Prairie Fires*, 49, 354; Laura Ingalls Wilder, *Little House on the Prairie* (New York: Harper Trophy, 1971), 41.
6. Qtd. in Fraser, *Prairie Fires*, 476. In my childhood version of Wilder, *Little House on the Prairie*, the sentence had been changed to "there were no settlers. Only Indians lived there . . ." (2).
7. Laura Ingalls Wilder, *Little House in the Big Woods* (New York: Harper Trophy, 1971), 4.
8. Wilder, *Little House on the Prairie*, 19–24.
9. Qtd. in Fraser, *Prairie Fires*, 393.

14. THE EFFICIENCY EXPERT: WILLIAM WORDSWORTH, FRANK AND ERNESTINE GILBRETH

1. See Frank B. Gilbreth and Ernestine Gilbreth Carey, *Cheaper by the Dozen* (New York: Harper Perennial Modern Classics, 2019), 84. For this chapter, I consulted a new copy of *Cheaper by the Dozen*, since many pages of my childhood copy ended up being eaten by my pet guinea pig, the same one who survived the trek up a snowy mountain in a ski cap (see chapter 13 in this volume, "Pioneer Girl").
2. Gilbreth and Gilbreth Carey, *Cheaper by the Dozen*, 30.
3. For other background on the Gilbreths, see Jane Lancaster, *Making Time: Lillian Moller Gilbreth—a Life Beyond "Cheaper by the Dozen"* (Lebanon, NH: University Press of New England, 2004).
4. William Wordsworth, "We Are Seven," https://www.poetryfoundation.org/poems/52298/we-are-seven. My childhood exposure to Wordsworth comes in part from John A. Hodgson, *Wordsworth's Philosophical Poetry, 1797–1814* (Lincoln: University of Nebraska Press, 1980).
5. Again, for the unsettling nature of classism or racism embedded in children's literature, see Claire Dederer, *Monsters: A Fan's Dilemma* (New York: Knopf, 2023); and Toni Morrison, on forgiveness, as cited in chapter 2 of this volume, "Reading to a Child." *Pidgin to Da Max*, coauthored by Douglas Simonson, Pat Sasaki, and Ken Sakata, is an illustrated glossary of Hawaiian Pidgin (Honolulu, HI: Bess, 2005).

6. Frances Ferguson writes on the spirit of efficiency in "We Are Seven" in "Historicism, Deconstruction, and Wordsworth," *Diacritics* 17, no. 4 (Winter 1987): 32–43.
7. The account of Mary Wollstonecraft being suckled by puppies appears in Fiona Sampson, *In Search of Mary Shelley: The Girl Who Wrote Frankenstein* (London: Profile, 2018), 22. I consider myself a dog lover, but—no.
8. For the shifting number of Gilbreth kids in print, see Elizabeth Tamny's article, "Cheaper by Eleven?," https://chicagoreader.com/news-politics/cheaper-by-eleven/. For the circumstances of Lillian's rarely mentioned stillbirth, which even Tamny doesn't cite, see https://www.findagrave.com/memorial/147168944/infant-daughter-gilbreth and https://www.thegilbreths.com/f_gen2.php.
9. See Elizabeth Tamny, "Something About Mary," *Chicago Reader*, November 13, 2003, https://chicagoreader.com/arts-culture/something-about-mary/.
10. William Shakespeare, *Hamlet*, ed. A. R. Braunmuller (New York: Penguin, 2001), 1.2.142, 3.2.136.
11. Gilbreth and Gilbreth Carey, *Cheaper by the Dozen*, 207.

15. INVISIBLE LABOR, INVISIBLE HANDS: ADAM SMITH, ZADIE SMITH

1. This chapter originally appeared in the *Los Angeles Review of Books*, April 16, 2022, https://lareviewofbooks.org/article/invisible-labor-invisible-hands/.
2. Jeanette Winterson, *Why Be Happy When You Could Be Normal?* (New York: Grove, 2011), 40.
3. For introductory biographies of Adam Smith, see Dennis C. Rasmussen, *The Infidel and the Professor: David Hume, Adam Smith, and the Friendship That Shaped Modern Thought* (Princeton, NJ: Princeton University Press, 2017); Mark Skousen, *The Making of Modern Economics: The Lives and Ideas of Great Thinkers* (New York: Routledge, 2022); Marie Bussing-Burkes, *Influential Economists* (Minneapolis, MN: Oliver, 2003).
4. See Adam Smith, *The Wealth of Nations*, ed. Adam Skinner (New York: Penguin, 1999); and Adam Smith, *The Theory of Moral Sentiments*, ed.

D. D. Raphael and A.L. Macfie (Oxford: Oxford University Press, 1976).

5. For more on absent-mindedness, see "The Detective's Mind," chapter 3 in this volume. For work on Smith and the invisible hand, see Eleanor Courtemanche, *The "Invisible Hand" and British Fiction: Adam Smith, Political Economy, and the Genre of Realism* (New York: Palgrave, 2017); Sarah Kareem, *Eighteenth-Century Fiction and the Reinvention of Wonder* (Oxford: Oxford University Press, 2014); Stefan Andriopoulous, "The Invisible Hand: Supernatural Agency in Political Economy and the Gothic Novel," *ELH* 66, no. 3 (Fall 1999): 739–58; Emma Rothschild, "Adam Smith and the Invisible Hand," *American Economic Review* 84, no. 2 (May 1994): 319–22. For work on hands, see Peter Capuano, *Changing Hands: Industry, Evolution, and the Reconfiguration of the Victorian Body* (Ann Arbor: University of Michigan Press, 2015).

6. Arlene Daniels, "Invisible Work," *Social Problems* 34, no. 5 (December 1987): 403–15.

7. I also consulted the *OED* for background on my ideas about labor. See "labor," https://www.oed.com/dictionary/labour_n?tab=meaning_and_use#39838660.

8. Smith, *Wealth of Nations*, 140.

9. Courtemanche, *The "Invisible Hand,"* 22; Smith, *Wealth of Nations*, 431.

10. Daniels, "Invisible Work," 403.

11. Zadie Smith, *Intimations: Six Essays* (New York: Penguin, 2020), 19–28.

12. Sophie Elmhirst, "Zadie Smith: Adventures in Paris, London, and New York with the Peerless British Novelist," *The Gentlewoman* 14 (Autumn–Winter 2016), https://thegentlewoman.co.uk/library/zadie-smith.

13. For the exhibit in Cincinnati, see https://freedomcenter.org/visit/permanent-exhibits/invisible-slavery-today/. For Adam Smith's views on slavery, see, for example, Spencer J. Pack, "Slavery, Adam Smith's Economic Vision, and the Invisible Hand," *History of Economic Ideas* 4, nos. 1/2 (1996): 253–69.

14. For the sociologist who coined the term "emotional labor," see Arlie Russell Hochschild, *The Managed Heart: Commercialization of Human Feeling* (Berkeley: University of California Press, 1983). For a

reconsideration of the term, see Julie Beck, "The Concept Creep of 'Emotional Labor,'" *The Atlantic*, November 26, 2018, https://www.theatlantic.com/family/archive/2018/11/arlie-hochschild-housework-isnt-emotional-labor/576637/.
15. William Shakespeare, *Macbeth*, ed. Stephen Orgel (New York: Penguin, 2000), 3.2.54; Horace Walpole, *The Castle of Otranto*, ed. Nick Groom (Oxford: Oxford University Press, 2014), 25.
16. Adam Smith, "History of Astronomy," in *Essays on Philosophical Subjects*, ed. I. S. Ross (Oxford: Clarendon, 1980), 49.
17. Smith, "History of Astronomy," 49.
18. Alexander Pope, *The Rape of the Lock*, in *The Rape of the Lock and Other Major Writings*, ed. Leo Damrosch (New York: Penguin, 2011), canto 1, 43.
19. Smith, *Theory of Moral Sentiments*, 184.
20. For discussion on this line, which appears in Book 4.ii.9 in *The Wealth of Nations: Books 4–5* (New York: Penguin, 1999), see Andrew Skinner, "Introduction," in *The Wealth of Nations: Books 1–3* (New York: Penguin, 1999), 84.
21. I'm much indebted to Katrine Marçal, *Who Cooked Adam Smith's Dinner: A Story About Women and Economics* (New York: Pegasus, 2016), and my student Sydney Ahmed, who recommended this book.

16. NO ROOM OF ONE'S OWN: HOMER, VIRGINIA WOOLF

1. This chapter originally appeared in *Air/Light* 1, no. 1 (Fall 2020), https://airlightmagazine.org/airlight/fall2020/no-room-of-ones-own/. I own an old paperback copy of Tom Stoppard's *Arcadia* (New York: Farrar, Straus and Giroux, 1993), which I had at the time of writing loaned out to a science friend and that was returned, unread. The epigraph appears on page 19.
2. The copy of *A Room of One's Own* (New York: Harcourt, 1929) that was on my table then was the one reissued in 1981 with a foreword by Mary Gordon; I liked the cover photograph. The essays on my dining-room table include Peggy Kamuf, "Penelope at Work: Interruptions in *A Room of One's Own*," *Novel: A Forum on Fiction* 16, no. 1 (Autumn 1982): 5–18; and Joseph Roach, "Viva Voce: The Efficacy of Oral

Interpretation," *Yale Review* 99, no. 4 (October 2011): 108–18. Thanks to Joe for reminding me that "there is something of the intimacy of lovers about teaching someone to speak poetry" (113) and for putting voice to the feeling that a "hands-on close reading . . . veritably pulses as it opens and closes, like a heart" (117). The Milne on my table was *The Complete Poems of Winnie-the-Pooh* (New York: Dutton Children's Books, 1998), which I had gotten as a gift for my ex-husband and from which I still read aloud to my children and to myself. I recommend "The Old Sailor" from this anthology for overwhelming days. I was using a hardcover edition of J. M. Barrie's *Peter Pan* that contained the original 1911 illustrations (Greenwood, WI: Suzeteo, 2019) (see "Shadow Work," chapter 11 in this volume). The particular issue of the *New Yorker* on my table in those months has been lost to posterity, unless it is still on my table, which may be the case.

3. I'm quoting now from Virginia Woolf, *A Room of One's Own*, ed. Susan Gubar (New York: Harcourt, 2005), 4, 8, which is the copy currently on my table.
4. Woolf, *Room of One's Own*, 66.
5. Woolf, *Room of One's Own*, 66.
6. I quote from the Edgeworth in my own *Eighteenth-Century Authorship and the Play of Fiction* (New York: Routledge, 2009), 131.
7. Woolf, *Room of One's Own*, 67.
8. David Hume's reference to playing backgammon occurs in book 1, section 7 of *A Treatise of Human Nature*; I own the version edited by David and Mary Norton (Oxford: Oxford University Press, 2000). The Wittgenstein biography I read was Roy Monk, *Ludwig Wittgenstein: The Duty of Genius* (New York: Penguin, 1991); Amazon tells me I have purchased this book twice, though I can't at the moment find either copy. In general, I recommend reading Wittgenstein or about Wittgenstein when one is delirious or suffering from the flu.
9. Ramona's fear of sleeping in her own room features in Beverly Cleary, *Ramona the Brave* (New York: Harper Collins, 1975), and the reference to Frances appears in Russell Hoban, *Bedtime for Frances* (New York: Harper Collins, 1960), also illustrated, like the Laura Ingalls Wilder books I read, by Garth Williams, and which I mention here so that any adult insomniac who has not stumbled upon the book can

avoid it. See too my preferred copy of Mary Shelley, *Frankenstein*, ed. J. Paul Hunter (New York: Norton, 1996), 32.
10. See Kamuf, "Penelope at Work."
11. On other ways to challenge the teleology of writing or reading, see my reflections on cross-referencing in note 16 to "The Detective's Mind," chapter 3 in this volume.

BIBLIOGRAPHY

Adams, Hazard. *Critical Theory Since Plato*. New York: Harcourt Brace Jovanovich, 1971.

Anderson, Emily Hodgson. *Eighteenth-Century Authorship and the Play of Fiction*. New York: Routledge, 2009.

———. *Shakespeare and the Legacy of Loss*. Ann Arbor: University of Michigan Press, 2018.

Andriopoulous, Stefan. "The Invisible Hand: Supernatural Agency in Political Economy and the Gothic Novel." *ELH* 66, no. 3 (Fall 1999): 739–58.

Aristotle. *Poetics*. Trans. Malcolm Heath. New York: Penguin, 1996.

Arnold, Morris. *The Soliloquies of Shakespeare: A Study in Technic*. New York: Columbia University Press, 1911.

Austen, Jane. *Emma*. Ed. Fiona Stafford. New York: Penguin, 2003.

———. *Northanger Abbey*. Ed. Marilyn Butler. New York: Penguin, 1995.

Austen-Leigh, Edward. *A Memoir of Jane Austen*. Ed. R. W. Chapman. Oxford: Clarendon, 1967.

Austin, J. L. *How to Do Things with Words*. Cambridge, MA: Harvard University Press, 1975.

Barrie, J. M. *Peter Pan*. Illus. Tasha Tudor. Greenwood, WI: Suzeteo Enterprises, 2019.

Beck, Julie. "The Concept Creep of Emotional Labor." *The Atlantic*, November 26, 2018. https://www.theatlantic.com/family/archive/2018/11/arlie-hochschild-housework-isnt-emotional-labor/576637/.

Beckett, Samuel. *Waiting for Godot*. New York: Grove, 1994.

Beer, Gillian. *Alice in Space: The Sideways Victorian World of Lewis Carroll.* Chicago: University of Chicago Press, 2016.

Behn, Aphra. *Oroonoko.* Ed. Paul Salzman. Oxford: Oxford University Press, 1994.

Bettelheim, Bruno. *The Uses of Enchantment: The Meaning and Importance of Fairy Tales.* New York: Vintage, 1989.

Bhabha, Homi K. "Of Mimicry and Man: The Ambivalence of Colonial Discourse." *Discipleship: A Special Issue on Psychoanalysis* 28 (Spring 1984): 125–33.

Birkin, Andrew. *J. M. Barrie and the Lost Boys: The Real Story of Peter Pan.* New Haven, CT: Yale University Press, 2003.

Blake, Victoria. "Shakespeare's Worst Line." *On Writers and Writing* (blog), January 8, 2016. https://victoriablakewriter.wordpress.com/2016/01/08/shakespeares-worst-line/.

Boone, Joseph Allen. *Tradition Counter Tradition: Love and the Form of Fiction.* Chicago: University of Chicago Press, 1989.

Brooks, Peter. *Reading for the Plot: Design and Intention in Narrative.* Cambridge, MA: Harvard University Press, 1992.

Bussing-Burkes, Marie. *Influential Economists.* Minneapolis: Oliver, 2003.

Capuano, Peter. *Changing Hands: Industry, Evolution, and the Reconfiguration of the Victorian Body.* Ann Arbor: University of Michigan Press, 2015.

Carne-Ross, D. S. "The Poem of Odysseus." In *The Odyssey*, trans. Robert Fitzgerald, ix–lxx. New York: Farrar, Straus and Giroux, 1998.

Carroll, Lewis. *Through the Looking Glass.* In *Alice in Wonderland*, 3rd ed., ed. Donald J. Gray, 99–208. New York: Norton, 2013.

Cavell, Stanley. "The Avoidance of Love." In *Must We Mean What We Say?*, 267–353. Cambridge: Cambridge University Press, 2002.

Chee, Alexander. *How to Write an Autobiographical Novel.* New York: Mariner, 2018.

———. "How to Write an Autobiographical Novel." *Buzzfeed*, February 8, 2016. https://www.buzzfeed.com/alexanderchee/how-to-write-an-autobiographical-novel.

Cleary, Beverly. *Ramona the Brave.* New York: Harper Collins, 1975.

Clemen, Wolfgang. *Shakespeare's Soliloquies.* Cambridge: Cambridge University Press, 1964.

Coleridge, Samuel Taylor. "Frost at Midnight." In *The Complete Poems*, ed. William Keach, 231. New York: Penguin, 1997.

———. *The Rime of the Ancient Mariner*. Ed. Martin Gardner. Illus. Gustave Doré. New York: Meridian, 1965.

Collingwood, Stuart Dodgson. *The Life and Letters of Lewis Carroll*. London: T. Fisher Unwin, 1898.

Cooper, Jilly. *Riders*. New York: Simon and Schuster, 1985.

Courtemanche, Eleanor. *The "Invisible Hand" and British Fiction: Adam Smith, Political Economy, and the Genre of Realism*. New York: Palgrave, 2017.

Cross, Wilbur Lucius. *The Life and Times of Laurence Sterne*. New York: Macmillan, 1909.

Dahl, Roald. *Boy: Tales of Childhood*. New York: Viking, 2010.

———. *Going Solo*. New York: Viking, 2009.

———. *Matilda*. New York: Random House, 2013.

———. *The Witches*. New York: Random House, 2013.

Damrosch, Leopold. *Eternity's Sunrise: The Imaginative World of William Blake*. New Haven, CT: Yale University Press, 2015.

Daniels, Ariene. "Invisible Work." *Social Problems* 34, no. 5 (December 1987): 403–15.

Davidson, Jenny. *Reading Jane Austen*. Cambridge: Cambridge University Press, 2017.

Davies, Mark J. *Alice in Waterland: Lewis Carroll and the River Thames in Oxford*. Oxford: Signal, 2010.

de Cervantes, Miguel. *Don Quixote*. Trans. Edith Grossman. New York: Ecco, 2005.

———. *Don Quixote*. Trans. John Ormsby. Overland Park, KS: Digireads, 2015.

Dederer, Claire. *Monsters: A Fan's Dilemma*. New York: Knopf, 2023.

Dickinson, Emily. "Pain—has an Element of Blank—." *All Poetry*. https://allpoetry.com/Pain--has-an-Element-of-Blank--.

———. "Pain Has an Element of Blank; Poem by Emily Dickinson." *Poem Hunter*. https://www.poemhunter.com/poem/pain-has-an-element-of-blank-2/.

Diski, Jenny. "Stinker." *London Review of Books*, April 28, 1994. https://www.lrb.co.uk/the-paper/v16/n08/jenny-diski/stinker.

Donne, John. "A Valediction Forbidding Mourning." Poetry Foundation. https://www.poetryfoundation.org/poems/44131/a-valediction-forbidding-mourning.

Doyle, Arthur Conan. *The Complete Sherlock Holmes*. 2 vols. New York: Barnes & Noble Classics, 2003.

Dyer, Geoff. *The Last Days of Roger Federer: And Other Endings*. New York: Farrar, Straus and Giroux, 2022.

Ellison, Ralph. *Invisible Man*. New York: Vintage, 1980.

———. *Shadow and Act*. New York: Vintage, 1995.

Elmhirst, Sophie. "Zadie Smith: Adventures in Paris, London and New York with the Peerless British Novelist." *The Gentlewoman* 14 (Autumn & Winter 2016). https://thegentlewoman.co.uk/library/zadie-smith.

Eugenides, Jeffrey. *The Marriage Plot: A Novel*. New York: Farrar, Straus and Giroux, 2011.

Everett, Percival. "Chemically Darkened Like Me." *Oxford American: New South Journalism Issue*, Fall 2012, 132–33. https://oxfordamerican.org/magazine/issue-78-fall-2012.

———. *Erasure*. Minneapolis, MN: Graywolf, 2001.

———. *James*. New York: Doubleday, 2024.

Fadiman, Anne. *Ex Libris: Confessions of a Common Reader*. New York: Farrar, Straus and Giroux, 1998.

———, ed. *Rereadings: Seventeen Writers Revisit Books They Love*. New York: Farrar, Straus and Giroux, 2006.

Felski, Rita. *Uses of Literature*. Oxford: Wiley-Blackwell, 2008.

Fielding, Henry. *Joseph Andrews*. Ed. Martin C. Battestin. London: Penguin English Library, 1985.

Fraser, Caroline. *Prairie Fires: The American Dreams of Laura Ingalls Wilder*. New York: Henry Holt, 2017.

Freud, Sigmund. "Family Romances." In *The Standard Edition of the Complete Psychological Works of Sigmund Freud*, vol. 9, *1906–1909*, ed. James Strachey and Anna Freud, 235–42. London: Hogarth, 1959.

———. *The Interpretation of Dreams*. In *The Basic Writings of Sigmund Freud*, ed. and trans. A. A. Brill, 149–520. New York: Random House, 1966.

Gallagher, Catherine. *Nobody's Story: The Vanishing Act of Women Writers in the Marketplace, 1670–1820*. Berkeley: University of California Press, 1994.

Garber, Marjorie. *Shakespeare's Ghost Writers: Literature as Uncanny Causality*. New York: Routledge, 2010.
Gentleman, Francis. *The Dramatic Censor: Or, Critical Companion*. Vol. 1. London: J. Bell, 1770.
Germano, William. *From Dissertation to Book*. 2nd ed. Chicago: University of Chicago Press, 2013.
———. *Getting It Published: A Guide for Scholars and Anyone Else Serious About Serious Books*. 3rd ed. Chicago: University of Chicago Press, 2016.
Gifford, James. "The Gilbreth Family." *The Gilbreths*. https://www.thegilbreths.com/f_gen2.php.
Gilbreth, Frank B., and Ernestine Gilbreth Carey. *Cheaper by the Dozen*. New York: Harper Perennial Modern Classics, 2019.
Ginzburg, Carlo. "Clues: Roots of an Evidential Paradigm." In *Clues, Myths, and the Historical Method*, trans. John and Anne C. Tedeschi, 96–125. Baltimore, MD: Johns Hopkins University Press, 1986.
Gopnik, Adam. "Grim Fairy Tales." *New Yorker*, November 18, 1996. https://www.newyorker.com/magazine/1996/11/18/grim-fairy-tales.
Gornick, Vivian. *Unfinished Business: Notes of a Chronic Re-reader*. New York: Farrar, Straus and Giroux, 2020.
Graham, Sarah, ed. *A History of the Bildungsroman*. Cambridge: Cambridge University Press, 2019.
Grahame, Kenneth. *The Wind in the Willows*. New York: Charles Scribner and Sons, 1908.
———. *The Wind in the Willows*. Abr. ed. Illus. Inga Moore. Eastbourne: Gardners, 2000.
Greenblatt, Stephen. *Will in the World: How Shakespeare Became Shakespeare*. New York: Norton, 2004.
Griffin, John Howard. *Black Like Me*. San Antonio, TX: Wings, 2004.
Gross, Kenneth. *The Dream of the Moving Statue*. University Park: Pennsylvania State University Press, 1992.
Gunn, Daniel P. "Free Indirect Discourse and Narrative Authority in *Emma*." *Narrative* 12, no. 1 (January 2004): 35–54.
Harman, Claire. *Jane's Fame: How Jane Austen Conquered the World*. New York: Henry Holt, 2010.
Hart, Sarah. *Once Upon a Prime: The Wondrous Connections Between Mathematics and Literature*. New York: Flatiron, 2023.

Hazlitt, William. *Hazlitt on Theatre*. Ed. William Archer and Robert Lowe. New York: Hill and Wang, 1895.

Heller, Nathan. "The End of the English Major." *New Yorker*, February 27, 2023. https://www.newyorker.com/magazine/2023/03/06/the-end-of-the-english-major.

Hemings, John, and Henry Condell. "To the Great Variety of Readers." In *The Norton Facsimile: The First Folio of Shakespeare*, ed. Charlton Hinman, 7. New York: Norton, 1996.

Hemingway, Ernest. *The Old Man and the Sea*. New York: Scribner, 1980.

Highfill Jr., Philip H., et al. *A Biographical Dictionary of Actors, Actresses, Musicians, Dancers, Managers and Other Stage Personnel in London, 1660–1800*. Vol. 10. Carbondale: Southern Illinois University Press, 1973–1993.

Hill, Pamela Smith, ed. *Pioneer Girl: The Annotated Autobiography*. Pierre: South Dakota Historical Society Press, 2014.

Hirsch, James. *Shakespeare and the History of Soliloquies*. London: Associated University Presses, 2003.

Hoban, Russell. *Bedtime for Frances*. Illus. Garth Williams. New York: Harper Collins, 1960.

Hochschild, Arlie Russell. *The Managed Heart: The Commercialization of Human Feeling*. Berkeley: University of California Press, 1983.

Hodgson, John A. "Arthur Conan Doyle (1859–1930)." In *A Companion to Crime Fiction*, ed. Charles J. Rzepka and Lee Horsley, 390–402. West Sussex: Blackwell, 2010.

———. *Coleridge, Shelley, and Transcendental Inquiry: Rhetoric, Argument, Metapsychology*. Lincoln: University of Nebraska Press, 1989.

———. "Decoding Poe? Poe, W. B. Tyler, and Cryptography." *Journal of English and Germanic Philology* 92, no. 4 (October 1993): 523–34.

———. *Wordsworth's Philosophical Poetry, 1797–1814*. Lincoln: University of Nebraska Press, 1980.

Hollander, John. *The Substance of Shadow: A Darkening Trope in Poetic History*. Ed. Kenneth Gross. Chicago: University of Chicago Press, 2016.

Homer. *The Odyssey*. Ed. and trans. Robert Fagles. New York: Penguin, 1996.

Hume, David. *A Treatise of Human Nature*. Ed. David and Mary Norton. Oxford: Oxford University Press, 2000.

Jonson, Ben. *Timber, or Discoveries Made Upon Men and Matter*. Ed. Felix E. Schelling. Boston: Ginn & Co., 1892.

Kamuf, Peggy. "Penelope at Work: Interruptions in *A Room of One's Own*." *Novel: A Forum on Fiction* 16, no. 1 (Autumn, 1982): 5–18.

Kareem, Sarah Tindal. *Eighteenth-Century Fiction and the Reinvention of Wonder*. Oxford: Oxford University Press, 2014.

Karim-Cooper, Farah. *The Great White Bard: How to Love Shakespeare While Talking About Race*. New York: Viking, 2023.

Koehler, William. *The Koehler Method of Dog Training: Certified Techniques by Movieland's Most Experienced Dog Trainer*. New York: Howell Book House, 1962.

———. *The Koehler Method of Open Obedience for Ring, Home, and Field*. New York: Howell Book House, 1970.

Kreider, Tim. "The Strange Situation." In *I Wrote This Book Because I Love You*, 115–48. New York: Simon and Schuster, 2018.

Lancaster, Jane. *Making Time: Lillian Moller Gilbreth—a Life Beyond "Cheaper by the Dozen."* Lebanon, NH: University Press of New England, 2004.

Leonard, William Torbert. *Masquerade in Black*. Metuchen, NJ: Scarecrow, 1986.

Lepore, Jill. "The Strange and Twisted Life of *Frankenstein*." *New Yorker*, February 5, 2018. https://www.newyorker.com/magazine/2018/02/12/the-strange-and-twisted-life-of-frankenstein.

Lerer, Seth. *Children's Literature: A Reader's History, from Aesop to Harry Potter*. Chicago: University of Chicago Press, 2009.

Lindfors, Bernth. *Ira Aldridge: The Early Years, 1807–1833*. Rochester, NY: University of Rochester Press, 2011.

Locke, John. *Essay Concerning Human Understanding*. 2 vols. Ed. Alexander Campbell Fraser. New York: Dover, 1959.

Looser, Devoney. *The Making of Jane Austen*. Baltimore, MD: Johns Hopkins University Press, 2017.

Lott, Eric. *Love and Theft: Blackface Minstrelsy and the American Working Class*. Oxford: Oxford University Press, 2013.

Lynch, Deidre Shauna. *Loving Literature: A Cultural History*. Chicago: University of Chicago Press, 2015.

Mack, Maynard. *Alexander Pope: A Life*. New York: Norton, 1988.

———. *Everybody's Shakespeare*. Lincoln: University of Nebraska Press, 1994.

Mannes, Marya. "Review of *Waiting for Godot*." *The Reporter*, August 1955.

Marçal, Katrine. *Who Cooked Adam Smith's Dinner: A Story About Women and Economics*. New York: Pegasus, 2016.
Marcus, Halimah, ed. *Horse Girls: Recovering, Aspiring, and Devoted Riders Redefine the Iconic Bond*. New York: Harper Perennial, 2021.
McGurl, Mark. *The Program Era: Postwar Fiction and the Rise of Creative Writing*. Cambridge, MA: Harvard University Press, 2009.
Mead, Rebecca. *The Road to Middlemarch: My Life with George Eliot*. New York: Granta, 2014.
Melville, Herman. *Moby Dick*. New York: Penguin, 1992.
Miller, D. A. *Jane Austen, or The Secret of Style*. Princeton, NJ: Princeton University Press, 2003.
Miller, Laura. *The Magician's Book: A Skeptic's Adventures in Narnia*. New York: Little, Brown, 2008.
Milne, A. A. *The Complete Poems of Winnie-the-Pooh*. New York: Dutton Children's Books, 1998.
———. *The House at Pooh Corner*. New York: Dutton, 1988.
Milton, John. *Paradise Lost*. Ed. David Scott Kastan. Cambridge: Hackett, 2005.
———. *Complete Poems and Major Prose*. Ed. Merritt Y. Hughes. New York: Odyssey, 1957.
Monk, Roy. *Ludwig Wittgenstein: The Duty of Genius*. New York: Penguin, 1991.
Morrison, Toni. "Chloe Wofford Talks About Toni Morrison." In *Toni Morrison: Conversations*, ed. Carolyn C. Denard, 98–106. Jackson: University Press of Mississippi, 2008.
———. "The Site of Memory." In *Inventing the Truth: The Art and Craft of Memoir*, 2nd ed., ed. William K. Zinsser, 83–102. Boston: Houghton Mifflin, 1995.
———. "This Amazing, Troubling Book." In *The Oxford Mark Twain: Adventures of Huckleberry Finn*, ed. Shelley Fisher Fishkin, xxxi–xli. New York: Oxford University Press, 1996.
Nabokov, Vladimir. *Strong Opinions*. New York: Vintage, 1973.
National Underground Railroad Freedom Center. *Invisible: Slavery Today*. 2024. https://freedomcenter.org/visit/permanent-exhibits/invisible-slavery-today/.
O'Connell, Lisa. *The Origins of the English Marriage Plot: Literature, Politics, and Religion in the Eighteenth Century*. Cambridge: Cambridge University Press, 2019.

Olsen, Tillie. *Silences*. New York: Feminist Press at the City University of New York, 1978.
Othon, Jack E. "Carl Jung and the Shadow: The Ultimate Guide to the Human Dark Side." *High Existence*, January 11, 2023. https://www.highexistence.com/carl-jung-shadow-guide-unconscious/.
Pack, Spencer J. "Slavery, Adam Smith's Economic Vision, and the Invisible Hand." *History of Economic Ideas* 4, nos. 1/2 (1996): 253–69.
Palfrey, Simon, and Tiffany Stern. *Shakespeare in Parts*. Oxford: Oxford University Press, 2007.
Pasanek, Brad. "Staging Thought." Lecture, American Society of Eighteenth-Century Studies, San Antonio, TX, March 2012.
Patterson, Ian. "Miss Dior, Prodigally Applied." *London Review of Books* 30, no. 10 (May 18, 2017). https://www.lrb.co.uk/the-paper/v39/n10/ian-patterson/miss-dior-prodigally-applied.
Perry, Christopher. "The Shadow." Society of Analytical Psychology, August 12, 2015. https://www.thesap.org.uk/articles-on-jungian-psychology-2/about-analysis-and-%20therapy/the-shadow/.
Phillips, Adam. *Winnicott*. New York: Penguin, 1988.
Piaget, Jean, and Barbel Inhelder. *The Psychology of the Child*. New York: Basic Books, 1969.
Plato. "The Allegory of the Cave." Trans. Shawn Eyer. Washington, DC: Plumbstone, 2016. https://scholar.harvard.edu/files/seyer/files/plato_republic_514b-518d_allegory-of-the-cave.pdf.
———. *Republic*. Trans. Paul Shorey. In *Plato: Collected Dialogues*, ed. Edith Hamilton and Huntington Cairns, 575–844. Princeton, NJ: Princeton University Press, 2005.
———. *The Symposium*. Ed. and trans. Christopher Gill. London: Penguin, 1999.
Poe, Edgar Allan. "The Murders in the Rue Morgue." In *The Collected Tales and Poems of Edgar Allan Poe*, 141–68. New York: Modern Library, 1992.
Pope, Alexander. "An Epistle to Dr. Arbuthnot." In *Selected Poetry of Alexander Pope*, ed. Pat Rodgers, 93–105. Oxford: Oxford University Press, 1998.
———. *The Rape of the Lock*, in *The Rape of the Lock and Other Major Writings*, ed. Leo Damrosch. New York: Penguin, 2011.
Raff, Sarah. *Jane Austen's Erotic Advice*. Oxford: Oxford University Press, 2014.

———. "Review of *The History of Sir Charles Grandison*." *Eighteenth-Century Studies* 57, no. 2 (Winter, 2024): 271–73.
Rasmussen, Dennis C. *The Infidel and the Professor: David Hume, Adam Smith, and the Friendship That Shaped Modern Thought*. Princeton, NJ: Princeton University Press, 2017.
Richardson, Samuel. *Sir Charles Grandison*. 3 vols. Ed. Jocelyn Harris. Oxford: Oxford University Press, 1972.
———. *Sir Charles Grandison*. Ed. Jocelyn Harris. Oxford: Oxford World's Classics, 1986.
Roach, Joseph. "Viva Voice: The Efficacy of Oral Interpretation." *Yale Review* 99, no. 4 (October 2011): 108–18.
Rose, Jacqueline. *The Case of Peter Pan, or The Impossibility of Children's Fiction*. Philadelphia: University of Pennsylvania Press, 1992.
Rothschild, Emma. "Adam Smith and the Invisible Hand." *American Economic Review* 84, no. 2 (May 1994): 319–22.
Sampson, Fiona. *In Search of Mary Shelley: The Girl Who Wrote Frankenstein*. London: Profile, 2018.
Schneider, Alan. "Alan Schneider in *Chelsea Review*." In *Samuel Beckett: The Critical Heritage*, ed. L. Graver and R. Federman, 3–20. London: Routledge, 1958.
Sehgal, Parul. "The Case Against the Trauma Plot." *New Yorker*, December 27, 2021. https://www.newyorker.com/magazine/2022/01/03/the-case-against-the-trauma-plot.
Serpell, Namwali. "Morrison Hall." *New York Review of Books*, August 18, 2023. https://www.nybooks.com/online/2023/08/18/morrison-hall-toni-morrison-princeton/.
Shakespeare, William. *Hamlet*. Ed. A. R. Braunmuller. New York: Penguin, 2001.
———. *King Lear*. Ed. Stephen Orgel. New York: Penguin, 2000.
———. *Macbeth*. Ed. Stephen Orgel. New York: Penguin, 2000.
———. *The Tempest*. Ed. Peter Holland. New York: Penguin, 1999.
———. *The Winter's Tale*. Ed. Frances E. Dolan. New York: Penguin, 2017.
Shapiro, James. *Contested Will: Who Wrote Shakespeare?* New York: Simon and Schuster, 2010.
Shelley, Mary. *Frankenstein*. Ed. J. Paul Hunter. New York: Norton, 1996.
Simonson, Douglas, Pat Sasaki, and Ken Sakata. *Pidgin to Da Max*. Honolulu, HI: Bess, 2005.

Smith, Adam. "History of Astronomy." In *Essays on Philosophical Subjects*, ed. L. S. Ross. Oxford: Clarendon, 1980.

———. *The Theory of Moral Sentiments*. Ed. D. D. Raphael and A. L. Macfie. Oxford: Oxford University Press, 1976.

———. *The Wealth of Nations*. Ed. Adam Skinner. New York: Penguin, 1999.

Smith, Zadie. *Intimations: Six Essays*. New York: Penguin, 2020.

Spacks, Patricia Meyer. *On Rereading*. Cambridge, MA: Harvard University Press, 2011.

Spenser, Edmund. "Amoretti LXXV: One Day I Wrote Her Name." Poetry Foundation. https://www.poetryfoundation.org/poems/45189/amoretti-lxxv-one-day-i-wrote-her-name.

Sterne, Laurence. *Tristram Shandy*. Ed. Howard Anderson. New York: Norton, 1980.

Stevens, Wallace. "The Snow Man." Poetry Foundation, 1921. https://www.poetryfoundation.org/poems/45235/the-snow-man-56d224a6d4e90.

Stevenson, Robert Louis. "My Shadow." In *A Child's Garden of Verses*, illus. Tasha Tudor, 24. New York: Simon & Schuster, 1999.

Stoppard, Tom. *Arcadia*. New York: Farrar, Straus and Giroux, 1993.

Tamny, Elizabeth. "Cheaper by Eleven?" *Chicago Reader*, January 1, 2004. https://chicagoreader.com/news-politics/cheaper-by-eleven/.

———. "Something About Mary." *Chicago Reader*, November 13, 2003. https://chicagoreader.com/arts-culture/something-about-mary/.

Tartar, Maria. *The Enchanted Hunters: The Power of Stories in Childhood*. New York: Norton, 2009.

Tennyson, Alfred Lord. "Ulysses." In *Tennyson's Poetry*, ed. Robert W. Hill Jr., 82. New York: Norton, 1999.

Treglown, Jeremy. *Roald Dahl: A Biography*. New York: Houghton Mifflin, 1995.

Twain, Mark. *The Adventures of Huckleberry Finn*. Illus. Scott McKowen. New York: Sterling Children's Books, 2006.

Ulin, David L. "Roald Dahl's Twisted, Overlooked Stories for Adults." *New Yorker*, July 21, 2016. https://www.newyorker.com/books/page-turner/roald-dahls-twisted-overlooked-stories-for-adults.

Vaughn, Virginia Mason. *Performing Blackness on English Stages, 1500–1800*. Cambridge: Cambridge University Press, 2005.

Walcott, Derek. *Pantomime*. In *Crosswinds: An Anthology of Black Dramatists in the Diaspora*, ed. William B. Branch, 130–61. Bloomington: Indiana University Press, 1993.
White, T. H. *The Once and Future King*. New York: Ace, 2011.
Wilde, Oscar. *The Importance of Being Earnest*. Project Gutenberg, 1997.
Wilder, Laura Ingalls. *Little House in the Big Woods*. Illus. Garth Williams. New York: Harper Collins, 1971.
———. *Little House on the Prairie*. New York: Harper Trophy, 1971.
Winnicott, D. W. "Transitional Objects and Transitional Phenomena: A Study of the First Not-Me Possession." *International Journal of Psychoanalysis* 34 (1953): 89–97.
Winterson, Jeanette. *Why Be Happy When You Could Be Normal?* New York: Grove, 2011.
Wittgenstein, Ludwig. *Philosophical Investigations*. Trans. G. E. M. Anscombe. Oxford: Blackwell, 2001.
Wood, James. *How Fiction Works*. New York: Farrar, Straus and Giroux, 2008.
Woolf, Jenny. *The Mystery of Lewis Carroll: Discovering the Whimsical, Thoughtful, and Sometimes Lonely Man Who Created Alice in Wonderland*. New York: St. Martin's Griffin, 2011.
Woolf, Virginia. *A Room of One's Own*. Intro. Mary Gordon. New York: Harcourt, 1981.
———. *A Room of One's Own*. Ed. Susan Gubar. New York: Harcourt, 2005.
Wordsworth, William. "I Wandered Lonely as a Cloud." Poetry Foundation. https://www.poetryfoundation.org/poems/45521/i-wandered-lonely-as-a-cloud.
———. *The Prelude*. Ed. Jonathan Wordsworth. New York: Norton, 1979.
———. "We Are Seven." Poetry Foundation. https://www.poetryfoundation.org/poems/52298/we-are-seven.
Young, Elizabeth. *Black Frankenstein: The Making of an American Metaphor*. New York: New York University Press, 2008.

INDEX

"absentmindedness," 52–54, 199
absorption, 6, 8, 34–36, 53;
   self-absorption, 25, 130
absurd, theater of, 128
"Act of Oblivion," 142–43
actors, 19–21; Black parts played by white men, 63–64; entire script not given to, 107; and likeness, 62; and loss, 19–20, 24, 28; and soliloquy, 107–8. *See also Hamlet* (Shakespeare); Shakespeare, William
Adventures of Huckleberry Finn, The (Twain), 78, 138, 142
"Adventure of the Abbey Grange, The" (Doyle), 51
"Adventure of the Cardboard Box, The" (Doyle), 46–47
Alcibiades, 100
Alice's Adventures in Wonderland (Carroll), 68–77; falls in, 69–70, 80; water in, 70–71, 73–74; water's role in composition of, 76–77

Allegory of the Cave (Plato), 95, 97–98
Amoretti (Spenser), 79
antiracism, 142
Arcadia (Stoppard), 213
Ariel (character, *The Tempest*), 140–41, 144, 201
Aristophanes, 100, 235n7
Aristotle, 101–2; *Poetics*, 52, 230n17
Arnold, Morris, 109
Ashcroft, Peggy, 64
asides, 105–7, 110–11; as mini-soliloquies, 107; as nonengagement, 115–16; "passive aggressive," 113. *See also* soliloquy
associative thinking, 15, 46–47
asymptote, 68–69
audience: for children's books, 29–32, 39; death of actors, response to, 19; reaction to *Waiting for Godot*, 128–29; and soliloquies, 107–10; theater, 19, 62–63, 107–8. *See also* reader

Augustine, Saint, 108
Austen, Jane: character vignettes, 120–21; "free indirect discourse," 120–21; impersonality of, 122; interruption of while writing, 216, 221; marriage plot, character fungibility within, 119, 121; similarities between characters, 118; *Works: Emma*, 118–22, 123; *Northanger Abbey*, 118–19; *Persuasion*, 117–18, 123–24; *Pride and Prejudice*, 118, 121–22
autobiography, 23, 27–28; Ellison's essays, 142; *Little House* books marketed as, 171; revision as, 25; Shakespeare's hidden personal life, 21, 225n8
avoidance, 34–36, 60, 65, 86

Baillie, Joanna, 109
Banquo (character, *Macbeth*), 138–39
Barrie, J. M.: *Peter Pan*, 135–41, 143, 145
Beckett, Samuel: *Waiting for Godot*, 127–30
Bedtime for Frances (Hoban), 218
Behn, Aphra, 21–22
Bennet, Jane (character, *Pride and Prejudice*), 122
Bennet, Lizzy (character, *Pride and Prejudice*), 121
Bettelheim, Bruno, 31
blackface, 63, 177
Black Like Me (Griffin), 59–60, 62–65
Blake, William, 27–28

blank slate metaphor, 46
blindness, 89–90
bodies, 152–53; constituted by water, 76; and shadows, 137, 139–40
books: carnal versus courtly lover of, 13, 224n14; children, analogy with, 26–27; as economic commodity, 12–13; motion of reading, 13–14; new, connection with, 56–57; as opportunity to talk about personal lives, 3. *See also* authors; children's books
Booth, Barton, 63
British boarding school system, 31–32
Brooks, Peter, 50, 159
Burton, Richard, 110

Caliban (character, *The Tempest*), 140
Carroll, Lewis, 11–12, 15, 68–80; associative quality of tales, 78; death of, 80; as mathematician, 68; role of water in composition of *Alice*, 76–77; *Works: Alice's Adventures in Wonderland*, 68–77; *Through the Looking Glass*, 11–12, 15, 68, 77
Castle of Otranto, The (Walpole), 208
castration complex, 113, 155
Cather, Willa, 33
cave, allegory of, 95, 97
Cavell, Stanley, 34
censorship, 142
Cervantes, Miguel de, 147–48, 152
Charles II, 49, 88–89
Cheaper by the Dozen (Gilbreth siblings), 185, 187–89, 191, 193;

deaths of siblings hidden, 193–94. *See also* economic calculation; pioneers
Chee, Alexander, 19, 23, 225n11
children: chores as preparation for future labor, 10; existential dread about being forgotten, 35–36, 38–40; importance of shadows to, 135–36, 144; lonely, as readers, 35–36; object permanence, 142; specialness, feeling of, 96; time and agency stripped away, 129–30; and trauma, 31–32, 68; violence as mark of departure from childhood, 35; writing by, 102, 175–76
children's books, 29–42; audience for, 29–32, 39; reading aloud, 30–36, 41–42; revisiting, 33, 228n19; and troubling life choices of authors, 32–33; truth claims in, 33; violence acknowledged in, 31–32
class attitudes, 189–90
Claudius (character, *Hamlet*), 106–7, 109, 111–15
Cleary, Beverly, 218
Cluchey, Rick, 129
clutter, 43–48, 83; necessary to scholarship, 47
Coleridge, Samuel Taylor, 25; *Works:* "Frost at Midnight," 40–41; "Kubla Khan," 218; "The Rime of The Ancient Mariner," 72–73
comparisons, 59–60. *See also* metaphor; simile
Condell, Henry, 21

Conrad, Joseph, 77
Cooper, Jilly, 150–51, 154, 158, 166; parodies of, 163–64
COVID-19 pandemic, loneliness during, 4–8
creativity: fluidity of, 79–80; and women's lives, 216, 220
Cromwell, Oliver, 88–89
cryptography, 47, 52

"Daffodils, The" ("I wandered lonely as a cloud . . .") (Wordsworth), 75
Dahl, Roald, 29–32; writing for adults, 32; *Works: Matilda*, 31–32; *The Witches*, 29–30
Daniels, Arlene, 200, 202–3, 206
death, 220; and loss, 19–21, 24, 28, 141, 172, 174; and pioneer families, 192–94; in pioneer families, 192–93; and tears, 80
Dederer, Claire, 32–33
desire (longing), 88, 99–100, 102, 159–60; absence of, 159; to be complete, 100; to be desired, 120; and detachment, 35, 41, 65; leading to insight, 96–97; for movement, 128, 163; "narrative," 159; Oedipal, 113–14; for perfection, 103; and physical exposure, 152; and trepidation, 3
detective's powers of observation, 46–47; academic thought compared to, 47, 52–54. *See also* Doyle, Arthur Conan

developmental psychology, 142
dialectical cross examination, 95
Dickinson, Emily, 239n8
disidentification, 121–23
Dodgson, Charles. *See* Carroll, Lewis
dogs, 84–88; gaze of, 88, 90; Platonic Dog Form, 96
domestic labor, 203–4, 220; housekeeping style, 44–45. *See also* parenting
Donne, John, 127
Don Quixote (Cervantes), 147–48, 152
Douglass, Frederick, 177
Doyle, Arthur Conan, 43–54; detective's powers of observation in, 46–47, 52, 54; as ophthalmologist, 68; scaffolding for stories, 47–50; *Works:* "The Adventure of the Abbey Grange," 51; "The Adventure of the Cardboard Box," 46–47; "The Man with the Twisted Lip," 53; "The Musgrave Ritual," 48–50; "A Scandal in Bohemia," 43, 46, 53

economic calculation, 189–91; factory model, 186, 189–91; free-market economy, 199, 210; productivity, senses of, 203–4
economic commodity, books as, 12–13
Edgeworth, Maria, 216–17
editing, 22, 25, 26, 171–72

efficiency, 186–94; and economic calculation, 189–91; as practice, 195
Elliot, Anne (character, *Persuasion*), 123–24
Ellison, Ralph, 9, 138, 141, 142, 201
Emma (Austen), 118–22, 123
Emma (character, *Emma*), 118–19, 121–22, 123
emotional labor, 207
endings, 166–67, 221, 249n11
erasure, 19, 79, 90, 142–43
Estragon (character, *Waiting for Godot*), 128–30
Everett, Percival, conversation with, 55–66, 138, 144

Fairfax, Jane (character, *Emma*), 121–22
fairy tales, 29, 31, 35
family resemblances, 61–62
"family romance," 96
fantasy: and horses, 147–49; sexual, 148, 156–57
Felski, Rita, 61
Fielding, Henry, 52–53
first impressions, 55–57
forgiveness, 32–33
forms: divorce process, 97–98, 102–3; Platonic theory of, 96–97, 235n1; as satisfying, 97–98
Frankenstein (Shelley), 14, 125, 126–27, 130, 143–44, 218
Frankenstein, Victor (character, *Frankenstein*), 14, 125, 126–27, 130, 143–44

"free indirect discourse," 120–21
free will, 83; and Koehler Method, 84; and temptation, 81, 86–87
Freud, Sigmund, 21, 113–14; "family romance," 96
Frost, Robert, 181
"Frost at Midnight" (Coleridge), 40–41

Garber, Marjorie, 139
Garrick, David, 24
Gilbreth, Frank Bunker, Sr., 185–90; death of, 194
Gilbreth, Lillian, 186–90
Gilman, Charlotte Perkins, 218
"Gold Bug, The" (Poe), 47
Gopnik, Adam, 30
Grahame, Kenneth, 74–75, 77
Griffin, John Howard, 59–60, 62–65

Hamlet (character, *Hamlet*), 194; as ashamed, 113–15; superciliousness of, 111–12
Hamlet (Shakespeare), 21, 80, 105–16, 192, 193; functions of soliloquies in, 108, 111–12; list of soliloquies in, 110; opening lines, 105–6, 110–11
hand, as idiom, 210–11
handshake, 55–59, 62–65; hug and kiss versus, 59; jazz permutations of, 63–64; physical closeness of manicures, 65
hardships, sought out, 171, 180–82, 190

Hazlitt, William, 28
Health, Malcolm, 230n17
Heart of Darkness (Conrad), 77
Heminges, John, 20
Hemingway, Ernest, 33, 78
Hermione (character, *The Winter's Tale*), 62
Hirsch, James, 108
"History of Astronomy" (Smith), 208–9
Holmes, Sherlock (character, *Sherlock Holmes* books): cocaine addiction, 44, 50; as detached, 53–54; as disorganized, 44–48; momentum of mind craved by, 44, 50–51; powers of observation, 46–47, 229n8
Homer, 27; *The Odyssey*, 27, 214, 219–20
hope, 3, 35, 128, 130, 221
horses, 149–50; and absence of desire, 159–60; and danger, 160–63; elimination habits, 152–53; English hunt seat wardrobe, 156–57; and erotica, 148–49, 156–57; and fantasy, 147–49; "hobby horse" metaphor for sexuality, 148–49, 157; obsession with, 157–58
housekeeping, as access to mind, 45–46
houses and homes, 176–79; return to, 176–77
How to Write an Autobiographical Novel (Chee), 19

human connections, 6, 64; handshake, 55–59; –inspired by reading and writing, 9; with new books, 56–57; words as way to avoid "real" reaching out, 65
Hume, David, 207–8, 218
hypervisibility, 140–41

identity, 23–24
infatuation, 164, 166
Ingalls, Charles, 172
intellectual labor: as antidote to loneliness, 8–9; changes in approach to, 6–7; done in the "shadows," 8, 20, 23; as hidden, 8, 10–11, 19–25, 27, 172; predicated on invisibility and isolation, 8; public defenses of private need, 9; "research" and sabbatical time, 203. *See also* labor; mind; reading; scholarship; writing
internet, 6, 117–18; dating profiles, 119–20
interruptions, 1–2, 216–17, 221
invisible hand, 200, 207–12
invisible labor, 197–98; acknowledgment of, 198–99, 211; emotional, 207; labor, defined, 201–2; "invisible work," 200, 202–3; ongoing labor as, 206, 220–21; parenting as, 5, 10, 206; preparatory work, 5, 198, 205; and psychological baggage, 198–99; service work, 205–6
Invisible Man (Ellison), 138, 141, 201

"Invisible: Slavery Today" exhibit, 205
isolation, 1–3; as choice, 220; during COVID-19 pandemic, 4–8; as maddening, 218; of ocean, 72; and pain, 126; potential perks of, 7; produced by writing, 15, 219; and stasis, 126–28; and women's writing lives, 216–17. *See also* loneliness; privacy

Jane Eyre (Brontë), 218
Jones, Ernest, 114
Jonson, Ben, 21, 26
Joseph Andrews (Fielding), 52–53
Jungian psychology, 142

King Lear (Shakespeare), 25, 29, 34, 36–38, 74; courage of Lear in act of renunciation, 37
Koehler, William, 83
Koehler Method, 82
Koehler Method of Dog Training, The: Certified Techniques by Movieland's Most Experience Dog Trainer (Koehler), 84
Koehler Method of Open Obedience for Ring, Home, and Field, The (Koehler), 86–87
"Kubla Khan" (Coleridge), 218

labor: defined, 201–2; domestic, 203–4, 220; hand as idiom for, 210–11; as idiom, 206, 211; of love, 206–7; productivity, senses of, 203–4; and time, 203; unpaid

work not counted as, 202–3, 206; Western concept of as separate from life, 203, 206–7. *See also* intellectual labor
Laertes (character, *Hamlet*), 80, 112–14
Lane, Rose Wilder, 171, 174, 176
language: as metaphorical, 65; as physical, 65–66; Wittgenstein's games, 55, 61
Liddell, Henry, 76–77
likeness, 55–56, 59–63; family resemblances, 61–62; mimicry, 62; racial appropriation, 63–65; word and gesture as separate and the same, 65–66. *See also* human connections
Little House on the Prairie books (Wilder), 169–78, 181–83; as acts of revisionist history, 171; cover illustration, 174, 177–78; homes, description of, 177–78; original draft, 173
Llewellyn Davies, Michael, 137
Llewellyn Davis, Peter, 137
Locke, John, 45
loneliness: aloneness versus, 6; artistic renderings of, 102; of children, 35–36; during COVID-19 pandemic, 4–6; intellectual labor as antidote to, 8–9; as love, 174; and mental illness, 218; and racing, 130–31; reading as counter to, 9–10; and smartphone use, 204. *See also* isolation

loss: and actors, 19–20, 24, 28; of childhood through parenting, 34; and death, 19–21, 24, 28, 141, 172, 174; of innocence, 35; and love, 166–67; and shadows, 19, 28
love, 99–100; artistic renditions of, 100–102; and endings, 166–67; infatuation versus, 164; labor of, 206–7; loneliness as, 174; and loss, 166–67; platonic, 99–102, 151; reading and writing as paradoxical, 192; and shadow work, 144–45. *See also* desire
Lynch, Deidre, 3

Macbeth (Shakespeare), 135, 138, 208
Mannes, Marya, 128–29
"Man with the Twisted Lip, The" (Doyle), 53
Marçal, Katrine, 212
marginalia, 52, 233n7
marriage plot, 119, 121
mathematics, 50, 67–68, 80
Matilda (Dahl), 31–32
Melville, Herman, 71–72, 105
Mendelssohn, Moses, 109
Metamorphoses (Ovid), 36
metaphors, 55. *See also* likeness
Miller, D. A., 122
Milne, A. A., 78–79
Milton, John, 6, 27, 81–83; blindness of, 89–90; as "reformed Puritan," 88–89
mimicry, 62

mind: "absentmindedness," 52–54, 199; absolute inaccessibility of, 45; academic, 52–54; blank slate metaphor, 46; as capacious and finite, 47; companionship requested by, 51–52; detective's, 46–47, 52–54; housekeeping as access to, 45–47; momentum craved by, 50–51; reverie, 51. *See also* intellectual labor

Mississippi River, 77–78

Moby-Dick (Melville), 71–72, 105

Momus's glass, 109, 120–21

Morland, Catherine (character *Northanger Abbey*), 119

Morrison, Toni, 9, 32–33, 142

motherhood, single, 1–5, 127, 155, 213–21

movement: in *Frankenstein*, 126–27; invisible labor as, 221; in racing, 125–26; of reading, 13–14; transience, 172–84, 191; waiting versus, 128–29

"Musgrave Ritual, The" (Doyle), 48–50

Musgrove, Louisa (character), 117, 123–24

Nabokov, Valdimir, 64

nakedness, 152–53

narrative desire, 159

National Underground Railroad Freedom Center, 205

Nightingale, Florence, 215

Northanger Abbey (Austen), 118–19

novels: antinovel sentiment, 39; "free indirect discourse," 120–21. *See also specific authors* "nuclear family," 6

obedience training, 84–88; and free will, 84

object permanence, 142

obsession, 157–58

Odysseus (*The Odyssey*), 214

Odyssey, The (Homer), 27, 214, 219–20

Oedipal desires, 113–14

Oedipus Rex (Sophocles), 52

Old Hamlet's ghost (character, *Hamlet*), 114, 139–40

Old Man and the Sea, The (Hemingway), 78

Olivier, Laurence, 64

Once and Future King, The (White), 35–36

opening lines, 105–6, 110–11

Ophelia (character, *Hamlet*), 80, 112, 115, 194

Othello (Shakespeare), 63, 64

pain: "beetle in a box" story, 61–62; as isolating and communal, 126; suffering, as requirement of attention, 89

Paradise Lost (Milton), 6, 27–28, 81–83, 87–90; God as corrective parent in, 90; predestination versus foreknowledge in, 87–88

parenting: competing interests and demands, 41–42; conversations about sexuality, 154–56; as

invisible labor, 5, 10, 206;
  parent-child chaos, 40–41. *See
  also* domestic labor
Paul Bunyan tales, 40
Penelope (*The Odyssey*), 214,
  219–20
"Penelope at Work" (Kamuf),
  219–21
perfection, 26, 95–104, 205, 217; and
  intellectual contests, 99–100;
  and Platonic theory of forms,
  96; as process, 98–99; and
  relationships to others, 102; as
  result of trial and error, 98, 104
performance studies, 23
performative utterance, 66
"personal space," 5
Persuasion (Austen), 117–18,
  122–24
Peter Pan (Barrie), 135–41, 143, 145
Pioneer Girl (Wilder), 171–73, 176
pioneers, 170–71, 185–86; housing,
  172–73; reproductive ethos of,
  186–87, 189, 192–93; stock,
  concept of, 185–86. *See also*
  economic calculation;
  efficiency; *Little House on the
  Prairie* books (Wilder)
Plato, 95–102; Works: *Allegory of the
  Cave*, 95, 97–98; *Republic*, 97;
  The Symposium, 99–100, 102,
  235n1
platonic love, 99–102, 151
Poe, Edgar Allan, 46–47, 229n8;
  Works: "The Gold Bug," 47;
  "The Purloined Letter," 47
Poetics (Aristotle), 52, 230n17

Polonius (character, *Hamlet*), 111,
  112, 115
Pope, Alexander, 20, 209; "The
  Rape of the Lock," 201
Pozzo (character, *Waiting for
  Godot*), 131
Prairie Fires (Fraser), 170
predestination versus
  foreknowledge, 87–88
Prelude, The (Wordsworth), 25
Pride and Prejudice (Austen), 118,
  121–22, 217
privacy, 108, 173, 178, 183; isolation
  as choice, 220; spaces of, and
  writing, 8; women's lack of, 215.
  See also isolation
Prospero (character, *The Tempest*),
  140–41.144
Protestant ideals. *See also*
  Milton, John; *Paradise Lost*
  (Milton)
Protestant ideals, and dog
  obedience training, 84–85, 86
psychological access, 45–47
Puritans, 88–89
"Purloined Letter, The" (Poe), 47
pursuit, 125–28

Quin, James, 63, 64

race: antiracism, 142; white
  appropriation of, 63–65
reader: invitation into plot, 47,
  49–50; narrator's addresses to,
  33; protection of from labor
  of writing, 24–25. *See also*
  audience

reading: as counter to loneliness, 9–10; internal, 8; as participation, 9; physical motions of, 13–14

reading aloud, 30–36; to adults, 36–38, 42; balance between cathexis and independence, 41; bedtime story, 39; as holding environment, 42; as transitional space, 41–42

Republic (Plato), 97

respite, books as, 12

Richardson, Samuel, 58–59, 230–31n2

Riders (Cooper), 150–51

"Rime of The Ancient Mariner, The" (Coleridge), 72–73

Roach, Joseph, 247–48n2

Robeson, Paul, 64

Room of One's Own, A (Woolf), 214, 220

Rosinante (horse, *Don Quixote*), 147–48, 152

running, 124–28, 145; connection and friendships through, 127, 131; and loneliness, 130–31; "out of my head" moments, 125–26, 131; "stopping moment," 126

"Scandal in Bohemia, A" (Doyle), 43, 46, 53

scholarship: designed to hide struggle, 27; as detective work, 47; disparity between research and life, 24–25; personal identity hidden within, 23

separation anxiety, 82

service work, 205–6

sexuality: conversations with adolescents, 154–56; "hobby horse" metaphor for, 148–49, 157; horses and erotica linked, 148–49, 156–57; sexual orientation, 100

shadows, 4, 50, 62, 135–45; of academic writing, 23; in allegory of the cave, 95, 97–98; and attachment, 137, 140, 142, 145; and bodies, 137, 139–40; and censorship, 142; emotional labor kept in, 207; ghosts, 138–39; importance of to children, 135–36, 144; in Jungian psychology, 142; lack of efficacy, 136, 139–40; and loss, 19, 28, 136, 145; negative connotations of, 141–42; and "object permanence," 143; in *Peter Pan*, 135–41, 143, 145; and Platonic theory of forms, 96; potential for erasure by, 90; sadness linked to, 139–40; as servants, 140; servitude linked with, 140–41; "shadow tag," 136–37, 139–40; shadow work, 241n21; writing process done in, 8, 20, 23. *See also* "invisible" labor

Shakespeare, William: authorship controversies, 21; deferral strategy, 106–7; ease of composition, myth of, 21, 25–26; hidden personal life, 21, 225n8; near-erasure of from cultural memory, 19; respite for offstage actors in, 107; *Works: Hamlet,* 21, 80, 105–16, 192, 194; *King Lear,* 25, 29, 34, 36–38, 74; *Macbeth,* 135, 138, 208; *Othello,* 63, 64; *The Tempest,* 140–41, 144, 2001; *The Winter's Tale,* 25, 62

Shelley, Mary, 14, 125, 141, 144, 218; pregnancies, 193, 194

Shelley, Percy, 101

Siddons, Sarah, 28, 62

Sidney, Philip, 101

similes, 55. *See also* likeness

Sir Charles Grandison (Richardson), 58–59, 230–31n2

slavery, 141, 205

Smith, Adam, 13, 199–200, 207–11; "invisible hand," 200, 207–10; *Works:* "History of Astronomy," 208–9; *The Theory of Moral Sentiments,* 199, 210; *The Wealth of Nations,* 202, 210, 211–12

Smith, Maggie, 64

Smith, Zadie, 7, 203–4

snowball, as synecdoche, 40, 228n22

"Snow Man, The" (Stevens), 37

Socrates, 95, 97, 99–100

soliloquy, 107–8; "alone speak," 109; and "free indirect discourse," 120–21; functions of, 108, 111–12; objections to realism of, 108–9; as "private talk," 110–11; self-addressed speech versus interior monologue, 108–9. *See also* asides; talking to oneself

solitude: interruptions of, 1–2, 216–17, 221; necessary for writing, 1–2; permitted by books, 12; of writing, 14–15

Spenser, Edmund, 79

Sterne, Laurence, 20, 79–80, 120, 135–36, 148–49, 156, 157; on his impending death, 166–67; on writing and conversation, 154

Stevens, Wallace, 37, 68

Stevenson, Robert Louis, 136, 138–39

Stoppard, Tom, 213

swimming, 58, 70–72, 75–76, 195

sympathy, theories of, 45

Symposium, The (Plato), 99–100, 102, 235n1

talking to oneself, 108, 199, 236n3. *See also* soliloquy

Tartar, Maria, 39–40, 228n19

Tempest, The (Shakespeare), 140–41, 144, 201

temptation, 81, 86–88, 91

Tenniel, John, 68

Tennyson, Alfred Lord, 51

Theory of Moral Sentiments, The (Smith), 199, 210

thoughts: academic, compared to detective's, 47, 52–54; detective's powers of reading, 46–47; "free indirect discourse," 120–21; as friends, 15; verbalization of in soliloquy, 108–9

Through the Looking Glass (Carroll), 11–12, 15, 68, 77

Tiger Lily (character, *Peter Pan*), 137, 141

Tristram Shandy (Sterne), 20, 79–80, 120, 135–36, 148–49, 156; "hobby horse" metaphor in, 148–49, 157 troubling life choices of authors, 32–33, 68, 79, 236n9
tuberculosis, 80, 166
Twain, Mark, 77–78, 138, 141, 142

"Ulysses" (Tennyson), 51

violence: acknowledgment of in children's books, 31–32; as mark of departure from childhood, 35
Vladimir (character, *Waiting for Godot*), 128–30

waiting, 128–29
Waiting for Godot (Beckett), 127–30; San Quentin performance, 129
Walcott, Derek, 62
Walpole, Horace, 208
water: amniotic fluid, 74; artesian, 73–74; and birth, 74, 80; bodies constituted by, 76; and creative movement, 79–80; creativity and movement of, 76–77; as disorienting, 75; erasure by, 79; humans as interlopers in, 78; percentage of on earth and in bodies, 80; rivers, 74–75, 77–78; saltwater and dehydration, 72–73; sea and ocean, 70–73; as source of buoyancy and peace, 75–76; swimming in, 58, 70–72, 75–76; tears, 68–70, 79, 80; in tuberculosis, 70
Watson, John (character, *Sherlock Holmes* books), 44, 48–50, 51, 53–54
Wealth of Nations, The (Smith), 202, 210, 211–12
"We Are Seven" (Wordsworth), 187, 188, 190, 192
weaving and spinning metaphors, 220–21
Wentworth, Captain (character, *Persuasion*), 123
Whale, James, 143
White, T. H., 35, 36
Wilde, Oscar, 121
Wilder, Almanzo, 174, 182
Wilder, Laura Ingalls, 169–78, 181–83; audience and editor pushback against topics, 176–77; biographies and annotated editions, 171–73; as farm columnist, 176; "On Ambition" essay, 175; *Works: Little House on the Prairie* books, 171; *The Long Winter*, 182–83; *Pioneer Girl* draft, 171–73, 176; *These Happy Golden Years*, 175
Williams, Garth, 174, 177–78
Williams, William Carlos, 68
Wind in the Willows, The (Grahame), 74–75, 77
Winterson, Jeanette, 198
Winter's Tale, The (Shakespeare), 26, 62
Witches, The (Dahl), 29–30

Wittgenstein, Ludwig, 218, 231n5; language games, 55, 61
Wollstonecraft, Mary, 193
women: isolating effects of writing life on, 216–17; lack of privacy, 215; literature of shaped by interruptions, 216
Woolf, Virginia, 80, 214–15; *Works: A Room of One's Own*, 214, 220
Wordsworth, William, 25, 218; *Works: The Prelude*, 25; "The Daffodils" ("I wandered lonely as a cloud . . ."), 75; "We Are Seven," 187, 188, 190, 192
working class, 198
writing: abandoning project, thoughts of, 19–20; as absolute expression of self, 23; by children, 175–76; as compulsion, 174–75; and conversation, 154; editing, 22, 25; flaws as reminders of dedication, 26; hidden work of, 5, 21–22; isolation produced by, 15, 219; and lived experience, 19–20; and pain, 126; parallels of lived experience with research, 19–20; and personal trajectory, 2–3; preparatory labor, 5, 198; in private spaces, 1–2, 8; process of done in shadows, 20, 23–25; seamless process, myth of, 21–22; self hidden within, 19–20, 25; as solitary, 14–15; starting a new piece, 57–58; transcendence of process as goal of, 22; weaving and spinning metaphors for, 220–21. *See also* scholarship

Yellow Wallpaper, The (Gilman), 218
yoga, 195
Yorick (character, *Tristram Shandy*), 148, 156

Zeus, 100, 101, 102

GPSR Authorized Representative: Easy Access System Europe, Mustamäe tee
50, 10621 Tallinn, Estonia, gpsr.requests@easproject.com

www.ingramcontent.com/pod-product-compliance
Lightning Source LLC
Chambersburg PA
CBHW022039290426
44109CB00014B/915